WHITE
FIRE

WHITE
FIRE

A Portrait of Women Spiritual Leaders in America

MALKA DRUCKER

PHOTOGRAPHS BY
GAY BLOCK

Walking Together, Finding the Way
SKYLIGHT PATHS Publishing
Woodstock, Vermont

White Fire:
A Portrait of Women Spiritual Leaders in America

Text © 2003 by Malka Drucker
Photographs © 2003 by Gay Block

For information regarding permission to reprint material from this book, please mail or fax your request in writing to SkyLight Paths Publishing, Permissions Department, at the address / fax number listed below.

Grateful acknowledgment is given for permission to use material from the following sources:

The lines from Poem XIII of "Twenty-One Love Poems," from *The Dream of a Common Language: Poems 1974–1977* by Adrienne Rich. Copyright © 1978 by W. W. Norton & Company, Inc. Used by permission of the author and W. W. Norton & Company, Inc.

"Human Family," from *I Shall Not Be Moved* by Maya Angelou, copyright © 1990 by Maya Angelou. Used by permission of Random House, Inc.

Library of Congress Cataloging-in-Publication Data
Drucker, Malka.
White fire : a portrait of women spiritual leaders in America / Malka Drucker ; photographs by Gay Block.
          p. cm.
Includes bibliographical references.
ISBN 1-893361-64-0
1. Women religious leaders—United States. I. Block, Gay. II. Title.
BL72 .D78 2002
200'.92'273—dc21   2002013691

10   9   8   7   6   5   4   3   2   1
Manufactured in Canada

SkyLight Paths Publishing is creating a place where people of different spiritual traditions come together for challenge and inspiration, a place where we can help each other understand the mystery that lies at the heart of our existence.

SkyLight Paths sees both believers and seekers as a community that increasingly transcends traditional boundaries of religion and denomination—people wanting to learn from each other, *walking together, finding the way.*

Walking Together, Finding the Way
Published by SkyLight Paths Publishing
A Division of LongHill Partners, Inc.
Sunset Farm Offices, Route 4, P.O. Box 237
Woodstock, VT 05091
Tel: (802) 457-4000   Fax: (802) 457-4004
www.skylightpaths.com

For our grandsons, Julian, Owen, Robert, and Solomon Ace, new men.
M.D. and G.B.

Contents

Acknowledgments

|REGRET THAT SPACE AND TIME DID NOT ALLOW THE PRESENCE OF ALL THE WOMEN
we interviewed. They all deserve acknowledgment for their contributions to the book: Shariffa Carlo Al Andalusia, Meinrad Craighead, Mary Lou Cook, Barbara Dobkin, Lynn Gottlieb, Blu Greenberg, Pat Jojola, Rabbi Sharon Kleinbaum, Eileen Lighthawk, Rabbi Emily Lipof, Ana Perez-Chisti, Starcross Sisters, Dawn Snell, Frances Townes, Rabbi Shohama Weiner, and Janet Walton. I hope that these women are consoled by seeing that they are in excellent company. My editor has suggested that perhaps we need a sequel, and I hope that it comes to pass.

Rabbi Judith Edelstein deserves special thanks for planting the germ of the idea for this book. Maggie Lichtenberg gave an enthusiastic response to the project in its early stages, as did Jane Enyeart, and Eugenia Parry strengthened the project by her careful reading and comments. Gail Glasser and Margaret Moore organized and propelled the project into being. Janet Zarem introduced me to several of these women by sending me chapters of books and suggestions for useful books. The Reverend Helen Cohen's survey provided many of the epigraphs for the sections. Ann McGovern came to visit us in Santa Fe and spent most of her time indoors giving the manuscript the final polish. SkyLight Paths' Jon Sweeney, Maura Shaw, and Emily Wichland supported, improved, and encouraged the project every step of the way.

To those who have nurtured my spiritual path, including Rabbi Harold and Malkah Schulweis; my teachers and colleagues at the Academy for Jewish Religion; my parents who taught me gratitude and wonder; my children, Ivan and Max, and their life partners, Caroline and Betsy; and my sisters, Pamela, Bonnie, Linda, and Gale (*z"l*), I thank you with a love and gratitude that is beyond measure. And always, Gay, whose open mind and heart gave everything I needed.

Finally, thanks to the One who has always walked with me. May You bless and keep all who live, bring us light and grace, and let us feel Your love by bringing peace.

Introduction

I have never found it possible to suffer a bearded priest so near my heart and conscience as to do me any spiritual good. I blush at the very thought! Oh, in the better order of things, Heaven grant that the ministry of souls may be left in charge of women! The gates of the Blessed City will be thronged with the multitude that enter in, when that day comes! The task belongs to woman. God meant it for her. I have always envied the Catholics their faith in that sweet, sacred Virgin Mother, who stands between them and the Deity, intercepting somewhat of his awful splendor, but permitting his love to stream upon the worshipper more intelligibly to human comprehension through the medium of a woman's tenderness.

NATHANIEL HAWTHORNE, A BLITHDALE ROMANCE

WHEN I BECAME A RABBI IN 1998, I WAS HARDLY A PIONEER. IN THE congregations I served, however, I was always their first woman spiritual leader. While some liked me for being more approachable and egalitarian, others left the congregation shaking their heads. Rabbis are men, not women. What does tradition mean, after all? And what does it mean that more women are actively entering religious life? Are they destroying tradition or resuscitating it? Do they wonder about what to wear when presiding? Are they often called by their first names, or do they adhere to more formal titles? What is their relationship with their male colleagues? Questions such as these have nagged me ever since I started serving. My curiosity led me to meet almost sixty women leaders of many faith paths to hear how they understood themselves in their work. This book, which is a collaboration with my work partner and life partner, Gay Block, is a result of this inquiry. The title of the book takes its inspiration from a cryptic description of the Torah, the Five Books of Moses, found in the Jewish commentary, the Talmud: "Torah is written with black fire upon white fire." Overlooked and absent from half of the human narrative, women are like white fire, the element upon which black fire depends: without white, you cannot see anything. One day, when there is no injustice or oppression, we will be able to read the often ignored, invisible white language surrounding the black text.

The very presence of women spiritual leaders implies a slipping away from tradition. Some remain within the bounds of an established faith but do it in a new way, such as Marianne Williamson and Beatrice Bruteau. Others practice syncretism, a mixing of practices, such as Sylvia Boorstein, who calls herself a Jew and a Buddhist. Ralph Waldo Emerson wrote, "When we have broken from our god of tradition and ceased from our god of rhetoric, then may God fire the heart with His presence."

Sometimes the Star of David weighs heavy on me, a wedding ring bearing ambivalence, obligation, and binding mystery. All-inclusive gatherings that blend the best ideas have a strong appeal, not only to those without commitment to a single path. I'd go back to Starhawk's Halloween and Jean Houston's Mystery Workshop in a heartbeat. I liked the people and the rituals and found myself renewed. But I always return to my tradition. When I ask myself why, I remember. Seder, High Holidays—each word is a thread in my life that attaches me to my people, and I imagine my infant grandson learning the prayers I taught his father. And then I sense magnitude as well as gratitude. There are many paths that go beyond the local, little self, and this one is mine. What the many different spiritual gatherings I attended gave me collectively was clarity about the message and the mission, no matter what the practice.

All that this work has to teach me is still in progress. This I know: bookstores have swelling shelves devoted to spirituality. Self-help books reveal our yearnings, interests, and needs, and they abound with titles full of the wisdom literature of our time: *soul*, *heart*, and *path* are words that most often catch the eye. The new religion is about human potential. Find God to actualize yourself. If you believe in God, you'll do better on earth. Despite the solipsism, the quest is good, because the limitation of everything on earth—science, technology, possessions, even relationships—can send us further and deeper into ourselves and toward God.

What does being a woman have to do with it? Many of these books are by women. Even today, women are vulnerable financially and socially. Choosing to become spiritual leaders doesn't help their situation. They are sometimes lumped with fundamentalists and occasionally wonder themselves whether they are indeed crazy to tilt at pragmatic materialism. They are on the edge, for better or worse, as Joan Halifax and others poignantly demonstrate. Women may be especially suited for this realm, because they are well acquainted with being outsiders. Women, because they know what it is to be the stranger. Women, because they love kindness. Women, because they are half of God's face.

I began the project by interviewing women whom I knew or had learned about from my research. Friends from many religious traditions responded when I asked for the names of women whom they respected and who inspired them. The subjects themselves suggested others I might interview. I don't think it is coincidence that most of the women are close to each other in age and are veterans of the idealistic and creative decade from 1965 to 1975, the days of peace and love. Many who chose to serve twenty-five years ago, such as Rabbi Laura Geller, awakened in the civil rights movement. While the flower children had lofty ideals, the structures remained patriarchal; now these veterans have taken the tender message of their generation and have made it their ministry. "All we are saying is give peace a chance," the Beatles sang. All these women are saying is, give women a chance.

I hope no one is offended when I say that regardless of their diverse practices, these women seem to preach the same thing: loving-kindness. I'm not so naive as to think that this means we will all gather together and create a spiritual revolution that shifts our culture from greed and violence to generosity and peace. But I know that we can. I'm grateful to be part of a group that will keep on trying.

When a woman chosen for inclusion in the book led or taught a group, Gay and I attended the gathering, and then we interviewed and photographed her afterward. Some serve in denominations, such as the Methodists, that have accepted women ministers for a hundred years; others are part of groups that still do not allow women full rights to the priesthood. Some, such as nuns, live in traditional communities; others are reviving and creating radical new forms of faith groups. Some are media stars; others struggle to gather more than a dozen congregants. Some have personal assistants to make appointments; others asked,

"Why me? I'm no big deal." Some are frank feminists; others bristle when I mention the word. What they share, besides gender, is a passion and a calling to serve.

While many of these women lead traditional or untraditional communities, not all are ordained. Some are writers or teachers with no liturgical function, and some look after abandoned children who know no prayer except the face of the one who feeds them. In this work, I define a leader as one who either has a following and/or is changing religion's path by her ideas and presence. Because this project was originally conceived as part of a survey to examine America at the start of the current millennium, it has narrowed the focus of this book to women who have a following in the United States.

Their disparate journeys reflect the narrative of the Five Books of Moses, and this book is organized similarly. The Five Books begin with the birth of the world and end with the Jews about to enter the mysterious Promised Land. Genesis ends just before the Israelites go down to Egypt, Exodus tells of their travail and liberation, Leviticus states the law, Numbers recounts the struggle to live the law, and Deuteronomy brings everything full circle, with Moses retelling the narrative the people must remember to survive as a people in their own land.

While the leaders' stories tended to place them in different sections of the narrative, no one belongs in just one section. Every woman in the book is a pioneer; all have left the comfort of the familiar; all have a practice; all have struggled to do their work; and all are the beneficiaries of the past twenty-five years of women entering spiritual leadership positions. Still, their stories tend to belong more in one book than another. The "Birth" section includes those who were the first to take a position formerly reserved for men, for example, the first ordained ministers. The women in the second section, "Exile," are writing a new page in their sacred texts and are helping to decode "white fire." When asked which of the Five Books best described their experience, most women in the book chose Exodus, the book of exile and liberation. The women in "Exile" are often theologians, writers who have changed the consciousness of both male and female congregational leaders.

The third section is called "Law" because these leaders closely uphold the tenets of organized religion and work within the confines of the law. While they may not transgress the familiar boundaries of gender, their feminine perspective still makes a difference. The fourth section, "Wilderness," contains perhaps the most poignant and heroic stories, for these are the women who often have more than gender to surmount. It is from this section that I regretfully omitted many women. Rabbi Sharon Kleinbaum, as spiritual leader of the largest gay and lesbian synagogue, wields power possessed by few clergy, let alone a lesbian. It is questionable that she would have the same authority in a mainstream congregation. Dawn Snell, a student at New York Theological Seminary because she has the gift of spiritual song, is middle-aged, African American, and poor. While she is a great asset to her church, they will not hire her, so she serves the only way she can—as a volunteer.

The final section, "Harvest," brings the bounty reaped from the feminist and spiritual movements of the past twenty-five years. Two groups of women emerge in this chapter. First are the women new to the work, beneficiaries of the pioneers who struggled to change minds and hearts. The other group is made up of the women in the foreground of what has been called millennial religion. Here we find women such as Jean Houston, who are creating new forms of religious expression by borrowing from many traditions.

At the end of the interview with writer Elaine Pagels, she asked me why I wanted to be a rabbi. She had already made clear her skittishness toward organized religion. My answer resembled that of John Donne, who writes hotly about the eros between him and God: I had to; I couldn't help it. After years of ambivalence, I enrolled in the seminary at fifty—not the optimal age to tackle the Aramaic language and Talmud, as well as other ancient texts. But when you're in love, you can do many things.

I had no intention of taking a pulpit, but fieldwork was an academic requirement. The congregation I first served was in Westchester, New York; it was small, well established, and proud of the distinguished rabbis who had served them. I was their first student rabbi and the first woman to lead them. They accepted my lack of rabbinic experience and were satisfied with what I did know, and we learned a lot together. I found new relationship with people as a rabbi. When my congregants came to me with their deepest questions about how to live, their quest lifted me to reach for all I knew from Torah and from life to be a bridge between them and the Holy. In short, I was hooked.

The women I met in researching this book gave me a sense of family in discovering a sisterhood of passion and commitment; the feeling was mutual. Many were grateful that I was working on the project, especially Dr. Nahid Angha, who connects Sufi women around the world. I needed all these women—contemplatives, teachers, writers, congregational leaders, and charismatic syncretists—to give me permission to see other ways to serve besides the pulpit. They taught me to look beyond the numbers of followers as a measure of success. Those who labor unknown in the world while doing God's work are the women who taught me what humility, dignity, and personal power look like. Women who have found new paths by blending traditions have shown me the possibilities of spiritual freedom, and women who reach millions have surprised me in revealing so much hunger for meaning. They helped me to respect the work I do and, most of all, to glory in the collective ministry of women.

Some, like Iyanla Vanzant, came to their work after terrible suffering. For many, teen pregnancies, bad marriages, tragic deaths, and drugs were the preparation for a life of faith. Of course, I spoke only to the survivors—those who had the stuff to fight. Many with gifts gave up, and their work was lost. Women, especially in mainstream denominations, put up with a lot.

Why do women bother challenging tradition and prejudice? Women have always sustained religious communities as wives and daughters of male ministers. Nurturing often comes easily to women, and now they are stepping into positions of authority for themselves. Many are in the forefront of the newest liturgy, the healing service. As Dorothy Day said, "I think there has to be a sort of harmony of body and soul, and I think that comes about, certainly for women, through those very simple things of 'feeding the hungry and sheltering the harborless.'"

A couple of years ago, an English newspaper, the *Express*, reported that women bosses have a different way of managing their jobs and employees than male bosses have. They are better listeners and better communicators. They tend to engage more closely with their employees, involving them rather than ordering them about. Tamara Ingram, joint chief executive of Saatchi and Saatchi, says, "Motherly skills make for a very effective management style." Women are used to multitasking—a skill all pulpit leaders need. We who have raised children, cooked, and held the house together do this very well. Balance and diversity, the yin/yang of things, makes for a better leader, and men are learning from women. At Mazda Corporation, men are now taking classes, in the face of competition from women: they're learning listening techniques, how to recognize feelings and understand relationships, and even stress relief. Mother may be a more palatable God-image right now than the bearded one. Yet, this is just another concrete, corporeal image: God is about energy, not form. Idolatry is natural; yet, the work and miracle are to defy this inclination and accept surprise in the universe.

Despite the attempt of most women to offer me a picture of their work and lives as smooth and successful, not all have survived the falls in a barrel. Maybe they focus on the "good news" to remind themselves that despite the bias and fear that continually challenge them, doing the work is worth it. The tiny number of clergywomen at the peak of their profession stands in stark contrast to the ranks of women coming out of seminaries. The Roman Catholic Church still doesn't ordain women, and the Southern Baptists voted to condemn their denomination's hundreds of women pastors. Their justification? "The Bible tells us that God does not give women authority over men." Many churches and synagogues regard the hiring of a woman as a risk, so they hire men. Women are still perceived as counselors and teachers who lack the ability to manage money or administer big congregations.

One aspect of God is transcendent; the other aspect, close and immanent. The women I met didn't hide behind robes or dogma; they revealed themselves in doubt and faith; in so doing, they revealed the One for whom they work. I invite you to look at and listen to these women of spirit up close, and to allow yourselves to be taken on a new ride. Notice how often one woman will refer to another found in this book, and you'll glimpse the importance of a sisterhood. Ma Jaya adores Jean Houston. Marianne Williamson raves about Iyanla Vanzant. They strengthen one another with their faith and shared experience as they begin to shift the patriarchy and hierarchy of normative religion.

What seems new—that is, the presence of women in spiritual life—is actually old. The pagan world of goddesses reminds us that we once lived in the world with a different vision of the feminine. Perhaps the increasing presence of women spiritual leaders comes from our deepest need to return to a world where women are respected as divine representatives. The names we call the feminine Divine—Kuan-Yin, Mary, Kali, Sophia, Iyanla, Shekhinah—reveal how every wisdom path wished connection to the feminine. How our children will understand the

Holy after taking Communion from a woman priest, and how that may change the world, is the answer that I eagerly await.

I imagine this book as a dinner party where women have eagerly gathered for a conversation about being a woman, a person of faith, and a leader. While some know each other, many do not, but it doesn't matter. Listening to them in ensemble reveals that all their differences are less important than how much they share as women of faith. Since community and interconnection tend to be feminine traits, sisterhood is important, and I hope the subjects of this book enjoy hearing themselves in concert. I also hope that upon finishing the book, the reader may feel that she or he has found a teacher that offers a new way to see women and the Divine.

Given the triple challenge of being a woman spiritual leader, it is a miracle that so many have persisted and prevailed. At least it demonstrates that dreams can come true. More deeply, the increasing presence of the feminine, coupled with the imperative to reconnect ourselves to the sacred, has given women the spiritual authority to show a new way. This may be the moment when the white fire reveals the path to peace and love.

1

Birth

The rules break like a thermometer,
quicksilver spills across the charted systems,
we're out in a country that has no language
no laws, we're chasing the raven and the wren
through gorges unexplored since dawn
whatever we do together is pure invention
the maps they gave us were out of date
by years . . .

ADRIENNE RICH

BIRTH, THE MOMENT OF EMERGENCE FROM DARKNESS INTO LIGHT, IS HOW THE Bible describes the first Creation, and it is how we experience the genesis of every being and every idea. The following portraits are of women pioneers, trailblazers, and veterans, because they have given birth to a new day in the spiritual lives of women. Either they have assumed positions formerly reserved for men, or they have broken new ground by heading projects devoted to cultivating the presence of women leaders in American spiritual life. The women in this section reveal persistence, creativity, and courage. They share strong commitment to

1

family: all are or have been married, they have children, and they describe their families of origin as wise, loving, and strong. These commonalities may be no coincidence. Pushing the boundaries of rules and customs within traditional communities may require "regular women" who could be anyone's sister, mother, or daughter.

Thanks to the women's movement launched in the 1970s, women have become a familiar presence in the once male-dominated workplace. But before women toast themselves on gaining acceptance, Rabbi Joy Levitt, one of the first generation of ordained women, wryly cautions, "When an institution is in decline, women finally get the invitation to join. Since mainstream religion hasn't been attracting the best and brightest men, they've stopped worrying about the negative effect women will have on the profession. It's also true in medicine and law." Spirituality may be on the rise, but most congregations are shrinking, and so is the male ministerial pool. Seminaries need students, and women are eager to fill the ranks.

Leontine Kelly, a Methodist minister, became the second woman and first African-American woman to be elected as a bishop in any denomination—although she did not feel called to the ministry until after her children were grown. Laura Geller, a Reform rabbi and one of the first women to be ordained, has broken the "stained-glass ceiling" by leading a congregation exceeding one thousand families. Suzan Johnson Cook, an American Baptist minister, became the first African-American woman to be elected as a senior minister in her denomination's two-hundred-year history.

Psychologist, scholar, and religious writer Nahid Angha is an Iranian Sufi who lives in San Rafael, California. She is the cofounder of the International Association of Sufism and the founder of Sufi Women Organization. Rebbetzin Esther Jungreis, the widow of an Orthodox rabbi, teaches traditional Judaism via books, newspaper columns, radio, and lectures to thousands weekly. Her followers come from myriad backgrounds, and her singular achievement is unique in the Jewish community. She is the embodiment of the title of her 1982 book, *The Jewish Soul on Fire*.

Cheryl Kirk-Duggan, a Christian Methodist Episcopal elder, is the executive director of the Center for Women and Religion at the University of California at Berkeley, a multicultural, interfaith organization that promotes justice for women in religious institutions, provides resources for ministerial leadership skills, and offers academic programs in women's spirituality, culture, and health. She writes for many audiences, and her subjects range from the recent *Misbegotten Anguish: A Theology of Ethics and Violence* to a study of African-American spirituals from a womanist perspective, called *Exorcising Evil*.

The Right Reverend Leontine Kelly

Mirror twins are different
Although their features jibe
And lovers think quite different thoughts while lying side to side
We love and lose in China
We weep on Englands's moors
We laugh and moan in Guinea
And thrive on Spanish shores
We seek success in Finland
Are born and die in Maine
In minor ways we differ
In major ways we're the same
I note the obvious differences between each sort and type
But we are more alike my friends than we are unalike
We are more alike my friends than we are unalike

What a world this would be if we could just remember these simple truths.

MAYA ANGELOU

Retired Bishop Leontine Kelly doesn't match the picture of a traditional bishop in a cassock and tall white hat. She is a kindly eighty-year-old grandmother who happens to be the second woman and first African-American woman to be elected bishop of any denomination. That the United Methodist Church, her denomination, is mostly white makes the achievement even greater. When I asked Rev. Cheryl Kirk-Duggan to recommend women spiritual leaders, "Teenie" was at the top of the list.

Bishop Kelly greets us at her garden apartment in a retirement home in a middle-class suburb near San Francisco. Wearing a tasteful sweater suit, she invites us to join her for tea in her living room. It is filled with family photos, black Madonnas, mother-and-son sculptures in both black and white, a sign proclaiming "Shalom" to visitors, and religious icons from Native American and Asian traditions. Before we sit, she takes us on a tour of the apartment with a running narrative explaining the significance of the mementos and who is in the photographs.

Her family is handsome and high-achieving. This began with Kelly's parents; her father, brother, and husband were all Methodist ministers. After showing us her children, including a little girl she brought up who is now an attorney, she holds up a picture of a beautiful young woman, her granddaughter. "Tiffany wanted to go to Colorado State, which is very white. She didn't care, but she's very brown and has not accepted herself really as a black person, and it upsets her parents. She was just graduated from a high school where she was the only black member of her class. Her father is in the corporate world, and she's always been in white neighborhoods and in a white world. She's seventeen and has never had a black friend."

I understand her well. Just as Judaism isn't simply a religion, being black isn't simply about color. It is a civilization of history, music, and literature that spans centuries and transcends geographic boundaries. Each generation bears a responsibility in transmitting tradition, and the best way is through community. Faith, family, and community form the bedrock of Bishop Kelly's life. We sit down to talk about her path to becoming a bishop, the position from which she retired at the mandatory age of seventy in 1990.

"When my husband suddenly died in 1969, he was minister to a little black church in rural Virginia that had never had a minister, and his family lived in their community for 130 years. In our two years there, the community poured out so much love on us—we didn't know how soon we were going to need it. My husband had said he would help them build a new church, but it didn't work out that way. At that time I was a high school teacher in North Umberland County, Virginia. That was my calling, my ministry. I was also a lay

The ordination of women in Methodism began with A.M.E. Zion in the late 1800s. The United Methodist Church began ordaining women in 1956, giving them equal status to men in the church. John Wesley, an early founder of Methodism, was strongly against slavery and was also an activist for miners, thus establishing a tradition of social action within the church.

speaker in the United Methodist Church, someone interested in sharing the good news of the gospel but not interested in ordained ministry.

"After the funeral, the district superintendent from the bishop's office came to me and said, 'Teenie, the people want you. They want you to be their pastor.' I

The United Methodist Church is a recent denomination that united a Methodist church divided by slavery. In the North, blacks encountered so much racism after the Civil War that they created the African Methodist Episcopal Church (A.M.E.). But there were blacks who stayed within the church, such as Bishop Kelly's father, who taught her that you don't win the battle by leaving the battlefield. In 1968, the Northern and Southern, as well as black and white, constituencies joined to create the integrated United Methodist Church. Still, in the South there are geographical jurisdictions that are made up entirely of black Methodists. "Racism is still very much alive," the bishop says.

said that I didn't want to be a pastor. I had no intention of ever being a pastor. 'You have the gift and grace for ordained ministry,' he said. I told him that I believe in a called ministry; you just don't choose a vocation. God has to call you, and you have to agree to go in that direction. So he said those famous last words: 'If you would just hold the position until we can get somebody.' That was March, and by June they were supposed to have somebody. I ended up being there for six years, and we finally built a new church and parsonage.

"When I did receive the call and entered the seminary in 1976, I had three children, the youngest of whom was in college, and another little girl whose mother left her with me when she was eighteen months old. My mother, who was ninety, also lived with me. It was completely impossible to do, but I made it through and got my Master's of Divinity. My kids said I'd be ordained and retired at the same time!" Since then, Kelly has earned nine honorary doctorates for her work and commitment to social issues.

"Back then, women only got rural appointments, and that was all right, because my choice was to work in our rural church. Like my father, brother, and husband, I have pastored only black churches." As Suzan Johnson Cook says, we talk best to those whom we know best, and if we don't serve our own people, who will?

"The only way I survived racism was through acceptance of the Divine and the Divine's acceptance of me. I was a child of God. I grew up in an apartment building [in Ohio] that was part of the Underground Railroad, and that shaped my life. God wasn't a ghostly creature floating around somewhere, but a God who answers through history with people who make a difference in the world. I was blessed that my parents helped us understand that we were children of God and that society was in violation of not understanding that about us. We went to segregated schools. We couldn't swim except on Fridays, before they drained the pool in the white school. In the ninth grade, I found the map of the Underground Railroad, and one of the stations was under the school. I took the map to the principal, and I ended up in trouble. By then I was in the junior NAACP.

"Our parents were clear that the law of the land was one thing—we couldn't go to movies—but there was another law, the law of God. It's so important to keep the self-esteem of a black child, and so many children have parents who don't have the educational and spiritual balance to give them that. They've battled it too much themselves.

"There were eight children in my family. My mother was fair, like a white woman. Her discoloration, as I call it, was a result of slavery. And my father was as brown as my mother was light. She always said that we were a mixture of coffee and cream. Once we were coming home from a concert in Cincinnati. It was ten at night, and I was asleep with my head on the door, and I heard this policeman's siren. My brothers always said my father never drove fast enough, so he couldn't have been speeding. The cop came up to my father and said, 'Pull over.' He shined his flashlight in the car and said, 'What are you doing with a white woman?'

"And before my father could answer, my mother flipped on the light and pointed to us in the back and said, 'I think you're a little late asking.' That cop started to blush deep in his collar, and he turned red as a beet and said, 'Go on.' I always think of that when I hear the term 'redneck.'

"Papa said to Mama, 'How did you think to say that?' And she said, 'Well, Baby, when you're born my color you think of all this stuff.' Afterwards, we all laughed and joked about the cop, but I couldn't go to sleep, because I couldn't find the white woman! There wasn't anyone but us in the car. I never thought of my mother as white. Was she one of them? I must have been about nine. It took me two years to ask my mother. She was combing my hair, and I asked, 'Are you a white woman?'

"She said, 'No,' and she told me the story of slavery. Her great-grandmother had been a slave who had been a seamstress on a slave plantation, and her grandmother had been a child of the master. The mistress of the plantation had no children, and she resented this little child with long curls. When the mistress threw her down a flight of stairs she learned how to hide in her mother's skirts and to be very quiet.

"My mother inherited her mother's light color. She was very strong. She was a very active early member of the NAACP, one of the organizers of the Urban League in Cincinnati. We grew up with parents who lived their beliefs, and we children were blessed. The biggest challenge in my life has come from my being a mother, because the difficulty of raising black children is racism." Bishop Kelly tells her story without anger. Raising children is a sacred, daunting task for any parent, but how do you raise children with hope and good hearts in a society so unequal in opportunity? That which does not kill us makes us stronger, Nietzsche wrote. Kelly learned from her parents how to keep her spirit alive in a white world. By making her ministry welcome to everyone, including the controversial group of gays and lesbians in the Methodist Church, Kelly has taken the wound of prejudice and has turned it into blessing.

The bishop may move slowly, but her mind and heart are audacious. "To see a woman in this work is revolutionary. It's like getting over the blonde, blue-eyed Jesus. Every Christian depicts Jesus in their image, so I have a black Madonna and a black Jesus. We each have the right to make these choices, and it's liberating to see the Divine in a new, personal way. Whether in the rural or urban church, or as a bishop, women bring a more humane feeling to structure and power. We cannot victimize others the way we have been victimized. I use team approaches because I'm a woman. I've been battling prejudice as a black all my life, so when I began working with women, I was ready. Being a woman pastor was an amazing way for me to pull women together and say that we are here and we have a right to the same appointments as men.

"When I was bishop I was invited to a convent in Schenectady, New York. They had sisters who wanted to be ordained, who even served churches, and who wanted to strengthen the movement to get the church to make them priests. I was the first woman priest those women had ever met. They asked me to have a Eucharist, because they had never seen a woman administer it. On Saturday afternoon we left the convent to go to First Methodist Church, and they invited other priests and nuns. So I preached and administered the Eucharist. There was not a dry eye. I now wear a cross the sisters gave me that I will wear until the church ordains women."

When she tells us how she went from rural pastor to bishop, she sits forward in her chair and loses twenty years from her appearance. "In 1980, fifteen hundred United Methodist women clergy came together in Glorietta, New Mexico, for a powerful outpouring of spirit and fellowship. I was co-chair of the conference; the other chair was white. We said if the church is going to become Christian and live up to what it's supposed to be saying, then it can't not only leave out women, it can't leave out anyone. And if we were to fight sexism, we had to fight racism, because racism is deeper than any other kind of hatred in this country.

"We decided that we needed women in high-steeple churches and heading educational institutions, and for this we needed women bishops. The women were battling for a woman who was not on a pedestal somewhere like a typical southern white woman, but for a woman who was involved in the humanity of the church and the world. When they asked me to run for the position of bishop, it didn't happen the first time, but it did the second try, and we made history." The black clergywomen of the United Methodist Church recently established the Bishop Leontine Kelly Justice Award.

"In the beginning I questioned whether I had the administrative ability to lead an area of this size, with over a hundred thousand Methodists in the California-Nevada Annual Conference. And, as a black woman, how could I help people grow in their acceptance of my leadership? Two ministers asked me right away, 'Are you the bishop who's going to have the guts to move Cecil Williams?' [the charismatic and radical pastor of Glide Methodist Memorial Church in San Francisco]. I asked them, 'Do you want to take over for him?' They said no, and I told them not to ask foolish questions. Cecil's not the problem; the problem will be who will follow that powerful ministry that touches so many.

"One of the things I'm proudest of—besides my children—is how I tried to humanize the cabinet [of ministers] and help them to come to know one another better as persons. For women it's more than getting something done; it's getting to know one another, being comfortable with each other. When I dealt with pastors as a bishop, I related to them as people.

"I also wanted to be a bishop who was not afraid to speak up and stand out. I was invited to a Good Friday service held by peace activists at the nuclear power plant at Livermore. I ended up in jail, and it was the best, most meaningful Good Friday I ever spent in my life.

"The leadership in black tradition has always come right out of the church. Look at Jesse Jackson and Martin Luther King, Jr. When I taught evangelism at the seminary [Pacific School of Religion], some of the pastors told me that evangelism and social action don't go together. I said that I'd have no reason to be Christian if I didn't believe that it all fits together, and the model for me is Jesus Christ. It was what he did that was important, not just what he said. My father was a pastor and also a member of the Ohio legislature who helped the passage of civil rights laws.

"When I was in Richmond, Martin Luther King came to organize the students for the civil rights movement. We were all outside when I saw a man flip his cigarette down the blouse of one of the girls at the sit-in. She jumped up, and I was close enough to get it out and try to make her feel better. And I'll never forget—a white woman gave every one of our students a little American flag and said, 'I know it's hard for you to respect it, but keep working until we can live up to what it is to be an American.'

"That's the kind of thing I preach. I've had enough experiences in my life to know that everything fits together. And when we talk about God and put on a coin, 'In God we trust,' that's not the problem. We have racism because God is waiting for us to do something to stop it. When we know this, we have amazing power.

"When I retired, I stayed here and taught at the Pacific School of Religion. I'm grateful to live in California; it's the first time I've ever lived in the West. I grew up in Cincinnati, which is racist, and I was born in Washington, D.C., which at the time was completely racist. It's not that there aren't problems here; it's just that more people know what you're talking about.

"Two years ago I had a stroke. And when I got over that, I found out that I had breast cancer. I prayed to be a preacher again. It's what I love to do. And now I preach about six times a year at the request of the church. It's a way to talk to people and get them talking to each other, whether they agree or not."

Gay and I live on a street in Santa Fe called Bishop's Lodge Road. When Bishop Kelly received her photograph from us, she wrote back to say, "You live on the right road!"

Rabbi Laura Geller

Rabbi Laura Geller's impressive offices at Temple Emanuel suggest stability and power, inviting the assumption that they belong to a rabbi who has served the large, prosperous Beverly Hills Reform congregation for many years, and we might assume the rabbi is male. Laura Geller is, in fact, Temple Emanuel's senior rabbi, the first woman rabbi to hold such a position in a major metropolitan city, but she did not ascend to the position step by step, moving up the ladder from smaller congregations. In 1994, she shattered the "stained-glass ceiling"—the de facto barrier to a woman serving a congregation of more than a thousand—suddenly and surprisingly.

After twenty years as rabbi of the University of Southern California Hillel, the Jewish college organization, and director of the Southwest American Jewish Congress, a civil rights group, Geller became rabbi of this prized pulpit. Despite her never having served a congregation before, she was well known nationally. Although she was not the first woman rabbi to be ordained—she was among the first, having been ordained in 1976—she received generous media attention. Living in the land of celebrity probably helped, but the real reason Geller became prominent is that she is articulate and personable, and she matches the physical ideal of what many Jews believe a woman rabbi should look like. Rabbi Geller, an attractive, well-dressed, well-spoken woman, could pass for a corporate attorney.

Her secretary ushers us into a large paneled room with a fireplace, a wall of books, and a view of a patio and garden. Only her desk chair doesn't fit the image of a traditional office. It's big enough, like everything in the room, but it is covered in a floral print that matches the other chairs in the room. Laura enters after us and, seeing me looking at the chair, laughs. "When I first came in, I didn't know what to do with the room. Reupholstering helped soften and warm it." She's cordial, but it's Friday, and I know what the day feels like when you have a service that evening. I suggest that we begin right away so that she can finish preparing. She nods and says that she still has to pull her sermon together.

Eschewing the desk chair, she pulls up a chair in front of me, crosses her often-photographed long legs, and starts by telling us that she was born in Boston in 1950 into a Reform Jewish family. "Being Jewish was just a part of my family. It wasn't something that I ever reflected on. I wouldn't have said it was particularly important. It was just part of the air I breathed. But I do remember when I was a little girl, my parents had a synagogue committee meeting in our living room, and there were a lot of people there. My brother and I were sent off to bed.

"I snuck downstairs and I listened outside the door to see what the grownups were talking about, and they were talking about selling houses as a straw. I had no idea what that meant, so the next morning I asked my father, 'What were you all talking about last night? What does it mean to be a straw?' And he explained that a straw was somebody who would buy a house from a white person in order to sell it to a black person, to integrate housing in an area that was segregated. I thought about this for a while. 'What does that have to do with being Jewish?' I asked. And he said, 'That's what it means to be Jewish.' That's a really important memory.

"I went to Brown in the late sixties and was very active in the antiwar and civil rights movements. The center of political activity there was through the chaplain's office, and there were two wonderful Protestant ministers, both men, whose politics flowed out of their spiritual commitment. The year after Martin Luther King was assassinated, I went with a group of students and community people to the Southern Christian Leadership Convention in Memphis. I'd never been so far from home before. I was in a very large assembly hall mostly filled with black people singing gospel. I felt incredibly out of place and left the hall to sit outside. The local organizer saw me and asked, 'What's wrong?' I told him that I didn't belong here, and he said, 'You're right. Go back to your own community and organize there.' I remember thinking, 'What is my own community?' It made me think about the extent to which my Jewishness was part of who I was.

"So I dropped out of college, lived in Israel for a while, and came back to school determined to understand what it meant to be Jewish. I graduated and went to Hebrew Union College [Reform seminary] in 1971 not because I wanted to be a rabbi, but because I wanted to learn to be Jewish. I put myself in a place where I was forced to confront what Judaism meant, and that's the study I was looking for. I had the good fortune of being smart at a time when they were looking for smart women.

"Even though I wasn't committed to being a rabbi, the school wanted me to have a pulpit. In my second year, I went to Vassar twice a month to be the campus rabbi, and it was wonderful. I decided that I didn't want to be a congregational rabbi, and from that moment on I was focused on a career in Hillel. I was ordained and came to work as the Hillel rabbi at the University of Southern California. For fourteen years I loved working with college students, the same stage of life as when my identity unfolded. I was the first student at Hebrew Union College to get credit for a noncongregational internship. I hadn't spent a day in congregational experience." The phone rings, and she excuses herself to answer it. While I'm waiting, I see a box of nutrition bars on her desk and realize that missing meals is part of her life. She returns to her story.

"I eventually got married, had children, and I couldn't find a synagogue good enough for my kids. So a few of us created our own *chavurah* [fellowship] to educate our children. That worked fine when we all had only one child. But when more came along, it was clear we couldn't do this on our own. The older I got, the more I realized that the synagogue was central to the creation of Jewish identity, and if you don't have synagogues that work, it's going to be hard to have a Jewish community that can sustain itself. It was time for me to try to see what it was like to be a congregational rabbi.

"Right around that same time, Temple Emanuel was looking for a rabbi. I threw my *kippah* into the ring, as it were, and much to my surprise, and I think to theirs as well, they chose me. The congregation had gone through incredible turmoil, an unbelievably split congregation that had almost been acquired by another congregation. So there I was, at forty-four, senior rabbi of a major metropolitan congregation and the first woman to be selected to head a congregation of over a thousand families. It's been an incredibly interesting ride. We have a day school, an early childhood center, a religion school, and it is in every way a typical mainstream Reform congregation. The Reform movement is changing, and I'm part of that change." A buzz saw being used for the remodeling of the waiting area drowns out conversation and illustrates her point.

"I'd been in Los Angeles a long time and was known as a politically

A *kippah* is a head covering. Also known as a *yarmulke,* it may be worn by both men and women in non-Orthodox denominations as an expression of honoring God.

correct feminist and a politically progressive person. This congregation didn't set out to hire someone like me; they were looking for someone who could heal the congregation. So it wasn't exactly a good match—a matchmaker would never have put this congregation and me together—and yet the match has worked extraordinarily well. The board was able to see that my skills were transferable.

"Still, issues of gender have been on the table from the minute I arrived. We have families from more traditional backgrounds than Reform, and some of them have resistance to women in religious leadership positions. Many people said that they were glad that I was here, they respected me, but personally they weren't comfortable with a woman rabbi." Geller appears unflappable, rational, and calm. She speaks matter-of-factly about almost everything, and I think of how reassuring her persona would be as a lawyer, doctor, or stockbroker. No doubt she comes to her work with passion and commitment. Yet, her intensity is private, and she doesn't appear to be someone with whom you must walk on eggshells. Many must have felt that her steadiness was the ingredient needed to heal and stabilize the congregation.

"I was middle-aged when I came to Temple Emanuel, thank God. I came with a strong sense of who I was; I am exactly the same person I was before I took this position. So, at this stage of my life, I hear criticism differently from the way a newly ordained twenty-

Reform Judaism emerged in the early-nineteenth century as a movement that would help Judaism be part of a modern world. Reform Judaism ordained the first woman rabbi, Sally Priesand, in 1972. Other denominations of Judaism include:

Orthodox Judaism, which teaches that Torah was divinely revealed to Moses at Mount Sinai and that *halachah,* Jewish law, is both divinely guided and authoritative. Thus, no law stemming from Torah can be tampered with even if it displeases modern sensibilities. Orthodoxy often rejects more modern forms of Judaism as deviations from divine truths and authentic modes of Jewish life.

Conservative Judaism, which began in the mid-nineteenth century as a reaction to what its founders perceived to be the Reform movement's radicalism. It teaches that while Torah as a whole is binding and that much of Jewish law remains authoritative, new ideas and practices have always influenced Jewish beliefs and rituals and should continue to do so.

Reconstructionist Judaism, which was founded in the 1930s and is the most recent of the Jewish movements. The founders believe the essence of Judaism is defined as embodying an entire civilization and not only a religion. At the core of this civilization is a people who have the authority and the responsibility to "reconstruct" its contents from generation to generation.

six-year-old might. When people say that they don't believe in women rabbis, I understand that they're telling me something about themselves, not me. I don't fret, I don't have low self-esteem, but I think if I'd taken this job right out of school, it would have killed me.

"Because I was a grown-up when I took this position, I saw it as an opportunity to experiment with what it means to create a congregation that can be really important in people's lives. It's like a giant laboratory and an adventure with little risk. The congregation was so badly split that it was clear that if I failed, everybody would say it was impossible, and if I succeeded, it would be my success. So whatever I did was going to be okay. My success as a person is not tied to my success in this job; I don't think I can be beaten down by the job because it doesn't have that power. If the leadership of the congregation thinks that I'm not the right rabbi at some time in the future, I'll find another job. I'm not worried about it. So I have freedom, and it's really fun."

The seminaries teach you never to refer to the work as a "job." It's a vocation, a calling, a pulpit, or a position. But the truth is that you are getting a salary, you have to answer to people, and you're expected to fit a job description. Calling her work a job reveals that, despite her strong leadership, Geller wears the mantle of authority lightly. By the look of the rabbi's offices, her predecessors took themselves very seriously as consecrated leaders of a large affluent congregation. Rabbis in such places are often inaccessible to their communities: an appointment with them may take six weeks to schedule. Not so with Rabbi Geller. When I recommended her to friends to officiate at their marriage, she saw them soon after they called and spent almost two hours with them.

She continues, "It was fun to be Hillel director, really fun to be the director of a civil rights organization, and it's fun to be a rabbi of a congregation. It's a lot of work—more than I thought it would be—the schedule is quite relentless, but everything that I do, really, is either fascinating or moving. It's great! I get to work with people of all ages, and I matter in people's lives. I get to think about things, and I get to read books, and I get to meet interesting people. I couldn't really imagine a more interesting life." If anything is going to get people to be joyfully Jewish, it's being around someone who loves the tradition and serving its people.

Geller says, "To be successful you need to be a good teacher, you need to be a good public speaker, you need to be a good political organizer, you need to be

Shabbos is the Yiddish word for Shabbat, the Jewish weekly day of rest, observed from sunset on Friday until nightfall Saturday. Shabbat was established as a day of sanctity and blessing on the seventh day of Creation (Genesis 2:1–3).

smart, and you need to be able to work with people. The hardest part of the job is the relentlessness of it. I never have time to prepare; I go from one thing to the next without a second between. I don't get to eat what I ought to be eating." My eyes stray to the nutrition bars, and she nods. "From the outside I look like a workaholic, although I don't see myself that way. The work isn't hard; it's long.

"My leadership style is collaborative, which I think has to do with gender. I've been lucky enough to find good colleagues. The Reform model with a senior rabbi and rotating assistants every three or five years is not what I want. We were really lucky to find a terrific assistant rabbi right out of school, and I hope he stays. At an appropriate time, I'd like him to be named co-rabbi, and when I retire he becomes senior rabbi. We share things. This is a different model. We split the B'nai Mitzvah. We alternate leading Shabbat services, so I have Shabboses and he has Shabboses at home.

"I get to have a life, take real vacations, and I have confidence that this is a team effort. Lay people are as much a part of the team as professionals, and the cultivation of lay people to be teachers and leaders is a high priority. It's an important part of my strategy for building the kind of congregation I want. The more people who can lead services, and the more people who can teach Torah, the more people who can mentor B'nai Mitzvah kids, the richer this community is, and the more flexibility I have to do other things that are challenging to me. My vision of the congregation satisfies my personal needs and my spiritual needs for a certain kind of community.

B'nai Mitzvah are the life-cycle ceremonies that mark adolescents' entry into religious adulthood and responsibility. For boys, bar mitzvah occurs upon reaching age thirteen, when, according to Jewish tradition, males are liable for their own transgressions. Bat mitzvah, the life-cycle ceremony for girls that was introduced in the twentieth century, is held at age twelve or thirteen. According to Jewish law, females attain religious adulthood and responsibility upon reaching age twelve and one day.

"Five years ago, this congregation was four million dollars in debt. It was close to being bankrupt. There was deep tension between the day school and the synagogue community.

Literally meaning "teaching" or "direction," Torah is the name for the Jewish sacred text, also called the Five Books of Moses, which includes Genesis, Exodus, Leviticus, Numbers, and Deuteronomy. The term is also used, by extension, to mean all Jewish sacred literature and all the commentaries and interpretations of the Torah.

Miraculously, we paid off the bank loan; nobody thought it was possible. And the way we were able to do it was by going person to person and raising money, not in millions of dollars. These gifts have been considerably smaller than any fundraising consultant would have predicted, but we've been able to get people to buy back a vision of a community that is compelling and meaningful. So now we're out of debt. Fundraising is harder for me as a woman than it is for a man. My male colleagues tell me it has to do with being a rabbi, not a woman—but no matter. We succeeded in the campaign in spite of it.

"Not everyone likes everything, but everybody knows that they can come and talk to me. After my first High Holidays here, I told the head of the Union of American Hebrew Congregations that I was sending out a survey to see what people thought of the holidays. The response was, 'Are you crazy? You don't want that feedback.' We did it anyway and got a stunning percentage of respondents; and every year now we send out a High Holiday survey. It's about continuing to grow and get better. The message is, 'I care what you think.' This has to do with gender. I don't think people necessarily talk to their male rabbis the way they talk to me; they are comfortable criticizing me, and I find that to be an advantage. I'm thick-skinned, and I don't personalize what I'm hearing. That gives people a sense of involvement and safety with their feelings.

"When I took this job, it was a news story, because until I took this position, no woman had broken the stained-glass ceiling. But the real news story was you can get to be the senior rabbi of Temple Emanuel by starting as a Hillel director. The real story is if you follow your dreams, if you do what makes you happy, you're going to end up in surprising places. You have to do what you want to do. Don't do anything because you 'should.' Women who are working part-time or doing chaplaincy, or nontraditional stuff—that's terrific.

"Women are searching for intimacy, balance, and empowerment in their careers. Many women rabbis who chose alternative paths perceived that you couldn't have these things in a large congregation. The truth is, you can find it in any setting. And when you're the senior rabbi of a major congregation, you get to decide what you're going to do. Some of my women friends who were assistant rabbis had such a bad experience that they couldn't imagine being senior rabbis. But it's really fun to be the senior rabbi! You can create an environment where there is intimacy and empowerment and balance." It helps to be good-looking, articulate, savvy, straight, and confident, I think to myself. "I get to help make this a congregation that I would like to join," Geller says. "That's the bottom line for me. I want the prayer to work, the learning . . . I have high standards. I wasn't satisfied before I came to Emanuel. It *is* possible for a synagogue to be a place of compelling worship. The intellectually interesting part of the work is how to get there. It has to do with a synagogue that's passionate, activist, and visionary: this is from our mission statement. When you can articulate it, you're part way there.

"We're part of the Experiment in Congregational Education, a synagogue transformation project of the Rhea Hirsch School of Education of Hebrew Union College–Jewish Institute of Religion. It has involved lots of congregants participating in discussions about synagogue life. These discussions led to four areas of concentration. One was to become a warm and welcoming congregation; second, to think about learning in a different way; third, to create compelling and meaningful worship; and fourth, to find ways to keep our young people involved. Now we have four

The Experiment in Congregational Education (ECE) was established in 1992 to make synagogues into congregations of learners, and to help synagogues become more consciously deliberative and develop shared leadership within them. After starting their work with two congregations, the ECE soon was working with a dozen more, making it a leader in the field of synagogue change. The work of the ECE is chronicled in *Becoming a Congregation of Learners: Learning as a Key to Revitalizing Congregational Life* and *The Self-Renewing Congregation: Organizational Strategies for Revitalizing Congregational Life* (both Jewish Lights Publishing), the first two volumes in Synagogue 2000's Revitalizing Congregational Life series.

working groups, and over the next two years they will look at other synagogues to find programs that work, and we'll test out ideas.

"The alternative minyan [a prayer group of at least ten people] on Shabbat morning is already part of creating compelling worship. I wanted an alternative to the 'Bar Mitzvah service.'" Geller is referring to the standard synagogue's Saturday morning service being primarily a Bar Mitzvah celebration instead of Sabbath worship. "One of my great strengths is that I am not threatened by other people's competence. I hired two really talented rabbis, a husband and wife, who created an incredible service. After they left, it continued. I lead it, my colleague leads it, and sometimes lay people lead it. It began monthly, and now it's weekly. We're experimenting with a meditation service once a month now. Some will like it, and some will say, 'What's going on here?' It will take a long time to change the way the main service is structured, but if you create a compelling alternative, the alternative affects change everywhere.

"I'm starting my sixth year, and for the first time I feel things are starting to change. I didn't know how hard change was. It's clearly turning; it's exciting but it's slow. It's a group of people working together, clergy and laypeople, not me doing it on my own. It's easier to create a synagogue from scratch than to come into an existing synagogue, like this, and transform it. Many are here not because of me but because their ancestors' names are on these walls. I want to make a difference in people's lives and create a place of community and spirituality, as opposed to simply providing Hebrew school, Bar Mitzvah, a funeral. But some want what they had twenty years ago, and I want to honor the people whose ties go back much further than mine."

The alternative Shabbat service that we attend reveals how much Reform Judaism is changing. Once upon a time, a man might be told to remove his *kippah* at a Reform service; yet, the room of two hundred mostly middle-aged adults is filled with men and women wearing prayer shawls and head coverings. Laura wears both. Her service is as traditional as that found in any liberal Conservative congregation, and many of the assembled are professional, knowledgeable Jews who twenty years ago would not have set foot in a Reform service.

Rabbi Geller appears to be the model of a Reform rabbi, dignified and well spoken. She also wants to bring a little emotion into prayer. Music is the best agent, and Laura closes her eyes and sways to the melody, perhaps as an invitation to the others to enter the prayer. Participatory song, prayer, and study distinguish the service from the main sanctuary's service. She facilitates gracefully with learned laity; they don't need fiery genius and instruction. They need someone like themselves: a little more in the head than in the heart, but willing to experiment. As she takes risks in reaching for the spirit, so do they.

"Coming to this congregation and struggling to create community where I can pray has liberated my own spiritual development. Also, as you get older, necessary losses also open up the spiritual realm. So I'm on a spiritual path, and yet being a rabbi here sometimes gets in the way of that path—I'd like to be home for Shabbos dinner! Still, the counseling I do around spiritual issues, creating ritual—all this has helped me clarify my own vision. I pray before I eat, I keep kosher, so I have daily practice. But between being a mom, a wife, and a congregational rabbi, finding time for friends, trying to exercise, it's a struggle. My next challenge is daily private prayer, and I haven't found a way to do that."

I ask her about other areas of incompletion in her life. "When I look back at my life and feel great about a lot of things I've done, the one sadness is that I haven't had time to write. I've done a lot of work around new rituals, such as baby namings for girls, and I wanted to write a book about it. Meanwhile, zillions of wonderful books have come out, so I don't need to write that book any more."

Only when I ask about the juggle of family with vocation is there a hesitation, perhaps a reluctance to talk about it. About her two children she says, "I have two children, a son who is seventeen and an eleven-year-old daughter. They don't come to services that often, and my husband is not particularly involved in the synagogue. He comes on the High Holidays and on important holidays, sometimes on Shabbos. That's okay. He's a lawyer and a writer. If my kids had grown up in the synagogue, if it were my social life, it would be much more of an issue. My kids go to public school, and their lives aren't so constrained by my work except that I work so much."

Rabbi Geller's marriage ended in divorce. Half the women whom I interviewed were in relationships, and they spoke with pride and gratitude about the support they received from their families. Those who were single described the blessing of being able to give all to the work that is endless. There are drawbacks to everything. According to Freud, love and work are the goals for everyone. In the spiritual realm, sometimes those two become one, and when celebrity is added, it becomes even more difficult to maintain a personal life.

Rabbi Geller recently married again, this time to a man who shares her spiritual commitments and is professionally the director of a national Jewish organization devoted to the nuturing of Jewish culture. "Having a partner who not only supports me but shares my passion is an extraordinary blessing. He is my *chaver* in the true sense of the word—my study partner and my intimate friend. Being with him has helped me go deeper in my spiritual life and has helped me become a better rabbi."

THE REVEREND DR. SUZAN JOHNSON COOK

When I asked the *New York Amsterdam News,* the primary newspaper for black New Yorkers, for the name of a woman spiritual leader, the religion editor gave me one name: "Suzan Johnson Cook. She's the pastor of Bronx Christian Fellowship Church, and she's red hot." He was right. Dr. Cook's résumé covers six pages of exceptional achievement in the past twenty years. Among her many distinctions is having been appointed in 1997 by President Clinton to the historic President's Initiative on Race. As one of seven appointees, she was the only religious leader and the only black woman.

Selected by *Ebony* magazine as one of the top fifteen women in ministry nationally, she made *Time Out* magazine's short list of New York's top five preachers. She is the first black woman to be elected to an American Baptist Church in its two-hundred-year history, and as the New York City Police Department's chaplain she is the first woman and the first African American to take the position. She now holds the distinction of having been elected by her peers and colleagues as the first woman to head the Hampton University Minister's Conference, the largest conference of African-American clergy in the world, in its eighty-eighth year.

At her first pulpit in 1983, she revived the oldest Baptist church in Manhattan, the Mariners' Temple, from a congregation of sixty elderly black people living in Chinatown to a thousand people of all ages. She started the Hour of Power, a forty-five-minute prayer break during lunch hour at the church; and the Multi-Ethnic Center, an after-school program for children that offers volunteers' help with homework. Cook noticed that many of her members couldn't read, and she knew that if they couldn't, their children probably would be illiterate, too.

After thirteen years of serving the Mariners' Temple, she founded the Bronx Christian Fellowship in the South Bronx "to meet the needs of African-American and Latino professionals and their families," as its brochure says. The church also takes care of its many poor single women, single-parent families, and the emerging middle class. Since high school, Reverend Cook's dream had been to pastor a congregation that would come alive in a faith setting, with people who were excited about God in their lives, not people who came to church out of obligation. This was the model she had grown up with, and she wanted to return to her roots and give something back to the community that had nurtured her. Besides, she was raising her family in the Bronx and wanted more family time than the three-hour commute to downtown would allow. The minute she announced her plans, everyone said, "What took you so long to come home?"

Whenever I want to turn up the emotional heat at my Friday night service, I remember the service at Bronx Christian Fellowship, with the imposing figure of Reverend Cook gracefully moving people to clap, sway, sing their hearts, and shout praise. In one hour she baptized six people, named a baby, gave a sermon, collected money, and had plenty of time for greeting newcomers.

Three hundred people, mostly women, wearing everything from slacks to beautiful African clothes with striking headdresses, fill the seating area, and there are a lot of children. Cook says about the gender disparity, "Women love singing and being free in the spirit, so I think it's reflective of congregational life. But we have more than other congregations, because we have a lot of single mothers and women who share apartments." Very few nonblack faces are here, but I did talk to one man, born Jewish, who loves the teachings and the spirit of the church and regularly attends services.

After a brief devotional period, Reverend Cook, dressed all in white, walks into the sanctuary and says, "We have a special guest here today! Jesus!" The congregation shouts "Amen." A trio of singers begins singing warm-up hymns. Then the pastor asks, "What day is this?" The people shout back, "This is the

day that God has made—Let us rejoice and be glad in it!" The baptistry is at the front of the sanctuary, and, one by one, people ascend in white clothes and step into the tub. They fall backward into Cook's arms and into the water; one of her hands pushes the forehead down, and the other hand, in the water, helps them up. She is a tall woman and manages to dunk six-footers as if they were babies. Each face emerges from the water with a slight smile, looking so relaxed that

Tithing is the donation of one-tenth of your annual income, either in kind or in money, for charitable purposes or due as a tax for the support of the clergy or church.

I can imagine the warmth of the water and the strength of her hands. During this time, a male singer leads the congregation in singing, "Take me to the waters to be baptized." By the end of the baptisms, Suzan is almost as wet as those baptized, and she leaves to change into a brilliant red robe with a black shirt bearing two large red crosses.

After tithing collection, a six-month-old baby boy is proudly brought to the pastor by his parents for a baby dedication. She cradles him in her arms and asks those assembled, "Whose baby is this?" And everyone answers, "Our baby!" Walking into the middle of the congregation, she cradles the baby, à la *Lion King*, on his back in front of her, and asks, "Who will care for this baby?" "We will!" is the fervent response. What a difference between this spirited question-and-answer dialogue and the flatly read responsive readings that one hears in some other congregations. The little boy, dressed in white except for a brilliant orange batik sash from Africa, is given his African name and returned to his parents.

The sermon comes near the end of the service, perhaps so that people will leave with the lesson fresh and clear. Cook says, "You've got to stick with it! That's what I'm talking about today, sticking with it. Say it with me, 'You've got to stick with it.'" The congregation repeats it several times. Using the Book of Ruth to make her point, she says, "Ruth sticks. She doesn't have to follow Naomi, but she does, because she knows that God hasn't forgotten her. And God isn't about to forget about you! So the first lesson is, hang in. The second lesson is, reach out. Hang in not just with your plan, but with God's plan. Hanging in is faith, and God rewarded Ruth. God will reward your faith, too, if you stick with it." If the Bible is a self-help book, Reverend Cook leads the workshop in getting the book to work. Giving up informs no part of Reverend Cook's consciousness. She spent her happy, high-achieving childhood in Harlem and the Bronx in the 1960s. Many, if not most, black children unfortunately did not share her experience. Her story offers us hope because it shows that even in a racist society, it is possible for a community to protect its children from being harmed by the ruling class.

We meet the pastor on Tuesday in her office at the church. Sitting behind her desk in the typically cluttered office of clergy, Cook is commanding yet relaxed. She's recently written a book called *Too Blessed to Be Stressed,* and she walks the walk. In answer to my first question, she begins: "I was born into the civil rights movement. Martin Luther King was hot on the scene, and the churches were just filled with energy and excitement. That was where we received not just spiritual foundations, but like the Jewish community, our place to socialize. That's where the building of community took place.

"My mother went to the Presbyterian church, and my father went to the Baptist church. They were nine blocks apart, and we'd go to Sunday school with my mother and then we'd go to my father's church and they'd be rocking," she laughs. "Any time a child arrived at the church, somebody would ask things like 'What are you going to do with your life? Where are you going to college? They were planting seeds of opportunity and hope for our future, and we were maybe six or seven years old. They were teaching us how to aim high from the beginning.

"We were in church with the first doctors and lawyers in the New York black community, and we could see the civil rights movement and affirmative action working. We were around achievers all of our lives, and we knew that if we failed, we'd be failing a whole community. Nobody wants that burden," she says, smiling. "When someone asks me what it's like to be a trailblazer in the ministry, I say that I have a legacy of trailblazers. What we hope is that the trails we are blazing will open the door for others to join us.

"I come from a schoolteacher mother who served in Harlem for twenty-two years. To this day, as I walk through Harlem I am Mrs. Johnson's daughter. That's the impact she had on three generations. My father opened his own detective agency, and he did well. My brother runs the business now. We started out with meager means, but we were the up-and-coming black middle class, and we understood how to save. Bankers came to classrooms—I was in the second grade—and they taught us to put something away out of every dollar.

"We were spiritually grounded and came from intact homes. I didn't know the word 'divorce' until I got up to Riverdale Country School with its upper-class students." Her first day on the bus in elementary school taught her about prejudice. She invited a girl to sit next to her, but the girl refused, saying that her mother told her that she wasn't to sit next to a black person. The girl was Jewish.

"The seeds of racism are planted at an early age," Cook says, the mother of two boys. "Every African-American person is face to face with racism at some point. You realize that there is a difference. But mostly I grew up a beneficiary, a recipient, of what Dr. King and our parents accomplished. Many worked, and I continue to achieve so that their work was not in vain." When you work not only for your own glory, you stand a better chance of keeping balance and perspective as you reap rewards. Cook knows whom she owes on earth: the people who made God manifest in her life.

"I'm trying to raise my family as my parents raised me. My husband and I are together, we have two wonderful sons, and we spend time with them. This past weekend I watched my son drive in three home runs at his baseball game! I'm not just pastor. I'm wife, mother, pastor, sister, and daughter. My life is 24/7, and there are many paradigm shifts, and it's all part of working to make a whole, wholesome life." When President Clinton invited her to the A-list prayer breakfast, she was thrilled and naturally wanted to attend, but it was the first day of school for her sons, and she didn't go.

When I looked at Dr. Cook's credentials, I was not only impressed but also surprised that she wasn't better known. The answer lies in her priorities: fame and motherhood often compete with each other. "Every August we go away," she says. "I don't talk to reporters, and my husband and I just spend time with the children. I always go back to my roots and the source of my strength, that spiritual center. My ministry is to share my life experience, to share wholeness with people who are broken, and to share family values with people who didn't have what I had. I try to touch people. I was touched, and I try to pass it on."

I ask whether the ability to offer the human touch might be a gender issue. "Nurturing is natural for us, but I'm in a traditionally male role where I bring my femininity. I'm not a female pastor; I'm a pastor who happens to be female. People look for a leader, and pastoring isn't divided by gender. They want a leader to guide them and also

Reverend Cook was the only African-American woman and faith community leader appointed by President Clinton to the historic President's Initiative on Race. The Initiative was founded in an effort to prepare the country to live as one America in the twenty-first century, and to firmly establish America as the world's first truly multi-racial democracy.

encourage them." She pauses and says, "But there are differences that have to do with my experiencing life as a woman, and that means I'm not afraid to touch. I'm not afraid to cry.

"Here's another difference. I took a sabbatical, a full year, in my seventh year of pastoring, and every guy I know in America pastoring called and said, 'Are you crazy? You can't be away from your church for a whole year! You'll lose your turf.' I said, 'I'm tired, burnt out, and human. If I don't do this, somebody's going to be dead!' I went to study at Harvard, got refreshed, came back, and the church was still there. If we're going to lead in the twenty-first century, we've got to be whole leaders. I take what I need, and I'm not afraid. I told my board, as my sons grow I'm going to want a weekend for myself, maybe once a month. I'm planting seeds here: just as you need time, I need time. Life is about balance. Recreation means re-creation. I want time to write and speak of my heartbreak as well as my joy."

"Balance" is a word I heard often in the interviews. Many clergy, including those with young families, work sixty or more hours a week. They tell their people that nothing is more important than spending time with family. They may do it because they think that they are the only ones who can do it; it's a noble form of codependence. It works like this: The hard-working minister wants everyone to love God and take the faith path seriously. The congregation likes the minister and is doing the best it can, but it isn't close to the minister's expectations; there is a lot of competing entertainment out there. The people feel guilty that they're disappointing someone who is sacrificing so much for them. If a leader leads by example, we're in trouble.

"God is certainly overall," Cook says, "but I won't do anything that will sacrifice family. I'm building a new ministry, one that I can handle as a wife and mother. When I began ministry, I was single and, as the first black woman in my denomination, I always had to be 'on' and showing that I could do the work. I had no paradigm, no model, no one even to tell me what a woman minister wore. There were no female robes!" The robe she wears is of her own design.

Explaining how she came to be the first black woman elected as a pastor in the American Baptist Churches, she says, "Mariners' Temple took me as an interim pastor, and God opened the door in the community. There was no salary because all they had left were fifteen people. Well, I come from a world where this is just another challenge, so I went door to door and said, 'I'm the new pastor. Would you come to our church?' In six months, a hundred and fifty people had joined us. The model I live by is that God rewards faithfulness. If you do something with the right heart and the right intention, and you do it long enough, something is going to happen.

"Within a year, the congregation went to the denomination and asked if I could be their pastor. I had on-the-job training right away. They'd ask, 'Can you baptize?' 'Of course!' I'd say, and then immediately call one of my advisers—older men who had taken me under their wing—and find out what to do." She says, "Whatever can be done, I can do." This trait can be the ruin of someone without boundaries, without God and her family to help her keep balance.

"As we began to have success I began to develop my own style and relied less on my advisers. I stopped imitating the male pastors and their long services. It's not the old days, when people came to church all day because they had nothing else to do. You don't have to take eternity to be eternal. It's about touching God. My television background [as a producer] taught me to cut to the chase. I also started to bring my own feminine illustrations to the pulpit. I taught about these wonderful biblical women who were obscure, never preached about. I talked about blood in a way men can't. I'd been an actress, and all the dramatic skills I had I put to work. Women were saying, 'My God, I never saw that in Scripture.' And I hadn't seen it either."

Her ministry's transformation is part of the great sea change occurring in American religion: the inclusion of women physically and metaphysically. Margaret Mead wrote, "Never doubt that a few committed individuals can change the world." The Reverend Dr. Suzan J. Cook is a committed individual.

"I'm most comfortable with a black church tradition. We can't go out and try to touch a world in which we don't have familiarity and comfort. The congregation knows that I'm one of them. I've seen more of the world than many in the community who didn't have the same opportunities I had, and I'm

In 1985, Cook founded the Multi-Ethnic Center, an after-school program for community youth and their families. The center promotes excellence in education, self-esteem, career/life skills preparation, and the building of neighborhood partnerships. Cook believes that by funneling the boundless energy of children into creative activities like drama and dance, the center has promoted inter-ethnic dialogue within the surrounding community and helped to introduce performing arts to a culturally deprived area.

hoping that I can give them something to aim for. There's a Scripture that talks about not withholding good from anyone that you can help. We have a common mission here in the church: to create safe space in the midst of a city that is unsafe, a place where drug dealers don't have a chance. What I see the ministry as is not just church and worship—that's a major component—but I see community life where wholeness can happen.

"I'd like us to be one-stop shopping here, where you come and get everything you need. I'd like to see our community have Christian psychotherapists, medical professionals, and social workers. My vision is to have a family life center with a pool and a basketball court. I want us to own franchises and be able to create jobs and create wealth, because wealth is created. Urban areas have been robbed of services, and the church must provide them. That slows the church's vision, but you must help people to have a basic quality of life.

"The major challenge right now is never having enough money to make the dreams real, and I'm a big-dream dreamer. So I delay them or downsize. This community is largely unchurched, so I'm teaching them what it means to be part of a community. It means we have a plan and we go towards it, and we've got to finance it. I have no patience for conflict, divisiveness, or chaos. If you want to go another way, this place may not be for you. Wanting something isn't enough—and everyone, including me, has had to go through struggles to get where we are. It takes discipline. To get there, we sacrifice. In a community we give up our personal agenda if we're moving toward a common goal. We have to be on the same page, and there is one leader, one chief of a community. In our tradition it is the pastor, and I'm the one who makes the final call. And I take whatever comes from making that decision. You have to be ready to put up as well as speak up; otherwise it's just a dream, and you're not ready to achieve it."

Does she ever have moments of feeling inadequate to such an awesome task? "That's not the right word," she says quickly. "Yes, there is a lot to be done, but I choose achievable dreams so that I'm not overwhelmed. With all there is to do, I can't save the world, but I can work with this community. When I was younger, I thought I wanted to be leader of the world. No, I don't feel inadequate, because I've set the boundaries we talked about before, and I don't put too much on myself. I say no to what I can't or don't want to do."

A year after we met Cook, the church stopped its frequent moves into bigger space and bought its own building on Pelham Parkway. The pastor has written a new book, *A New Dating Attitude: Getting Ready for the Mate God Has for You*, and the church now has a web site.

Dr. Nahid Angha

Finding Muslim women spiritual leaders in America was a challenge. Religions in America, including strongly patriarchal traditions, have become more inclusive of women because of the generally egalitarian attitude of our society regarding gender. Islam is relatively new to the United States, and many American Muslims have come from countries that do not share the same consciousness regarding gender. To meet Muslim women required me to look at leadership in a new way: Islam reveres study and its teachers, who include both women and men. Since leaders are teachers, I went in search of women scholars and found a good sampling of teachers. I also included Sufi leaders, because Sufism, the mystical branch of Islam, regards the pursuit of knowledge and the quest for the Divine as identical.

At the University of Creation and Spirituality in Oakland, California, where we met Luisah Teish, we met another member of the faculty, Ana Perez-Chisti, a Sufi, who gave us a book to which she was a contributor: *Sufi Women: The Journey towards the Beloved*. The collection of essays included a piece by Dr. Nahid Angha, codirector of the International Association of Sufism and founder of the Sufi Women Organization, who had also edited and published the book. A search on the Internet helped me to find Dr. Angha in San Rafael, California, a Silicon Valley town, and she accepted our invitation for an interview.

Although we met long before September 11, 2001, I thought of Angha days after the attack. I e-mailed her assurance of my friendship and the hope that she, a native Iranian, and her family would not suffer prejudice from her fellow Americans. Rafael is the angel of healing, and I felt sure that she could use some. She responded warmly, letting me know that she'd received many supportive calls from friends and neighbors. The wound of September 11 remains fresh, the Middle East is on fire, and Israel is fighting for its life. Recalling Angha's interview helps me to keep heart and mind open to Islam and its followers.

One wouldn't expect to find a mystic in an industrial park surrounded by software companies, but that is where Dr. Angha asked us to meet her. The

In 1993, the Sufi Women Organization, "a humanitarian, non-political, nonsectarian organization, was created to introduce, disseminate, honor, and acknowledge, with Divine Guidance, the contribution and service of Sufi women to the world civilization; to come together free from human prejudice to share the knowledge, wisdom, experience, and concerns of Sufi women of the past and present with our societies and time. We remember how teachers of humanity have regarded the essence of the human being, regardless of gender or color, time or place, as reverent, dignified, and respectful. Such magnificence is the gift of Being; recognizing it is learned. Sufi Women Organization has come together to support, protect, and educate for such learning."—Nahid Angha, *Sufi Women: The Journey towards the Beloved*

headquarters of her organization look like a real estate agency, but once we walk through the reception area into a large room carpeted with Persian rugs rimmed with cushions and decorative Arabic text on the walls, the space becomes quiet, focused, and serene, like Nahid herself.

Although not a tall woman, she stands regally in a full-length velvet robe that connotes her status as a teacher. When she was eighteen she received her first robe; it was her father's. Her hair, face, and hands are uncovered. When I remark that Islam seems like Judaism in the range of interpretation concerning wardrobe, she responds, "Well, Islam is similar to Judaism, but not to Christianity. And the Prophet allows us to choose our way." We follow her into the prayer room and arrange ourselves on pillows.

An author and translator of fourteen books, Dr. Angha has studied philosophy and has earned a doctorate in psychology, but that only describes the surface of a mind that began formal learning from her father when she was still a small child. In slightly accented English, she says, "One of my first memories is when I was around three years old; I think I was that age because I was sitting on a step and my legs didn't reach the next step. I was outside, beside some fruit trees, and it was sunset, not dark. My father was sitting on the next step, and he said, 'So what do you think about this God, and where do you see yourself?' I don't remember my answers, but then he told me to go to the middle of the back yard. The stars were beginning to come out, and he told me, 'Look at the stars, feel yourself attuned with all these.' Sweeping his hand across the sky, he said, 'They are looking at you, so you are as big as this whole world.'

"That night stayed in my heart; I saw myself as united with the Divine, and everything was part of the Divine. I remain conscious of being in oneness, in wholeness with the universe because of that lesson. My spirituality began not with dogma, not with God's force, but with the beautiful face of God. My father taught me to meditate by looking at the stars. When you focus on something and try to see, you concentrate the energies, and your mind does not wander. When the mind wanders, you don't see. He told me, 'Everything is looking at you the same way that you look at them, so be with honor and reverence, and be respectful.' That is how I learned."

The story helps me to know her father, and it also explains how Nahid became a teacher. This is very much like Judaism: we are commanded to honor our parents and teach our children, so that we are worthy of being revered. Her formal, deliberate speech offers a glimpse of the lost world of learned, civilized, prerevolution Iran.

"My parents were in their twenties when I was born. My birth coincided with the beginning of my father's quest for inner traveling. So I was not only his first child but also his first spiritual student. He taught me how to be and how to stand for my being; he led me and guided me along the road towards achieving the knowledge of the self as a doorway towards greater understanding. Seeing my searching soul, he would take me to the gatherings of his father to listen to his teachings. My grandfather also had a great influence in my life, giving me treasures that can only be given by a teacher. My father, a Sufi master, came from a family of scholars who traced their lineage back to the Prophet of Islam. He was a very respectful man, who had the ability to think as a free spirit about all religions and all people. This had great influence on my way of looking at the world and religion. If this great, beautiful Being gave someone the chance of life, everybody has to honor that life."

Wouldn't the world be amazing if every Muslim lived by this precept and every Jew lived by "You shall love your neighbor as yourself"? Wouldn't everything be very different if each of us lived the Holy Scriptures of our respective paths? Meeting Nahid and other women in the book leads to a fantasy of getting them all together, all these spirits who speak about loving and healing, to see if they can sound the wake-up call that the world needs if it is to survive.

Nahid continues, "My father was reverent to Buddhism because he saw the religion as a divine message to humanity as a path of ascent without limitation of gender." Amazing, because Islam regards Buddhism—and Christianity, for that matter—as pagan. "The Qur'an has no limitations for women," she says. "It is open for all with purity and heart; the Prophet was one of the greatest advocates for women's rights, human rights. Muhammad made the pursuit of knowledge and religion everyone's responsibility, regardless of gender, color, or nationality.

"This is not practiced in some Muslim countries. Iran is Muslim, but it wasn't fundamentalist, as it is now. What Islam is and what politicians practice are two different things, as Judaism taught by Moses is very different from politicians in Jewish or Christian communities. Some Muslim countries are just taking advantage of the teachings and turning them to their own benefit; they call it Islam. The true Islam teaches people to learn, to understand, and to serve."

She turns to speak of her aristocratic maternal grandmother. "Though she was not a Sufi, she supported, understood, and respected Sufism; her mansion remained a place of Sufi gatherings for many years. She was strong, educated, wealthy, and forward-looking for her times. As with many women, she helped to build foundations for civilization and was an architect behind history, yet to the majority she was unknown." The tone of her quiet voice hints at protest. "From her I learned the art of living gracefully, and also being firm and strong in a world controlled by men."

Playing with the catch on her robe, she says, "Being born into a spiritual family has its blessings and blessings in disguise. While it's very suitable for my personality and mentality, there are sacrifices I inherited at birth as a practicing Sufi. From childhood, you're always trying to be older than you are. And when your father is a great teacher, you share him with many people. You hope that those people will know that you're sharing, but they don't always know. These experiences make you mature. You learn to overlook small things that aren't important. You set goals for yourself at different ages, and that becomes your own mission. I saw how hard my father worked and learned that you have to work hard.

"In 1994 I was invited to speak at an international Sufi symposium. I sat in the circle of *zikr* and led a *zikr* together with all my spiritual brothers; perhaps it was the first time in our history that a woman sat together with all those imams [prayer leaders] and scholars. I set my ground immediately by letting them know that I was a

A *zikr* is a Sufi ritual devoted to praising Allah and is intended to bring forth an ecstatic state.

scholar, and that's how I created an equal relationship with them. That's number one. Second, believe it or not, these men really trust their mothers, and a woman represents that. A mother is the first teacher of humanity and has taught every world leader. The Prophet said, 'Paradise lies under the feet of mothers.' No man has that power over another man. I can turn to one of these huge imams with a million followers and say, 'Come on, please, you have to do it,' and he listens. A man can't do that with another man, because it wouldn't look right."

When I ask about women's leadership possibilities in Islam, she retorts, "Who said women cannot do certain things in Islam? A woman can be an imam, and there are many women leaders in Islam and Sufism. There have been many powerful women and their names eminent, but they are mentioned only as foot-notes. It's not the religion; it's the society. It's always been this way in different cultures and times. I don't know the basis of it—rivalry, competition, maybe—but women are put aside. My mission is to make sure that the teachings, services, and contributions of Muslim women are known. That's why I write, teach, and pub-lish: it's all about education. I want a daughter a thousand years from now to know that there were women teachers who struggled and survived.

Gesturing to the headquarters, she said, "What we do here is have tradi-tional Sufi gatherings. We have teachers for meditation, Islamic studies, and I teach Sufism." Nahid is active in a variety of interfaith groups, including being the International Association of Sufism representative at the United Nations, a nongovernmental organization and Department of Public Information.

"The project that I care most about these days is the international dia-logue among Sufi women that I've been able to create through the Internet. We talk to each other, and when their media is distorted, we verify it from women outside our countries. Sometimes we collectively take action as an international community. A few years ago, when there was rioting in Indonesia, people were killed, homes destroyed, and businesses lost. We sent e-mails all over the world requesting contributions. All trusted the mission and gave generously. They repaired an orphanage and took care of old people, no matter what their religion was. I'm more human-focused than religion-focused these days." That may be another shared char-acteristic among women.

In Islam, women may not lead prayer in the presence of men.

"We don't know each other face to face, only by name, and still we trusted each other to do something useful for a group of women. One thing happened—and I try not to cry when I tell it. On the night of the riot, one of our women was trapped in her office. She sent a message for help to our dialogue all over the world: 'I'm trapped, people are fighting, and tanks are everywhere. My son is in the university, and the revolution took place there tonight.' Before you knew it, she received thirty messages offering help, suggestions, and prayers for her son. The next day she wrote that her son was all right. This kind of support makes you think that you are not alone, because many friends in the world care about you. Some of these women are not even Muslim."

Nahid, along with her parents, husband, and children, came to California in 1979. "The revolution in Iran began with a few incidents here and there, and we didn't think it would last that long. We had a house in England, and we thought we'd go there and wait. Then the revolution became very serious—you cannot imagine what it is like to live in a war zone. The mentality of the mob is a dangerous thing.

"We left England and decided to come to California, where we had a few friends. All the time we kept hoping that the next week, the next month, the next year, we would return. Twenty-two years have passed. I no longer wish to return any more, because my memories are good, and if I go back, I'll see them destroyed. Life is too important, and it passes so fast, that you must not turn back. You must make the best decisions, live to the fullest possible, and you can't waste time."

The importance of life and how it cannot be wasted comes up again and again. Dr. Angha's husband is a professor of philosophy and Islamic studies, and her daughters both have advanced degrees, one in psychology and the other in Islamic studies and law.

"We were the first Sufis coming from the Middle East here. In a few years my husband and I established a publishing company that became a good venue for Sufism. We introduced the ideas and became the voice for many other Sufis. Now we're quite known. But don't think I'm satisfied yet. I wouldn't work so hard if I were satisfied! I must educate many of my brothers and sisters, children, fathers and mothers, to become leaders and to continue this work of human rights. I don't want the whole thing to depend upon me and end with me." The day is short and the work is long, and Dr. Angha pushes all that work with her.

"When I was gathering the essays for the book about Sufi women, I kept calling this one woman for her essay. She'd always apologize, saying she was so busy. One day I said, 'When we all go to heaven and we're having coffee and cookies with God and talking about the good times on earth, no one on earth will know that you existed.' She sent the essay the following week," Nahid says, laughing. "I wish there were ten of me. Sometimes I work on three or four computers at the same time. But I also believe that the East can teach us the need to go deep, to wait, and to stop running. Much of the problem in this world has to do with so much doing and producing. We don't have time to listen or to speak our truth."

After a full day in the office writing hundreds of e-mails and editing manuscripts, she says, "When I get home, I'm not tired actually. I don't get tired of anything I do for Sufism. In the evening I spend time with the children and my husband. Sometimes we discuss ideas or pray together. We take turns leading, but I always refuse—I want to be in the background. Women are teachers of leaders; they teach future leaders. Only we have the nourishment of life; we have been given life to take care of. Nothing is higher than being a teacher. Some leaders are teachers, like my father. The teacher knows and gives information selflessly, while the leader takes the information and applies it to action. I always want to be called teacher, not leader. I want to motivate, encourage; I don't need to stand in front of anyone. This is a personal preference. Some people call me a leader, but I hate that word; it often comes with ego. I'd like to live in a peaceful world, and for that I don't want to call myself a leader. You have to serve in this life.

"Every human being deserves to be protected, and we are all responsible. We can't live in our little homes and say, 'I have what I need, I have a good life.' That is not a definition of humanity. Women need to be empowered to do this work."

Gay sets up the portrait, which Angha accepts with stoic forbearance. Afterward, she invites us for tea. I almost say no, but when I see a samovar and painted glass teacups in the kind of room that usually has a coffee machine and Styrofoam cups, I change my mind and imagine myself, just for a moment, in Tehran. She is unhurried and relaxed. I gather a few of her publications to buy. She refuses money and insists that the books be gifts. She asks me about the project, and I tell how much I'd like to get these women together. She nods and says, "I'd be glad to help organize it." We're working on it.

Rebbetzin Esther Jungreis

As leader of Hineni, the international Jewish outreach center she founded thirty years ago, Rebbetzin Esther Jungreis, widow of an Orthodox rabbi and a Holocaust survivor, is doing what no other Jewish woman has ever done. Personal, dynamic, and passionate, she may be the first Jewish woman evangelist who has single-handedly brought thousands of Jews back to Judaism. *Hineni* means "Here I am." In her mission to expose Jews to old-time *Yiddishkeit* (common-sense humane values), Jungreis wants them to know that she is here, God is here, the Jewish people are here, and everyone will be delighted when they come home.

Arriving in New York from Bergen-Belsen in 1947 at twelve, Jungreis got her first taste of how little American Jews know about their religion when neighborhood children mistook her white-bearded father for Santa Claus. She became angry and shouted, "Don't you know what a rabbi is?" But her father said, "Be patient. We must teach them. We must explain. That is our task."

And that is what Esther Jungreis has been doing for forty years, beginning with her talks at her father's synagogue. In addition to speaking to two thousand young people on Tuesday nights as Hineni's spiritual leader, she writes a weekly column for *The Jewish Press* and teaches the Bible on the Hineni cable show, broadcast weekly to "eight million homes coast to coast." She has also written a best-selling book, *The Committed Life*, a wise manual for a good life. This information comes from an impressive press kit that includes an eight-by-ten glamorous photograph of the rebbetzin ("rabbi's wife" in Yiddish), many articles from newspapers and magazines, and passionate letters of gratitude from people whose lives she has touched.

Since Orthodox Judaism is the most patriarchal of Jewish denominations, her accomplishment is all the more remarkable. Jungreis travels all over the world and somehow always gets back for her weekly teaching. It takes a while before we can arrange an interview, which finally takes place in the Hineni Heritage Center on the Upper West Side of Manhattan. Built in 1989, the narrow, gray stone

Bergen-Belsen was a concentration camp used by the Nazis to exterminate the Jewish people. All of Jungreis's paternal family, except her father, were murdered in Auschwitz.

structure stands out because of its centuries-old Eastern European architecture. Inside, it is a state-of-the-art multimedia museum of Jewish history, whose exhibits conclude with a film about the Holocaust using documentary footage taken in the concentration camps.

Jungreis's office is black and white, spacious and stylish. It contains a wall of books, the Jungreis family tree (she and her husband were third cousins and had the same family name), plaques from all persuasions of Judaism, and photographs of her family, including her revered father and her late husband. She is diminutive, thin, and well dressed, but she seems fragile. Her executive director and personal assistant, Barbara Janov, explains that the rebbetzin is ill, but she knew we'd made a special trip to see her and didn't want to cancel.

After expertly threading the video mike under her jacket, Jungreis faces me, hands in her lap, poised and ready. The building is a wonderful space, and I ask if she helped in its design. "Every nook and cranny. It all began in 1972, when I was speaking at a Hillel group. I told the young people that I was very much concerned that American Jews are disappearing because of the spiritual holocaust of assimilation. They asked what I proposed to stop it. I said that I'd take Madison Square Garden and I'd bring in kids from all over the country to call for a Jewish awakening. I wouldn't go to the synagogues because these kids weren't into synagogues."

The rebbetzin and I may represent different interpretations of Judaism, but we are in complete agreement about the spiritual crisis of our time. Who can deny the increasing consumption, vulgarization, and inhumanity of our society? Jungreis talks about walking down the street and seeing a child kick his mother as if "it were the most natural thing in the world." This is a culture that worships youth and disdains age. Antidepressants abound. When Jews desperate for meaning and belonging, and hungry for authenticity, attempt to practice their tradition, they have to start at ground zero with nursery school Judaism. Even if they went to religious school, they know nothing. It's easy to lose them in their frustration and ignorance. That Jungreis has brought so many to so much knowledge is admirable.

Jungreis continues the story of her ascent. "That next Saturday night, Shlomo Carlebach was giving a concert, and he started to make up a song about the rebbetzin going to Madison Square Garden. Then he invited everyone to his house to plan it. He was kidding, but many came, and just for fun we went to the Garden to see what it would take. I signed a contract then and there, and I became terrified. How can I get the people? What am I going to say? But my father and husband kept encouraging me, and it happened. We filled the Garden for two nights in a row, and that was the beginning. Overnight, Hineni became a household word; all the outreach movements came afterwards." She smiles and shrugs slightly. "Perhaps God wanted a woman to start this organization with this lost generation." But not just any woman. Rebbetzin Jungreis is larger than life. Many may yearn to bring people back to Judaism, but few have had her success. Charisma is useful, and so is a vision of a completely moral universe.

"There isn't a continent we haven't had Hineni programs," she says. "The back of my book [A Committed Life] has my e-mail and address. The publisher questioned me because it would be demanding. Of course it is! I try to help people as much as I can. I get to sleep at 3:30 in the morning because I answer every e-mail. What's the purpose of writing and doing if you can't interact with the people—that's what you're writing for.

"I speak in secular schools. In fact, I just spoke at the largest naval base in the country. They ask me to speak about my experiences in the Holocaust and how it impacted on our time and what our responsibilities are as human beings. Everything in Torah is applicable to everyone. Morality, decency, honesty, compassion, justice is universal. I'm committed especially to speaking on college campuses, and it's never limited to Jewish students.

"Hineni has a national cable television show, but what I'd love to see would be Torah programs on all the major networks. And I'd like to see branches all over the country with people we've trained for leadership. I'd like to reach as many people as possible, and then God will show me the way. There is a quest for spirituality today, and things are moving very quickly. No one could have predicted it.

"We have fifteen hundred young single people coming every week to study Torah. Anybody can go; we don't ask for birth certificates. We ask for a donation for our events, and if people pay, good. If not, we don't make a fuss about it. We never ask anyone for a membership fee. Anyone who wants to come is welcome. We have contributors. Everyone who comes is a member."

Having children is important to a small community that worries about its dwindling population. Hineni actively encourages creating families, and she works hard to get people together. "Introductions happen in two ways. Sometimes they meet on their own, and sometimes I make the introduction. I love making matches. We have a big party once a month for all the matches made in that month. They may meet at one of our parties, and after they marry, they join the young couples group that meets once a week in different homes. We have High Holidays at the Plaza Hotel, so we function as a synagogue for these families. My two sons are the rabbis, and my son-in-law also participates.

"Since the beginning, we've always tried to get Jews involved in Judaism, not converts. We've reached hundreds of thousands over the years. We are not interested in going outside Judaism, and we're not interested in converting. I am not here, nor is any other Jew here, to make the determination of who is a Jew. You are a Jew if you are born of a Jewish mother, no matter what you do. You may be unethical, immoral, adulterous, and you're a Jew. That's it.

"There is not one page of Torah that says anything about being Orthodox or Reform. These modern-day manifestations have only created disharmony. I believe that every Jew is a Jew, we have one Shabbat, one God, one Torah, and one faith. Some of us make compromises here and there, and God loves all of us. I'm not here to judge anyone. I'm here to help everyone as much as I can, and I hope that God doesn't judge me, either. We all have to look at each other with compassion, as God looks upon us."

Born in Hungary in 1936 to an illustrious rabbinical family that claims its lineage back to King David, she says, "I grew up in a home that practiced outreach. My father and grandfather were great rabbis who saved lives in the Holocaust—I could do no less here. When we came to this country in 1947, the dynamics changed. We no longer had to save physical lives, but now we had to save spiritual lives.

"My father always had us reach out to every Jew, because a Jew seeks to connect the pieces of his identity, and all people always want to return home. The home of the Jews is Torah, and unfortunately over the years they've lost it. At Hineni, we open our doors to the spiritually orphaned, and we allow people to connect." I ask whether this might be maternal behavior.

"I don't think that my being a woman has anything to do with it, with being inclusive. Jewish leaders from the beginning have been *haimish* [unpretentious] and accessible. Jewish leadership has always been warm and loving. The king of Israel counted

the people by their names. Can you imagine that? God knows me; God knows my name. That was thousands of years ago when our leaders embraced the nation with love and concern. We were more than numbers; we were part of a family, and that way has marked our leadership. My father and my husband would shed tears if they heard of someone's suffering, even if they didn't know the person. Still, they felt their pain, and that's what leadership is about, not politics.

"I'm not a feminist. I'm a Torah teacher, and I never think about it as a woman. My priorities have always been very clear: To reach my people with Torah, to make it available to every person, so that everyone should find that wonderful gift that God gave us to elevate our lives to make a difference in the world. It doesn't matter if it's a man or a woman I'm teaching. Everyone is here to make a difference, because God didn't create the world at random. There's a purpose to my life, to your life, and you only have to discover that. Torah opens the windows through which we can discover our ultimate goal and ourselves. Everyone can bring healing to the world."

I can bring healing to the world, but not as a lesbian rabbi. Because of my respect and admiration for her work, it saddens me that she does not accept my vocation as a rabbi and my identity as a lesbian. Modern Orthodoxy has been wrestling with the issues of the ordination of women and homosexuality for several years. The rebbetzin objects so strongly to the questioning of the traditional place for women in Jewish life that she has refused to be on a panel with Blu Greenberg, a respected writer and Orthodox feminist.

During the Passover seder, the meal that commemorates the Jewish people's liberation from slavery in Egypt, four questions are asked:

Why, on this night, do we eat only unleavened bread?
Why, on this night, do we eat only bitter herbs?
Why, on this night, do we dip the bitter herbs twice?
Why, on this night, do we eat reclining?

The answers narrate the story of the Exodus from Egypt, and help to illustrate the freedom that Jews have in asking questions as they are no longer slaves.

"I've never found that being a woman is a hindrance," Rebbetzin Jungreis says. "I grew up in a great rabbinical home, and women were always highly respected. My father, bless his memory, had the highest admiration for my mother, grandmother, and me. They always encouraged my work. I never thought it was something unusual that I, as a woman, was reaching out. Maybe our society thinks what I am doing is unusual, but it has nothing to do with Judaism. We've had great leadership from women—Miriam and Deborah, for example. I have, thank God, enjoyed great support from all the rabbis, and I speak all over the world without difficulties.

"I don't subscribe to the idea of the female rabbi, because I'm very much committed to the wisdom that has been granted us from Sinai." While Torah may not say anything about women rabbis, it also says nothing about male rabbis. There is no legal reason for a woman not to be a rabbi; what she may not do is serve as a legal witness to a wedding, a divorce, or a crime, just as a minor or a gambler may not be a witness. Jungreis's clear blue eyes command attention as she asks, "What is it I would be doing as a rabbi that I'm not doing now? I'm teaching and touching hearts, bringing people back. I've never felt a stumbling block. Women can do more because they are women. A woman has a way of touching the heart and souls of people. Whatever I do, I do with God's help and with the understanding that I'm following the path of our tradition, the Torah, as it was handed down to us. I don't need a title to reach out. I'm happy with my title of Rebbetzin, and I wear it proudly.

"I'm one hundred percent a Torah Jew, totally subservient. I'm not a perfect human being, but I'm remorseful if I'm not. Every dot, every comma, every word that came forth from Sinai was given to us by *Hashem* [God]. Torah is Torah. The whole world could change; Torah doesn't change. If you want to study Torah, study with a person who hears it the best. Torah has to enter from one heart to another heart. It has to be infectious. Find someone who lives it, breathes it, believes it, and is committed to it. It's not an intellectual subject; it is a way of life. You have to live and breathe Torah. When you study Torah, you become Torah. And if you don't, you really didn't study Torah.

"At the beginning of the twentieth century, people were convinced that they would be able to resolve all their problems through education and culture. They thought science and technology would solve the ills of society. The most brilliant people on this planet Earth engineered the Holocaust. With all the therapy and psychiatry, our families are more dysfunctional than ever. We have fax machines, computers, and yet we have less time than our forefathers did. We have new incurable diseases.

"And now we are entirely lost, and people are beginning to see that the answer is only through God. That's why there is quest, yearning, even in the secular world with people like Madonna. They are seeking something, and it's from the frustration, failure, and collapse of false deities."

We attend a Tuesday night teaching. At first it seems more like the church social revived, a safe place where singles can find one another. The foyer of the staid Upper East Side Orthodox synagogue, Kehillat Jeshurun, teems with young people who have paid a bargain price of five dollars for refreshments, learning, and a place to meet people. While they wait they schmooze over coffee and cookies and check out the scene. There will also be time after the lecture to socialize. A friendly man sits at a card table, offering information about Hineni, and takes the names of those who want to be invited to a Sabbath meal. When the rebbetzin enters and sits down at a table to sign books, many people approach her, asking for a blessing for a sick loved one or advice about a job, a move, or a boyfriend. She listens carefully to each one, offering warmth and concern.

The sanctuary is nearly full. Despite her title and traditional beliefs, there is nothing old-fashioned about Rebbetzin Jungreis. She ascends

During the Passover seder, the four different characters of children are defined as: the wise, the wicked, the simple, and the child who does not know how to ask. To the questions, the Haggadah provides religious instruction geared to each child individually. The types of children can be viewed as the four types of people who approach religious life.

to the lectern usually reserved for the male prayer leader and begins the evening's teaching about Passover. She looks at those assembled with great love and says, "Why don't we all go to Israel for Passover?" Enthusiastic applause greets the suggestion, and she laughs. She speaks without notes, urgently, intimately, and with impeccable timing.

About the four questions asked at the Seder table, she says, "Questions tell you more than answers. If you're dating a girl and she asks about where your parents live, where you went to school, how much money you make, you know her values." She moves on to the four sons in the ritual and what makes for a good child. "I made my children cry," she says, surprising the listener. "My husband was a rabbi, and people came to our house all the time with their problems. One day my son saw a woman come out of the rabbi's study, her eyes red with crying. He asked me why she was crying, and I said, 'That woman has cancer and she has three little children.' When he cried for her, I told him how to pray for people who were suffering. It's not good to protect our children from what makes them human beings.

"The toddler doesn't understand why his mother is so cruel, why she takes him to a horrible man in a white jacket who injects him with needles. The mother makes him eat things he doesn't like, take baths when he doesn't want to, and makes him go to sleep when he doesn't want to. Yet, this two-year-old knows that Mommy is the most wonderful person in the world. It's instinctual. We are not even toddlers next to God; yet, just as we say, 'Mommy, hold my hand,' so we say to God, 'Hold my hand.'" The room is silent as we imagine what it feels like to be held by God.

Jews are not so much the People of the Book as the people of the commentary—and the commentary never falls into a singular

---

"People of the Book" refers to a people who have based their behavior and understanding of things upon the word of God as found in the Hebrew Bible, with the Five Books of Moses being the most important part. In their "books," Jews learn their history and their future through stories and laws. Because the text is ancient, metaphysical, and concentrated, it often needs and is always enriched by interpretation. We find the first commentaries in the Pentateuch itself, when Deuteronomy retells the earlier stories not the same, but with important differences. "People of the Book" also derives from a tradition that sees study as a holy act.

dogma. Torah has always been open to interpretation, and the rebbetzin and I rely upon different commentaries that are both correct. I see in the faces around me that she is answering profound, existential questions and setting forth practical and noble ideas for living. She knows that these people do not primarily come to learn about Judaism; they come because they long for authenticity in their lives. They leave with a new respect for Judaism, a possible date, and the hope that they are finally on their way.

THE REVEREND DR. CHERYL A. KIRK-DUGGAN

Although we interviewed leaders all over the United States, almost half were from California. Because the state is often a trendsetter, it wasn't a great surprise that many new forms of religion and spirituality began there. In addition, mainstream faiths are also undergoing revolutions. Of the eleven Christian seminaries in the Bay Area, women outnumber men in six of them, and they are gaining numbers even in the patriarchal Catholic and Baptist ministries. *Shopping for Faith: American Religion in the New Millennium,* by Richard P. Cimino and Don Lattin, based much of its study in northern California, where we found a remarkable amount of spiritual energy in churches, ashrams, and retreat centers. The Reverend Dr. Cheryl A. Kirk-Duggan, Director of the Center for Women and Religion in Berkeley, California, since 1997, figures prominently in the book as an example of the changing face of ministry.

Dr. Kirk-Duggan was one of our first interviews because she organized "Soul to Soul: Women, Religion, and the 21st Century," a national conference for women spiritual leaders representing many faiths. We hoped that she would be a good resource to connect us with many women spiritual leaders, and she didn't disappoint us. I cannot imagine how we would have found so many of our subjects without Dr. Kirk-Duggan's suggestions, which spanned the country. The conference, which took place with Senator Hillary Rodham Clinton as honorary chair, included Bishop Leontine Kelly offering a keynote preaching event, along with Luisah Teish and Janice Mirikitani as speakers.

An academic program unit of the Graduate Theological Union, which has a cooperative relationship and some joint degree programs with the University of California at Berkeley, the Center for Women and Religion is a living community of the varieties of women encountered in this book. As director of the center and an ordained elder in the Christian Methodist Episcopal Church, Kirk-Duggan is a powerful and articulate representative of women clergy. We meet her in the

Founded in 1970, the Center for Women and Religion [CWR] is an interfaith and multicultural organization that "promotes diverse women's voices in cutting-edge theological education for spiritual growth and social change." CWR provides a critical pedagogy for ministerial leadership skills, academic excellence, women-oriented resources, and academic programs, particularly in the areas of women's spirituality, women's ways of knowing and teaching, and women's culture and health.

center's office, which is in an old house a few blocks from the university's campus. The space is homey, with plants, photos, and books. Kirk-Duggan, wearing a minister's collar, gestures us into her office. Her multiple degrees include a doctorate in religion with a concentration on theology and ethics from Baylor University. Many awards and pictures, including an array of butterflies, adorn her walls.

Like Suzan Johnson Cook and Leontine Kelly, Cheryl Kirk-Duggan describes a childhood that gave her the strength to grow up strong and confident in a racist society. All three women welcome the chance to talk about their origins, not only out of pride but because their stories melt stereotypes.

"I am the eldest of three children. My mother's name was Naomi Ruth Mosley Kirk, and my father's name was Rudolph Valentino Kirk." Names that blend Bible and show business may have something to do with Cheryl's having sung her first solo in the church at the age of four. "From eleven on, I played the piano or organ every Sunday. I didn't aspire to perform or have an audience," she says, smiling, and turning up her hands. "I was born a performer.

"My parents were remarkable people. They were partners, so I never went to my father to change something my mother did. We had a lot of moral and emotional support at home, and we had a lot of family prayer. God was the head of our household. My father was the first African-American deputy sheriff in the state of Louisiana since Reconstruction. He and my mother were very active in church, so we were part of a larger community. I never knew we didn't have money because we had so much love. I don't know how they did so much for us—I even had piano lessons.

"Every Thursday, which was the day my grandmother had off—she was a maid—we would gather at her house for dinner. Her house was down the street from the church, and it was an essential part of my growing up. We had rituals with her, like moving from the kids' table to the adult table, and we learned social graces. We set the tables and shared in cleaning up."

As in-residence and core doctoral faculty member and professor of theology and womanist studies at Berkeley, Kirk-Duggan teaches graduate courses, and her students learn more than what is in the book. "I grew up with self-assurance, which sometimes overwhelms people. My persona gets misinterpreted for self-absorption, which is ultimately cutting oneself off from God. My life is set in the opposite context. My reality is about where God is calling me to be in a given moment. That's why I took this job. Clearly, God was calling me to be here and do this work.

"When people think I'm self-absorbed, it's usually because they're projecting their issues about themselves onto me. And I'm not going to apologize, and I get on my students about that. I tell them not to write in their papers 'I will attempt . . .' You can say 'I will explore, critique, or examine.' 'I will attempt' says 'Please have mercy on me because this may not be up to your standards, and I'm just a pitiful little student,'" she says in a child's voice. "I want them to work and quit doing the traditional female apologizing."

I ask how she feels about current trends in religion. "I have mixed feelings about the feminization of religion. On the one hand, it grieves my heart that there are women who feel called to do ministry and their faith traditions won't allow it. I also respect that many women need to stay in those traditions, because that is where they feel nurtured and where their own sensibilities lie." Kirk-Duggan touches on an important point that Mary Farrell Bednarowski makes in *The Religious Imagination of American Women*: "Women write of the many ways their traditions have been more imprisoning than liberating, more stultifying than transforming, more death-dealing than life-giving. Yet, they write as well of their love for their traditions, their almost visceral connections with them, and their hopes for the transformed futures of these same communities."

While women may feel ambivalent—even angry—toward their religions that are patriarchal and hierarchical, they may decide not to leave but to fight for change within. They may be the hidden revolutionaries, the

Founded in 1962, the Graduate Theological Union is a consortium of nine theological schools, representing the Roman Catholic and Protestant traditions, three institutes of Jewish, Buddhist, and Orthodox studies, and seven research centers.

quiet women like Bishop Kelly who don't give up or go away but continue to press for a worthy place within their traditions.

"It's great that women are taking more leadership roles as heads of congregations," Kirk-Duggan continues, "because their ministries focus on women's needs. On the other hand, at one time men were secretaries and social workers were men; now they're mostly women. When a vocation becomes primarily women, it is no longer held in the same esteem. What will happen if many more women become clergy?

"Of course, a person's gender should not affect a job. If a woman is called to do it and she has the gifts and graces that allow it, why not? But I don't want a woman to do something just because she is a female. The point is not about getting women here for the sake of getting them here, but for the sake of getting the most qualified, most passionate person for the job."

Kirk-Duggan, ordained in an African-American denomination that has allowed women ministers for decades, acknowledges that many black churches don't want a woman behind the pulpit. "The world is spinning out of control, and people want church to be safe and unchanging. They say, 'A man baptized me. A man married me. My parents were baptized and married by a man. By God, I want a man up there in the pulpit!' Or, for some women, that male figure behind the pulpit is the husband they fantasized about and never had, or the son they never had.

"There is a sexual energy people don't want to talk about, but it's there. It's 'I desire you but cannot have you.' That makes the preacher more desirable and allows women to fantasize." Her words spill out. "It's fascinating! Notice the mannerisms of some male preachers. There is posturing, flexing in that pulpit—with or without the robe on. It's a sexual thing, and when you change who is behind that pulpit, you change the dynamic, which takes away the romance, the myth." Maybe it's time for another Audrey Hepburn

"**W**hat we have clearly become is an advocate for women in religion and in serving as leaders. We make conscious the oppression of women and hope that education will transform that. At first the issue was only gender; now we deal with race, class, and whatever else adds to the oppression of women. We help men to see that this is not only women's issue, because it is a societal issue. We do programming, teaching, and advocacy." —Cheryl Kirk-Duggan, *Soul to Soul*

playing a nun or, better yet, a minister to make women clergy as desirable as their male counterparts. "Some don't want a woman there because of their reading of Scripture. When Paul says women shouldn't speak in the church, let's remember that early Christians were Jews and Greeks; in both societies women were second class, and were not taught to read.

"**O**ne thing drawing women to the ministry is they are socialized to be caring and nurturing toward other people. So it's a natural. Many are also drawn by deeply felt political commitments to revise social institutions, like churches and synagogues, that have been entirely designed and administered by men, and to wonder what these institutions would look like if women had thought them through."—Margaret Miles, *Shopping for Faith: American Religion in the New Millennium*

"To those who think that women can't serve because they don't look like the Father, I go back to Scripture and point out that nowhere is there a picture of what God looks like. God is not a white male with a beard sitting on a throne taking people's names and writing down everything they do. And people get so hung up on the maleness of Christ, or the maleness of his apostles! If you go that route, then all the priests in the church should be Jewish and in their thirties. Jesus was male, so you have to be male to serve, some might say, but Jesus broke rules. Martha wants Mary to come back and help her clean, but Jesus says no, she can learn.

"Women outnumber men in nearly all religious congregations. Women have always had a lot of power, but some don't know it, and some are afraid of it. This is not a new phenomenon. A woman would have an idea, and she would give it to her husband, who would introduce it as his idea at a temple or church board meeting. And the response would be, 'Oh, what an excellent idea.' The woman would suck it up and never say, 'Guess what? That was my idea.' Things are changing—but not everywhere. What would happen in one of these churches that don't ordain women, if on Sunday the women didn't show up or stopped paying their tithes. Just watch how quickly a new revelation would come down from above!" she laughs.

"Women are more willing to deal with controversial, difficult issues. For example, I have no problem talking in the pulpit about sex. I say that sex is good if you believe that God made people good. At the same time I say to the boys and girls, unless you are ready to be a parent and in a committed relationship, then you don't need to be sleeping with anybody! And to the parents I say, a penis is a penis and a vagina is a vagina. Don't teach your children that sex is nasty, because the curiosity of children is always there. I've had male colleagues say that you couldn't pay them to talk in the pulpit about sex. But congregations give women permission to talk about it.

"It's because the very presence of a woman raises the subject. I am an icon-oclast and instigator. We are often in so much denial in our lives. Look at how we raise our children. We teach our boys that men don't cry, to suck it up when you're hurt, and we teach our girls that it's okay to cry; they get the idea that they can get their way when they cry. And the boys learn as toddlers that they have no right to feel pain or share their feelings. Then we wonder why, at thirteen or fourteen, they go off shooting folks with Uzis. What are they supposed to do with the rage? They have twelve years of pent-up anger!

"Women can talk about feelings, and that's the way relationship and empathic response is developed. I taught a class in entrepreneurial ministry. We talked about male and female leadership. Many—both men and women—described male leadership in terms such as forthright, even negative, and the other as more nurturing and feeling; we call it positive. We started to see that good leadership requires a blending of the two. For example, some women are earth mothers who try to love and to give to everybody, which is clearly not possible.

"Like everyone else, I'm trying to squeeze in a twenty-eight-hour day. We can't do it all, and we have to choose our burdens. A friend of mine, a woman minister, came to me saying that she was feeling heavy with the many burdens of her con-gregation. I suggested that she imagine each issue, each problem, as a brick, and to take that brick out of herself and put it in a box. Then she should take the box and put it on the altar. She felt a hundred times lighter after she did this exercise."

In addition to being the director of the Center for Women and Religion, Kirk-Duggan is an associate pastor at Phillips Temple Christian Methodist Episcopal Church, where she preaches. "My whole life has been interfaith," she says. "I was ordained from a Presbyterian seminary, my faith is Christian, my church is Methodist, and my husband is Roman Catholic. We share chores, and we attend each other's churches. We do not convert each other." She is step-mother to seven children.

We talk about the direction in which religion is headed. She sits back in her chair and looks toward the ceiling, and after a moment she says, "There are no good old days. The only thing that is different now is that we have more people and more technology. More crime, yes, but also more joy with more people. I wish that once a week, all the news would be good news, because I think we're programming ourselves into thinking that the world is going to hell in a handbasket. I do not see that. There are a lot of apocalyptic thinkers, and that element needs to be exposed. There is much yet that God wants to tell us, if we can stop long enough to be quiet and listen.

"I think it would be very interesting if the denominations would collapse into one. This may be the world to come in Christianity." She rocks forward and looks straight at me. "What I would love to see is that people can be mutually accepting. You have your family and I have mine; yet, we can sit at the same table, agree to disagree on certain things, and that would be okay. If we understand that God is who empowers us, then maybe in a thousand years we might have one religious institution that would be all-encompassing." The leaders independent of mainstream religion, such as Jean Houston, Iyanla Vanzant, and Marianne Williamson, are already there.

2

Exile

God said to Abraham: Go you forth from your land, from your kindred,
From your father's house, to the land that I will let you see.

GENESIS 12:1

EAVING HOME—THE PLACE OF FAMILIARITY, COMFORT, AND POWER—IS A MYTHIC requirement for heroes. Writers must also leave behind all that has been written to write a new page, and the way they do it is by looking at traditions and their texts as a child might, with no assumptions. The women in this section are writers who have changed the consciousness of both male and female spiritual leaders. Writing about religion from a historical, sociological, or philosophical perspective is not as difficult as writing about the spirit. Describing what is ineffable, nameless, and inexpressible is humbling. For some of us, we know that we are close to this realm when we cannot find the words for it. Writers like control; yet, to do this work requires letting go, a renunciation of one's own thought to listen to the voice, hidden and powerful, within the text and within oneself.

The women in this section have accomplished the profound task of finding the words to bring forth a new vision of spirit. Like Abraham and Sarah, they have been called to go out of the expected, the comfortable, and the established and to go into themselves to imagine and uncover what has never been seen before. This is the hero's journey—to chart the new place—and these women are charting the change women are making in spiritual expression.

The Talmud, a commentary on the Torah, describes the Five Books of Moses as being written "with black fire upon white fire, sealed with fire, and swathed with bands of fire." This suggests that there are two potential texts: one with black fire and one with white fire. The black letters we understand as the text that begins "In the beginning God created heaven and earth." But what about the space between the letters, words, and verses? What divine message does it carry? Perhaps one day we will be able to read the subtle white language that surrounds the prominent black letters. One way to understand the Talmud's cryptic description is to see the black fire as masculine and the white fire as feminine. Like the white background surrounding the black letters, women's language and lives are often overlooked, unread, and rendered invisible. The women below are beginning to break the code that will include the whole voice of humanity and the sacred in all faith paths.

Luisah Teish, author of *Jambalaya: The Natural Woman's Book of Personal Charms and Practical Rituals,* is a Yoruba priestess teaching traditional voodoo practices to largely Anglo students. Lauren Artress, author of *Walking a Sacred Path,* is canon for Special Ministries at San Francisco's Grace Cathedral. Her resurrection of the labyrinth at Chartres Cathedral as a ritual and a tool for contemplation has led to the creation of thousands of labyrinths, which, like meditation, have led many into the realm of the spirit.

Dr. Sylvia Boorstein reaches beyond her tradition, which is Jewish, into Buddhist principles of mindfulness and claims both paths for herself. She is the author of several books, including *That's Funny, You Don't Look Buddhist: One Being a Faithful Jew and a Passionate Buddhist.* Elaine Pagels, professor of religion at Princeton University, is best known for thoughtful and adventurous scholarship demonstrated in *The Gnostic Gospels* and *The Origin of Satan.* Dr. Beatrice Bruteau, a practicing Christian, wrote her dissertation on "The Reality of the World in the Philosophy of Sri Aurobindo." Drawing on many traditional religious practices such as Hinduism, Buddhism, and Judaism, she offers a way for

Christians to deepen their understanding and practice. Starhawk, an early leader in the Wicca movement, has written many books about worldly spirituality that include ecology, feminism, and social action, beginning with *Spiral Dance: A Rebirth of the Ancient Religion of the Goddess*.

LUISAH TEISH

Voodoo practitioner and Yoruba priestess Luisah Teish, author of *Jambalaya: The Natural Woman's Book of Personal Charms and Practical Rituals*, has invited us to attend her class at the University of Creation and Spirituality, located above a piano store in an industrial section of Oakland, California. So many unlikely places become sacred space in America, a nation more obsessed with matters of the spirit than any other. We consecrate this country with many expressions of faith.

Born and brought up in New Orleans in the 1950s, Teish, whose name means "adventurous spirit," is conducting a five-day intensive workshop in African-American ritual. The majority of her students are white. Of the six classrooms named for sages of the world, we enter the one called Sojourner Truth, the room between Abraham Joshua Heschel and Jose Hobday. In the center of the room is a bright carpet upon which a communal shrine offers photos of departed loved ones, little figurines of goddesses, candles, shells, and special rocks.

Teish has transformed the cement-block room into a sensual tentlike space with rich batik fabric and archetypal objects that students may use for their shrine. Students sit in a circle around the shrine. Women create sacred space roundly, in either a horseshoe or a circle, rather than in straight rows. While the class begins with drums and dancing, Gay and I are invited to take off our shoes and socks. A light-skinned black man receives us into the "village" by washing our feet.

The class of fourteen middle-aged people discusses a myriad of subjects, among them voodoo ritual (the word *voodoo* means "life-principle," "genius," and "spirit" in a West African language), building a communal altar, race relations, and circumcision. Other than the two of us, there are no other Jews in the room; we hear many opinions about circumcision. Teish calls upon me to explain the reason for this "physical mutilation." I explain that it's our way of marking the people and connecting them to their first spiritual father and mother, Abraham

and Sarah. They don't buy it. I feel myself tensing, unprepared to be in the hot seat. After an exchange that suggests contention, Teish moves the discussion to another topic.

As she begins the lesson the class listens carefully to her forceful words: "People, especially in university, tend to talk themselves to death and never get around to feeling what is being talked about. My scene is having you experience the essence of what I'm trying to put forth. Then you can do all the peripheral talking around it. Dealing with sexual dysfunction is my specialty. I don't believe in hiding my sexuality, neutering myself like a nun.

"Women who neuter themselves as spiritual leaders take away their power to heal. They do it because they don't want to be identified with sex the way it is in our society. People who just accept sexuality as natural are called savage, uncivilized, and animal. We have a culture that smashes, commercializes, and demonizes it. I tell stories from the African diaspora that are about sex and romance, and you can bring your children to it. There's no vulgarity and violence."

Teish does more than condone sex; she sanctifies it and uses it to connect to the spirit. Like Starhawk, she celebrates the sexual feminine, and like Walt Whitman, she celebrates the discovery of God in the beauty of one's self.

Exultation does not remove the discipline required to become a priest. Teish explains, "To become a priest, you have a period of celibacy to solidify energy before you go through an initiation. For three months you don't look in a mirror, sit in a chair, or have sex. We don't have monks and nuns."

She chuckles. "When we try to rebirth our ancestors, we go in the opposite direction by using sex as a vehicle. In Mali, when a young man marries and makes love to his wife on the wedding night, he whispers the names of his ancestors in her ear in hopes that one of them will come into her uterus." What a wonderful way to keep loved ones spiritually alive. Imagine your great-grandchildren praying for

"**A** religion of immanence celebrates the erotic, the sensual, and passionate. It is rooted in the concerns of everyday life. The rituals and charms that Teish includes speak to our senses. They can be seen as a path of psychological transformation rooted in things that speak to us deeper than the level of words."—Starhawk, in the preface to *Jambalaya*

your best qualities to return in a new life. The class is collectively nodding, taking in new information like sponges, hungry for more affirmation of their deepest selves. She speaks the truth!

"The erotic is a component of creation. Yesterday when we were dancing, a gay man bumped up against a big woman who had twins. I instructed him to do that because he and his partner want to have children. The energy between him and the woman stimulates fertility; it doesn't mean they're going to bed together later. No. She is the vehicle of that energy, and he takes it in." The man she is talking about is smiling shyly.

"Yesterday, when I taught you the dance steps, I didn't warn about how it was going to open up energy centers in your bodies. Last night, your muscles were hurting, but more than anything, you were aware of the sensuality in the dance and how that isn't allowed in normal worship." Several students nod vigorously.

David, king of Israel, was so in love with God that he danced naked in front of the Torah. Teish brings back that old-time, passionate religion when she connects the dots between sex and spirit. However much her students may enjoy listening to Teish talk about sex, they don't want to talk about it themselves. When she asks the class indignantly, "Who taught you that sexuality and spirituality don't go together?" only two people respond.

Teish continues, "We live in a society where they want to arrest nursing mothers for nursing in public. But they don't arrest porno queens for plastering their pictures on billboards." To make her point, she cups one of her large breasts and says, "I love my body! These feed my babies!" A few students laugh nervously, and Teish smiles, knowing that she has reached them. She has real authority here—the students have given it to her—and she takes the best possible advantage of it by teaching important lessons to white people from the wisdom of a black culture.

We meet with Teish in the tiny office of the school administrator, the only space that is quiet enough for videotaping. Faculty members continually enter the room with a perfunctory knock to get something or, without apology, to ask Teish a question. In class she was a priestess. Here she is just another teacher getting special attention. Teish never shows annoyance and is even deferential and apologetic to the intruders. Would this be happening if she weren't a woman and if she weren't black?

Quieter and less dramatic, she is no longer the performer with us and gives us a behind-the-scenes look at her creative process. She speaks as a master teacher explaining how she awakens her students to their internal power. From a few feet away I notice a stain on her gold satin priestly garment. Teish looks a little tired, but she glows with the pleasure of a well-taught class. She begins, "I want to teach people how to change themselves, how to feel natural and sacred. Self-acceptance is a big part of what I do, helping people to remove those layers. Everybody's suffering under secrets—family secrets, cultural secrets, society secrets—and I put my hand in the dirt that no one else has wanted to touch, until they reach the power that's caught up in there."

Twelve-step programs have taught many of us this inescapable, liberating lesson. How she does this involves many skills. First, she is an adept psychologist, who understands the pain of her students and knows how to treat it. Second, she is a stage designer and creates a welcoming space for people to feel safe enough to speak their truth in a group. Finally, as a healer she reconnects them to their rich and powerful erotic selves, the part that creates and loves.

Teish says, "The first day of class, I asked them what they hoped to get out of the class for themselves and their communities. They said everything from 'I took this to see if African-American culture and spirituality has meaning for me as a white American' to 'I'm a white American who lives around African Americans, and I want better understanding of how to relate.' From what I witnessed in class, when they heard the question they either weren't ready to speak their truth of why they were really there—that is, to feel whole in their lives—or they had no idea that the class would touch them so intimately.

"I establish the class as a safety zone. No one gets attacked for what they say. In here every offense will be addressed. We will contemplate every question and attempt to soothe every hurt and celebrate every joy." Whether she can accomplish this is less important than that she knows what her students need. "After I learn everyone's name I need to know what their family ancestry is—who's Italian or German or Jewish or Pentecostal—so I can reach into my reserve and find their definition of things. Then I explain definitions in my culture, and the real work begins.

"At the beginning of class, I give them guidelines for designing their personal ritual, and I go outside the room. They invite me in after they've done a personal opening ritual, and they add to it each day of class. As they call upon the energies through the objects they choose, they move towards their independence and their interdependence with each other. The sense of kinship you feel in the room has to do with my removing myself as the authority, and it's been building by people who don't know each other." The kinship that she describes was palpable; this was a group that would end with the exchange of phone numbers.

"They'll be in our West African 'voodoo village' for this week. I practice the voodoo of New Orleans, which blends African ancestor reverence, Native American worship, and European occultism. By teaching them voodoo, I'm showing them how to re-sacralize the everyday, and I'm bringing some kind of understanding that will lead to respectful cultural exchange."

Offering an example of her teaching, she says, "Yesterday when they danced, they talked about feeling energy coming into their bodies, and I told them they were on their way to possession. This has nothing to do with Linda Blair [the young actress whose character was possessed by a demon in *The Exorcist*] and her spinning head—nothing. This is not about a lone woman in a dark room messing with things she doesn't understand. Suddenly she is seized by the personality of a maniac and throws up split-pea soup, and shoves a crucifix in her vagina. This is ridiculous," she scoffs.

Teish calls New Orleans "the city of voodoo, a psychic seaport, like the San Francisco Bay Area. Visitors to New Orleans become 'tipsy' after a short time. 'Tipsy' is the name given to that state of mind that precedes possession, a welcome and heartwarming occurrence. It happens in communal

Magic is the art of using the forces of nature in the manipulations of symbols to manifest a desired change in people and things. As Dion Fortune writes, "Magic is the art of changing consciousness at will."

"Thealogy" is a word coined from *thea,* the Greek word for Goddess.

---

rituals where an ancestor, embodying holiness, resides in the devotee. I grew up tipsy," she says matter-of-factly. Suzan Johnson Cook speaks of "getting the spirit" in her Baptist church. The difference with voodoo is that the spirit takes the form of a loved ancestor.

Teish learned early that there was an unseen world below the surface of everyday life. It was common practice to scrub steps with red brick dust to protect the home from human and spiritual intruders. Magic abounded everywhere, especially in the word. Teish observed her mother successfully invoking rain by speaking to the clouds, heard older folk speaking of visiting "two-headed" people (that is, spiritualists), eavesdropped on old women interpreting one another's dreams. Home remedies for physical and mental illness, along with incantations and candles, were what she knew to be medicine.

No one taught Teish about these mysteries, perhaps because voodoo had become a capital crime during slavery, and it became a hidden practice among African Americans. Her mother refused to teach her how to "work the spirits," saying "I ain't gon' teach you nothin', yo' temper too bad." Nevertheless, Teish always knew that she had a spirit guide, but not until 1974 did the voice that she calls her Goddess guide her to learn how to be a priestess and to teach others, especially women, from her powerful tradition.

Teish says, "What I try to do here is demystify what African spirituality is about and take the fear out of it. I'm teaching people whose tradition has encouraged them to ascend so much that now they're out of their bodies and disconnected from the earth. By sharing some of what we do, I hope to reawaken in them the sense of connectedness, the sense of the spiritual, and that the sexual is connected to all of it. When that basic thing is awakened and they've been exposed to this essence, they can go back to their communities and create rituals that are relevant to who they are.

"The African observed the voluptuous river, with its sweet water and beautiful stones and surmised intuitively that it was female. They named the river Oshun, Goddess of Love . . . the river came before the woman, and . . . the woman's stride is affected by the flow of the river."—Luisah Teish, *Jambalaya*

"The thing I'm most proud of in my life is my book *Jambalaya*. Since the fourth grade, I've known I would write a book. I was very glad that the ancestors and spirits saw fit to use my hand to put what they had to say down on paper. I've written at least three books and burned them." The book is personal and, like the books of other leaders described here, tells a story, both rich and sad, of a childhood that brought her to where she is today. But it is much more than that. In her book, Teish offers recipes and rituals for such things as how to spiritually clean a house, make a bed for sound sleep, ensure domestic tranquillity, and stop gossip. The last piece of magic calls for a cheap, whole beef tongue; a fountain pen; and Dragon's Blood ink. Alice Walker has proclaimed *Jambalaya* "a book of startling remembrances, revelations, directives, and imperatives, filled with the mysticism, wisdom and common sense of the African religion of the Mother. It should be read with the same open-minded love with which it was written."

Yet, Teish says, "Writing is agonizing for me because I'm a pleasure seeker and love performance." I can sympathize—I don't know anyone who loves to sit down and face the blank screen. "I love conducting ritual. There is that moment when everybody is on, participating, and blending energy. I feel like the queen of the festival in that moment because I've stirred the pot and it's really cooking. Once I did an opera for the rain forest, and a little girl points at me and asks her mother, 'Is that Mother Earth?' For her I was the planet. I get chills when I think of it!"

Teish went to live in California at fourteen, and there she met people who saw her gift. Two of her teachers inspired her to write and to dance. For the first time, she had "white women friend-sisters." Before that she had only been a maid, cook, or babysitter to Anglos. She began writing and dancing, and secretly studying voodoo in the libraries of Los Angeles.

"At a young age I was fortunate enough to dance with Madame Katherine Dunham [a pioneering black choreographer] in Illinois and to rub shoulders with celebrities. I was one of those cute things who thought she was going to get herself

"**B**lood has been used in traditions all over the world because it is the life force. We cannot live without it. But Nature in her kindness and wisdom has provided woman with easy and regular access to this force, and all people receive life through the red flow of woman."—Luisah Teish, *Jambalaya*

an Oscar. But that's not what happened. I tried to be the perfect black woman and perfect dancer, but I knew I wasn't succeeding. It was 1975, and I was miserable. I looked out my window one day and the wind was blowing the grass the wrong goddamn way. I said, 'I don't have to take this shit. I can get out of here.'

"I took a bunch of pills, but I didn't die. Instead, I had an out-of-body experience. I saw myself sitting on the ceiling looking at me in the hospital bed, and a woman's voice said nicely, 'Cut the crap. You got something to do here. I'm coming back to you, and you're going to get it together.' I had a vision of the Goddess." Other women in this book, such as Maryanne Lacy and Iyanla Vanzant, touched bottom before they began to rise. Their experiences were strong enough to tell them that there was a guiding hand in their lives.

Teish talks about her challenges. "Right now you're looking at the balanced Teish, but I have two personalities. Sometimes there is the amazing Amazon who thinks she can fight anybody. She just can lift her foot and kick out that wall and it's going to move. Now when that Amazon kicks and her ankle hurts, then my 'Poor Pitiful Pearl' takes over. She cries, 'Teish, look what Amazon did to my foot. Why do you let her do that?' And I say, 'Pearl Baby, come on, we're going to put something on it.' I mediate between those two. When I am most successful is when the ego-identity Teish gets out of the way and lets the big woman in." This is the only glimpse I have of Teish's inner life, her struggle to do the work. She has come a long way, as she tells us, and she likes to share the inspirational lessons that has she learned from her life and voodoo traditions. Her wrestling with anger doesn't diminish her authority in my eyes.

"It took a couple of years to clean away the habits of being reckless or hanging with this one and going here and there. Step by step with various trials, I kept going through processes until I came to my rebirth ritual. I began to study the stories that impact my life, and I changed my personal mythology. The old mythology was a decaying goulash that was killing me. Catholicism gave me only two choices: either you're the virgin or the whore. I was the good little girl who polished statues in the church and the good little slave who ironed the nuns' habits. She's the virgin, right? The dancer, actress, fashion model, she's the whore. And in between there was a warrior who was trying to fight off the forces she felt. I resisted becoming a priestess for eight years—I was afraid. I moved to the Bay Area with fifteen dollars in 1971. By 1974 my spirit guide became my steady companion, and women black and white, women yellow, red, and brown, were asking me to teach them the little I knew.

"A lot of people don't know that they are co-creators of their life. My life has given me knowledge that it can be done, and my tradition has given me tools and the assignment to be a spiritual and cultural ambassador to the world. I'm very grateful. I started as a black nappy-headed little girl born in the segregated South to a longshoreman and a maid-cook. Now I'm somebody who is invited to sit in a circle with Australian Aborigine women in the bush, who can walk into the pyramids in Egypt, who can go to the mountains of Venezuela, and who can sit at a coffee shop in San Francisco." She has also become a healer in the world with her creativity, generosity, and faith.

In Teish's multigenerational, multicultural, sexually expansive "village," we glimpse how citizens of a new world might live. They recognize one another's gifts, and it demands letting go of old biases and fears. In such a place, a mother of twins does bumps and grinds to help a gay man have a child with his lover.

THE REVEREND DR. LAUREN ARTRESS

The Reverend Dr. Lauren Artress's home, a simply furnished condo in a modest neighborhood in San Francisco, provides a balance to her workplace, the ornate and majestic Grace Cathedral. As canon for Special Ministries since 1992 (and canon pastor since 1985), she has distinguished herself as an innovative priest who has created many transformational events in a traditional setting.

Her best-known work by far is her resurrection of the labyrinth as a tool to connect spirit with Spirit. The five-millennia-old practice must have been waiting for Dr. Artress, because from the time she put two labyrinths at Grace Cathedral in 1991, a tapestry labyrinth in the sanctuary and a terrazzo stone labyrinth outside in the interfaith meditation garden, a movement was born.

In 1998, the *New York Times* wrote, "In an age when many Americans are looking beyond the church pulpit for spiritual experience and solace, a growing number have rediscovered the labyrinth as a path to prayer, introspection, and healing." Labyrinths lie on church floors and community plazas, and in private gardens, spas, retreat centers, prisons, and hospitals. They also appear in diverse religious settings, including synagogues, ashrams, and Buddhist temples.

The appeal of the labyrinth may be felt by people who would like to attain a quiet mind but find meditation impossible because they cannot sit still. The labyrinth brings stillness with deliberate movement, like yoga. If entered with a tired, confused mind that needs to make a decision, the circular path rests the mind by giving it a focus in watching where one walks. In giving the mind a simple yet absorbing task, the labyrinth takes us out of the sometimes never-ending labyrinth within. Studies have suggested that the eleven-circuit pattern at Chartres Cathedral, which was the model for Artress's labyrinth, has neurological benefit. However it works, when I enter with a question or a plea, I exit feeling answered.

Several years ago, I awakened dry-mouthed and in a panic before the High Holiday services that composer and musician Debbie Friedman and I were conducting together for the first time. I entered the labyrinth in my backyard to calm myself down, and as I took the first step my fears became questions: How on earth am I going to hold my own with Debbie's charisma? How will I not disappoint so many with high expectations of the services? As I walked I began to think about the first walkers, Abraham and Sarah, and all that followed them on a labyrinthine journey of forty years. And then I got it. It will go well because of the goodness of my ancestors. Just to be sure, I reminded the One who answered me: "God, not for my sake, but for the sake of the great ones whom you chose to carry a new idea, help me." My nervousness and doubt disappeared, never again to return for any event with as much force. I've also used the labyrinth ritually to aid in the introspective preparation for the Jewish New Year.

Like the labyrinth, Lauren Artress first appears deceptively simple: a devoted Episcopal priest serving in a powerful, mainstream institution. A little time spent with her reveals far more. One of the few women to hold a position of such authority in her church, she is a psychotherapist with a divinity degree from Princeton Theological Seminary. Born in 1945 in Cleveland, Ohio, Artress spent her childhood in the country along the Chagrin River. While she describes her family as "emergency Presbyterians," going to church only when necessary, she experienced transcendence through nature early in her life.

She says, "At around twelve years old, the world began to open up for me. One day I climbed to a high cliff over the river, and something like a mirror caught my eye. Looking closely, I saw a school of fish with the sun reflecting off the silvery sides of the fish. I watched them in different formations for hours. I'd stumbled onto a great mystery, but I didn't know what to call it. I had seen a sacred dance and had stumbled onto a divine secret: there are invisible patterns throughout all of nature. Once you have a mystical experience you're open, but it might take years to catch up with it." When she discovered the labyrinth many years later, she remembered her experience with the fish as her first encounter with sacred pattern.

A labyrinth is not a maze. There is no puzzle to solve in a labyrinth. It has one path that leads into the center and back out. The labyrinth can be painted on the ground or on a large canvas, or it can be constructed with other materials such as stones or bricks. You can see all of the path all of the time.

Death is part of a pattern but difficult to discern, especially when one is young. "When my grandmother died between my freshman and sophomore years at Ohio State University, it was my first confrontation with death. It was just unbelievable that someone could be here one moment and not the next. In my searching for comfort and meaning, I found the pastoral ministry there, the United Campus Christian Fellowship. My interest was so intense that a member of the group suggested that I go to a seminary.

"I went to Princeton Theological Seminary because it had a good department in pastoral theology. It was a relief to be at a much smaller school than Ohio State University and tucked away in a more pastoral setting. There are no barriers between God and nature, but the church has boundaries, and if you're working in a traditional setting, you have to know them." She knew God through nature, and Princeton helped her focus her passion to bring together psyche and spirit. Trained to be a pastoral counselor and pastoral psychotherapist, Artress searched for the nexus between mind, body, and spirit, and that exploration ultimately became key to her ministry at Grace Cathedral.

"Because I worked as a therapist for seventeen years in New York, I have a sense of the longing of the human soul. Most of the people I work with now have the longing without any tradition and are looking for it. I'm identified as a Christian and an Episcopal priest; yet, I also work with seekers of all kinds. I'm a bridge. I welcome all people into the church, and I connect the regular Sunday goers with the alienated types. The consciousness of each helps the other.

"It is not my goal for people to become Christian, but I do think it's important that everybody find a path and move along on it. Christianity is one way of healing, about finding one's way. It's about being an awakened being that's hopefully growing and deepening in compassion, able to do service in the world in some way."

It was "restless uncertainty," as Artress describes in her book *Walking a Sacred Path: Rediscovering the Labyrinth as a Sacred Tool*, that moved her along the path. "In 1985 I went to Jean Houston's Mystery School. It prepared me to take the jump from the East Coast to the West, to start my work at Grace Cathedral as the canon pastor. I hadn't worked in a church; I had no administrative experience. It was a real risk. I was making this major change, giving up my practice, ending things, moving here. The Mystery School gave me the energy to leave New York and work in a new way. I found myself being a transformational person in the midst of Christianity."

After five years of serving in the cathedral, Artress was exhausted by its demands and decided to return to the Mystery School in 1991 to gain clarity. "Something important was supposed to happen, and something gentle was being born. Jean showed us this little-known medieval pattern that she said was a powerful spiritual tool whose path would lead each of us to our own center. I walked the labyrinth three times by myself after everyone had left it. Something important was supposed to happen, but I didn't know what it was.

"I came home and literally kept walking around my apartment in circles, saying, 'What is it?' over and over. Three months later I had the answer: I knew that I had to put a labyrinth in Grace Cathedral. I'd already done crazy things, women's retreats, singing for your life, lots of transformational events, but this was different.

"This was more than me. It was a women's issue. Women have to bite the bullet—if we don't know what we're doing, we don't do it. So that's the bullet to bite. Do it no matter what. If you don't know where you're going, that's fine. I'm lucky; I don't have perfection in me. My colleagues describe me as somebody who's willing to jump off the high diving board, and when I'm in midair, I'll check whether there's water in the pool. I see a lot of women crippled by low self-esteem and perfectionism. One criticism sends them running out of the room. You can't do that when you're working in the public world. This is not about perfection; it's about doing it. 'If it's worth doing, it's worth doing poorly.'" Artress goes on, "A lot of women, even with feminist consciousness, get stuck doing spiritual work in their living rooms. They should be moving on into big spaces, creating spiritual fermentation, getting people thinking, aware that there's a new concept out there called awakening. Grace Cathedral is a large institution, and I feel deeply that I'm working directly with the Holy Spirit.

"Marian Woodman says that it is our task 'to release new spirit from old stone, however painful that will be. Then, and only then, will we be free.' That's why working in a tradition is important for me. I have two parts to my personality. I can work well with structure, and then I'll turn around and be a bridge to life's dynamic nature. I can negotiate with the cathedral to have an overnight retreat for women in it. I can do transformational things within the church when I interface with it and speak a common language. I like working in the Cathedral because we can do bigger things because the vision is larger than a traditional parish.

"At Grace Cathedral, we're changing our language and our vision, but I don't think Christianity overall knows where it is going. Of course it's about healing, but even more important is birthing the creativity of the people. We have a suffering God dying on a cross, and people are so mesmerized by that image and so caught by it that they don't understand the Christ of glory, the Christ transformed. It's safer to stay with that suffering man on the cross. I'm not trying to say we shouldn't pay attention to suffering. I'm saying we can't envision ourselves beyond suffering, and if we don't do that, then we're in a repetition compulsion," Artness explains.

I'm so relieved because I thought that suffering was a Jewish thing. Sylvia Boorstein says that pain is inevitable; suffering is optional. Creativity happens when we don't sap our energy in suffering. God is the Creator; let us be like God and create. Artress says, "I love Jesus as an archetype for transformation and new creation. He's the imprint for the immortal and the mortal. What the church has done borders on dangerous in making him a weak milquetoast. Who says it's better to give than receive? I don't think Jesus said that. He didn't have those kinds of dualities. I also see how radical Jesus was—that it takes guts, just like with Moses. It takes guts to stand present, fully in the moment, and say who you are and say the way you think things should go. Leading people into the wilderness was no small deal.

"Christianity was a countercultural movement, and it's becoming that again. The more we lose membership in our churches, the more Christianity is going to have to realize the message doesn't fit people's needs today. Plenty of people go to church like it's an inoculation against what you're really afraid you're going to get. Christianity could radicalize you. But for many, going to church doesn't mean change or deepening their compassion. Transformation is what feminist theology does; it's based on your experience, not someone else's. That's what the labyrinth is doing."

Artress continues, "I often joke that it's fine to introduce the feminine in the church as long you don't talk about it. People get incensed if you talk about it, but not if you introduce the feminine as an experience. The labyrinth is an example of moving into a different state of receptive consciousness and allowing a flowing of movement. When you're in it, you're internal, you're contemplative, you're releasing, and you're letting go. You receive in the center, and then you go out and take it into the world. You're bringing what you received back into everyday life.

"Everyone, including Alan Jones, the dean of the Cathedral, agreed that we should take a trip to Chartres as part of our research in planning a labyrinth for the cathedral. I was embarrased and turned beet-red when I first presented the labyrinth to a clergy colleague. But it so happened that six of the Grace Cathedral congregation were going to be in France at the same time, including Alan Jones. I asked them to meet me in Chartres. I wanted to walk the labyrinth there to verify the idea about introducing it to our congregation. When we arrived, we had to move chairs that had covered it for two hundred and fifty to three hundred years. The walk was powerful for all of us, and we felt an awesome, mysterious sense of grounding and empowerment. The mood in the dark and quiet space became light, fluid, and joyful. I felt like I received the embrace of Mary. I had ventured into her glorious web.

"Labyrinths became hidden because the church is ambivalent about the imagination, about creativity, and it doesn't like artists or mystics. Alan [Jones] and I often joke that the only good mystic is a dead mystic. That's the only time the church will recognize a mystic, because they're afraid of them, can't control them. Look," she says, gesturing at herself and me. "A lot of us are called into the other world, and we're scared to death of it. Women, especially." Called is the right word; we don't exactly choose. Just as sexual orientation affects your life, so does spiritual orientation.

While Artress is at home in the traditional liturgy of the church, she knows that many are alienated from it and need a different way of being close to God. "There are thousands of labyrinths now; millions of people have been transformed by them. For instance, many people come with terminal illnesses. People who are in grief from a major loss, such as a child. A lot of grief work takes place in the labyrinth because you can talk to the person on the other side. A lot of healing is around saying good-bye, saying thank you; saying, 'I take in me that gift you've given the world that I see in you.'

"People are intuitively drawn to the labyrinth. We train people to present the labyrinth. It needs a brief explanation because the experience can be subtle. Most of the people I've trained are women. Out of thirty, five will be men. Maybe it's because I'm a woman. Certainly the spirit is moving in the heart of women. We come from a consciousness that we know what we have is not good enough, it's not addressing our human needs. Male consciousness doesn't know this all the time, but a lot of men are aware of it and those are the ones who come to the training as well. Things are changing everywhere; the feminine is appearing everywhere as large, old institutions are breaking up.

"I don't have a partner or children, so I'm free to do the work. I've traveled almost every weekend since 1996. I had a longtime relationship when I moved to San Francisco, but now my work would make that difficult. The energy that's coming for me through my life and work now is coming from the labyrinth. It's not a time to settle down or to be connected in that way. It's a time to be called out into the world and to be connected to many people." This may explain the sparseness of her apartment.

"My biggest struggle, on the most personal level, lies with working with the projections that you get from people. The more present you become, the more people project on you what they expect you to do for them when they should be doing it for themselves. I'm well trained and I know who I am, so I can sort projection easily. A lot of my work is helping people find their soul assignments. People need to know they have their own light to show in the world. We as women need to know this so we feel secure when issues of envy and competition come up, as they inevitably do.

"They don't have to do it my way, and they don't have to do it like me, but if they do, I'd like acknowledgment of my work. It's good to speak of the lineage of teachers.

"People who train with me sometimes want to do the same thing I am doing but they get confused about it. Sometimes people get envious and it is very uncomfortable to feel that kind of energy coming toward you. It's a specific problem for a woman spiritual leader. Women want to steal your light because they don't know they have their own." Joan Halifax told me that she read a recent study about women's leadership being challenged by other women; Artress is the only leader who speaks directly to me of this.

"People don't have an image of a female spiritual leader in a patriarichal setting. Everytime a woman celebrates the Eucharist we break open the frozen consciousness that God is a man. People are getting more used to this possiblity, but are still pretty attached to God being of masculine gender.

"Women priests challenge everyone's conception of God at some level. What I'm going to say is controversial. God is in process and evolving, too. We human beings are like brain cells in the mind of God. The more we open up pathways, the more God can evolve and mature as well. We're part of a huge, amazing creation that is beyond the human imagination. Compassion, patience, tolerance, and being open will lead us through this evolution."

Lauren Artress breaks the traditional mold of what one would expect a female priest to be. She is less a nurturing mother than a creative catalyst and visionary. Had they lived at the same time, the biblical Deborah and she might have commiserated about the problems a woman warrior faces.

SYLVIA BOORSTEIN

In her book *That's Funny, You Don't Look Buddhist: On Being a Faithful Jew and a Passionate Buddhist*, Sylvia Boorstein writes, "I am grateful that I know two vocabularies of response. I think of one as my voice of understanding and the other the voice of my heart." That is why she regrets accepting an editorial suggestion for the title of the book. Besides flirting with stereotypes, it makes light of her work. A better title for the book might be *The Art of Living*, because to be with her is to witness presence, warmth, insight, candor, and a zest for life.

Boorstein attempts to answer the question "How is it possible to be both a Jew and a Buddhist?" by telling her own story of having, as she calls it, "dual citizenship." Born in 1936 in Brooklyn, she describes her parents as mild-mannered, cheerful, and loving. Sylvia calls Judaism her "karma, and it's good." A relaxed and buoyant demeanor suggests that her wisdom has come from the felicitous combination of a blessed childhood, a good marriage, a satisfying career, and meditation for half an hour each day. Not quite.

While these elements are part of her story, they overlook the wild ride that awakened and transformed her. Some women in this book describe epiphany under strange circumstances: Ma Jaya was in a bathtub, Jean Houston was in a closet turned into an altar, and Joan Halifax had a nervous breakdown. While a few, such as Nahid Angha and Lauren Artress, describe gentler paths to enlightenment, many describe drama and trauma—perhaps essential in birthing anything, including oneself.

In the mid-1970s, Sylvia was a practicing psychotherapist, a wife, and the mother of four children. Her life was excellent, and yet she wasn't at peace. In fact, the more abundant her blessings, the more frightened she became that something, sooner or later, would happen to take them away. Life felt "too hard, too fragile, to accept without despair." As she approached forty, the fear that anyone could die at any time overtook her. "I wish I could tell you that this awareness made me cherish every moment," she writes. "The truth is that it simply terrified me." After a neighbor's two children were run over by a car, Sylvia would send her children off to school saying not only "'I'll see you later" but "I love you." "I was overwhelmed at realizing what a gift it was to have them return," she says. While Sylvia was falling into "agitated depression," she saw that none of her friends seemed worried about the same things she was, so she kept silent, not wanting to appear "weird with a morbid preoccupation."

Her husband, Seymour, a psychiatrist, believed that spiritual paths should have answers to such dilemmas, and he became the family's "advance spiritual scout." After attending a two-week Buddhist meditation retreat, he suggested that Sylvia try it. It was July 7, 1977, in Toledo, Oregon. There she met her friend and teacher Jack Kornfeld. It wasn't love at first sight. Although she was teaching yoga by then, she was in great pain from sitting still with her mind going everywhere. She had headaches, she says, because, "every story of my life was replayed for two weeks without escape." But when Sylvia learned the first of Buddhism's Four Noble Truths, she heard an answer. The First Truth acknowledges that life is painful and unsatisfying, unreliable even when pleasant because it is always changing. "I stopped being mad and anxious at life," Sylvia says, "and I learned to get up in the morning and say 'Thank You.'"

She became an enthusiastic meditator, practicing at least an hour daily and going on long retreats. Gradually she sensed that her fear of loss and change had diminished, and she was enjoying life in a new way. One day while meditating she experienced her entire body streaming with what felt like lines of energy. Although Kornfeld warned her about getting "captivated" by intense experience, she liked it, and soon she was having out-of-body experiences and images of Genesis. At first it was wonderful. But her body began going into awkward spasms unexpectedly. She didn't sleep for days, and she wasn't thinking much about anything except mystical energy experiences. She consulted Buddhist teachers, Western doctors, and acupuncturists. Finally, after a period of months, perhaps as much as a year, of accepting the energies as "just what was happening" rather than struggling with them, they disappeared.

While Sylvia describes a tantalizing adventure, the kind usually heard from people who took LSD in the sixties, she stresses that she doesn't believe it was necessary for what she learned and characteristically admits that she

"Pain is inevitable; suffering is optional."—Sylvia Boorstein

was hooked on the trip. It took three or four years for her body to relax, and when it did, two things had changed. She found herself with a deeper understanding of suffering, and she began to read Scriptures and Jewish prayer with new interest.

No longer simply her club or family, Judaism now offered ecstatic expression for the delight and gratitude she felt for her life. She began to find herself a little like a fiddler on the roof, mindful of floating music and steady feet to keep the balance. Her equanimity with two paths is rare, because most of us see identity in black-and-white terms: you are this or you are that, not both. Sylvia's work is of special interest to Jews because so many of us are practicing and teaching Buddhism. Unlike Sylvia, however, many of the teachers—Jack Kornfeld, Sharon Salzburg, and Joseph Goldstein, to name a few—are born Jews but are otherwise Buddhist in belief and practice.

The door post of her woodsy, light-filled house in northern California displays a mezuzah, the public mark of a Jewish house. Greeting us at the door, Sylvia appears older than her book jacket photograph, but her voice and movement, along with her reddish blonde hair, suggest a woman far younger than her sixty-five years. When the heart stays young and joyful, it is evidence of the highest wisdom. She exemplifies the ending verses in Psalm 92: "The righteous shall flourish like a palm tree, grow tall like a cedar in Lebanon. Planted in the house of the Eternal, they shall flourish in courtyards of our God, bearing new fruit in old age, still full of sap and still green, to declare that the Eternal is upright, my rock in whom there is no wrong."

On the sunny morning when I sit across the dining-room table from Sylvia, eating a pastry that she's prepared, I become tranquil by contagion. She is congenial and cheerful; yet, it isn't only temperament as much as a reflection of intention and practice. Her five grandchildren probably fight for her lap; as an archetypal grandmother, maternal experience informs her leadership. She is also very smart. Her ideas, expressed simply and personally, are sophisticated, and her reconciliation of Judaism and Buddhism is brilliant.

I attempt a linear beginning with Sylvia by asking about her background. She nods, thinking, and looks at me. "Your question reminds me of two things, and then I'll tell you my story. I asked someone at a dinner party the same question, and after he told me, he said, 'Of course this answer would be different depending upon when you asked me.' I find that continually true. I've done one particular exercise dozens of times where you write about the twelve stepping-stones of your life. Birth is number one; where you are now is number twelve. You're asked to consider the remaining ten steps in a contemplative way, and you don't plan it in advance. You sit down, write, 'I was born . . . ' and then you number up to twelve. It's never been the same any time I've done it.

"I used to think that some things will change on the list, but I'll never leave out the death of my mother. It was a huge event when she died—I was twenty-three—and I'd worried about her weak heart since I was a child. Her illness shaped who I became, and her death is what confronted me about the frailty of life. But seven years after I 'knew' this, I did the list and my mother wasn't on it! Everything that we do matters, but sometimes we remember different events.

"When I see that everything we do has an effect, it makes me careful when I teach—not like tight, tense careful, but careful in the sense of impeccable. When we see clearly, we behave carefully. Nothing is wasted, not even wasting time! If I've wasted today, it doesn't need to upset me. I've learned that I won't do that tomorrow." Sylvia enjoys talking and teaching, leaning forward as a good teacher and therapist does.

"Intention is what corrects me. It's important to have a practice, it's important who taught you, but what is most important is intention. Why are you doing it? What do you hope will happen? My intention is to be alive and awake in my life so that I manifest myself as clearly as I can. It makes for a better life because it gives me the peace that is available to all human beings.

"The meditation that makes me aware of the great peace available to all of us is to name the people I'm thinking about. Maybe I'm thinking about my grand-children; then I think of their parents, my husband, my friends, my nearest friends; and then I remember their partners and their extended families. It's a pleasure to sit there, and you can sit for a long time with this. Right now I think of Malka, and I think about Gay," she says, looking at each of us. "And I think about Gail [our assistant, who set up the interview]. Everyone's name reminds you of somebody else; you just sit there and make a long list of names. It's a great practice because while you do it, you think about how many people live in your heart and how blessed you are. It picks up your whole mood."

She refills our teacups, and I'm reminded of the Zen tea ceremony. You can't pour until the cup is empty. A heart has to be empty to be full; a heart full of self-absorption cannot take much in. "Sometimes I do this in groups and ask people to softly say the name of who they're thinking about. And someone will say Pearl, their Pearl, but then I say to myself, 'Ah, I forgot *my* Pearl,' and then Pearl reminds me of Glenda. The other day I started this, and I thought of all the people in Los Angeles, and then Turkey, and categories of people. So you begin close and small, and look where it can take you.

"It's a great way to cultivate a heart that holds all beings without hesitation. It's about the oneness. We can ask ourselves if we can be in a place where we're in touch with everyone's struggle. No selection, my sister-in-law but not my brother-in-law, this one who is in the hospital but not that one who snubbed me." I wonder how this exercise works with people who had terrible parents, no partner, and no friends.

In describing her life in the 1930s as an only child living near Coney Island with her parents and grandmother, Sylvia says, "My community was observant, but it wasn't a sophisticated religious understanding; it's just what they did in Europe. Being kosher was a given. Sticking together as a community was a given. My parents didn't go to *shul* [synagogue in Yiddish], but I went with my grandmother and had a wonderful time. It was a *shtibl* [a small, modest synagogue] with a little entry room where you hung your coat and then a main room where everybody sat on folding chairs. Men and women weren't together, and my grandmother always sat in the same seat, from 8:30 to 12:30, with the same old ladies in the row.

"There wasn't a lot you could do on Shabbat—you couldn't draw or write— but after I flipped baseball cards and played tag, I'd come back in and squeeze into the row. The women had orthopedic devices, ace bandages, crutches, and I'd have to creep by them. They would mumble into their prayer books in Yiddish about the child who is creeping in and out too much. My grandmother would say, 'Leave her alone.' That's all that I remember. The rabbi gave frightening sermons on Yom Kippur about the Book of Life and the Book of Death, but I was never frightened because I was so well loved.

"This is 1940, and anti-Semitism was terrible. I wasn't well loved in school, I was the only Jew in my class, and kids said really terrible things to me. My mother worked hard to have me moved to another school. Even though I had to walk very far and couldn't go home for lunch, my mother's effort to keep me comfortable and my parents' kindness told me that it's all right to be alive. The sense of God I have is my mother. Abraham Joshua Heschel wrote, 'I cannot see God's face, but I can see my mother's.'

"The God of my father's parents didn't work for him, and he didn't figure out how to get another one. But somehow, even though Judaism wasn't quite up to speed, my parents didn't get mad at it, and I love them for that. They showed up appropriately for major holidays, they were ardent Zionists, and my mother, despite her socialism, loved religious form. They sent me in the summers to Camp Kinderwelt, which was a labor Zionist camp. I had a great time. There was always a lot of religious differences and debates, but the camp was traditionally observant and *kashrut* observant [of Jewish dietary laws]. We kept Shabbat and sang songs every morning, and we said the Pledge of Allegiance in English."

She says, "I would love for my children and grandchildren to have a religious, spiritual practice as Jews. Periods of quiet awaken the natural capacity of mindfulness. Meditation is one way, and so is Shabbat. I gave the grandchildren a translation of the morning prayer like this: 'Good morning, God, this is Erik, I'm up again.' My children have strong Jewish identity through ritual and community, and they take a lot of pleasure in it, as I do. I'd also like them to use Judaism as a practice for mindfulness. Jews are returning from other traditions to discover that their religion teaches nondual relationship, nondual presence, ideas that they found useful in Eastern thought. I've even begun to teach rabbis how to meditate," she says, looking at me. I meditate and like it, but, unlike Sylvia, I don't feel Jewish in the lotus position.

How do we reconcile the idea of the One with the idea that there is no transcendent figure? Sylvia says, "I really like using the name of God. We were lying in bed at night, my youngest grandchild and I, saying prayers. 'The Spirit of God will take care of you all night long,' I began, and half way through he asked me, 'Grandma, is God a boy or a girl?' His older brother said, 'Erik, it's not a person, it's not like that.' So, we talked about how when you feel good, have a good idea, or when you're happy, that's how you know there is God in the world. When you're not frightened, then you know God is in the world."

She spreads her arms and looks around the room. "When I'm not frightened and I'm paying attention, I might look around and say that the whole world is filled with God's glory," she says. "It's completely amazing that you and I are sitting here in this moment. We met just once before, and we're talking like old friends.

> **A** minyan is a prayer group of ten people. A minyan is required to say certain prayers and to read the Torah.

I'm talking in the air, and magic is happening; it's being recorded." Abraham Joshua Heschel's answer to those who asked him about what it means to believe in God was "To have radical amazement."

Sylvia describes a "best day" scenario of practice: "I get up in the morning, say whatever I'm going to say, and I sit for maybe twenty minutes. Three times a week I drive to the minyan. I like being with the community because I like praying and also because I know they need me. We need ten people, and I count."

"My mother's father retired at sixty-five and came to live with us. He slept in my room. The phone would ring early in the morning, and I'd grope for the phone to hear somebody in Yiddish say, 'We need a tenth person for a minyan.' My grandfather wasn't religious and had long ago given up the practice, but they knew he wasn't working. He'd jump out of bed, get dressed, and run out the door. He didn't have a big consciousness about prayer, but he did have a big consciousness about showing up for people if they needed him.

"I have that consciousness. When my grandchildren were here for a couple of weeks, they went to camp. One morning I wasn't sure if the group would have a minyan, so I woke the children early, got everything packed for the day, and we went to *shul*. The youngest children asked why, and then the twelve-year-old grandson said, "Grandma, you're the tenth person here." That might have been the most important thing that happened while they were here. I told them about my grandfather, and that they can pass it down to their children. Now they have a five-generation story about showing up when people are needed."

When asked about that for which she has the most gratitude, she answers as do most mothers in this book: "My family. And I'm grateful for the work I've done. I teach people how to pay attention, and I teach it the same way, no matter who it is or where I am. I teach a lot of retreats at Spirit Rock. I'm away teaching about eighteen to twenty weeks a year." Sylvia is a founding teacher of Spirit Rock Meditation Center in Woodacre, about an hour and a half from her home. Describing a retreat, she says, "Posture isn't so important. Watching the mind work is the point: how it creates suffering and can get out of it, how it ties itself in a knot by telling a story, and how when things leave the story, you can get out of the knot. A retreat shows you the pattern of your habitual stories. The Buddha was a tremendous psychologist!

"My grandfather used to say that it's hard to be a person, very hard to be a Jew. It's hard to be—that's all there is to it. He was motherly, as is my husband, in that he likes to take care of people. That, I think, is a woman's trait. The other trait is that we have invincibility about things. I never doubted that I'd be able to meditate, maybe because I had babies and got through tremendous discomfort and distress. Women just do things."

Before I can question this, she goes on, "Of course there are women who have an opposite attitude and have to get over it. Malka, because you're a small woman as I am, I'll tell you a story about when I was thirteen or fourteen and very interested in [the movie actress] Virginia Mayo, who wore big, beautiful hats. I said to my mother, who was smaller than I, 'I feel bad that I'm not going to be a tall woman and I won't be able to wear one of those hats.' My mother said, 'If you absolutely know that you're fine, you can get an enormous hat, walk into a room, and everybody will say, "What a good idea, an enormous hat on a small woman." You'll just do it.' My parents didn't push me, and they never told me that I did anything wrong, so I always thought I could do everything. I have way more confidence than talent. My degree of confidence has sustained whatever talent I have."

She says, "I love writing, and when I'm in the middle of it, I am pregnant, like this," she says, holding her hands over her womb. "I can't put it down, like you can't be pregnant only when it's convenient. I'm always thinking about it, and that gets alive in my body and mind. I love to write, and I write a lot in my mind while I'm driving. I work a long time on a sentence."

Sylvia is a wonderful storyteller, finding the perfect example, usually from her own life, to give abstract, slippery concepts a form. My favorite is one that I heard at a Jewish meditation workshop she gave in New York. I imagine her sitting in a comfortable chair in front of five hundred people, speaking as if she were talking to a friend.

"Just ten days ago, I was provided with a timely example of constricted mind," she begins, laughing. "I was preparing to go to the second Seder at the home of one of my adult children, and I heard from another of my children about some misunderstanding in my family. I became miserable.

"Before the phone rang with this news, I had been buoyant. The first Seder had been wonderful, and I was really looking forward to the second one, and all of a sudden, I began to

tell myself unhappy stories. 'How could my children do a thing like that? They're all grown up, and what does this mean about their respect for each other? Didn't I teach them that? I've made a mess of raising them!' I watched myself telling a story that was making me miserable, unhappy, and depressed.

"I began to rehearse how I would arrive at this Seder, not saying anything about it, of course, thereby assuring that the guilty party should feel guilty. All of a sudden, luckily, it was a miserable enough story that I told myself, 'I am enslaved. I am about to go to a Seder and say the words in the Haggadah, "Do not tell this story as if it happened a long time ago. Tell it as if you were there right now."' So, I decided to make an exodus. I said to myself, 'Sylvia, wait a minute. Relax. Take a breath. What is true? Truth is, your feelings are hurt. Truth is also that these are really wonderful and remarkable people, and they're also regular, normal people. Every once in a while they hurt each other's feelings, and every once in a while, they hurt my feelings. What's also true is, thank God, we're all in relatively good health, we're all going to a Seder together, and we're happy about it.' I watched the walls of my closed-in mind push out again as I said to myself what's true.

"I fell in love with my whole family again. I went to the Seder, and when I got to the line about 'Don't tell this story as if it happened a long time ago,' I got it. What we are called to do is to keep pushing back the walls of a closed-in mind, because that's when we get frightened, worried, hurt, mad, or disappointed. The challenge is to keep the vision wide."

Dr. Elaine Pagels

The Harrington Spear Paine Professor of Religion at Princeton University, Elaine Pagels has long been interested in early Christianity's creation of a world struggle between good and evil. Awarded a MacArthur Fellowship in 1981, her book about the Gnostic gospels won the National Book Award in 1980. After reading her book *The Origin of Satan*, I finally understood how anti-Semitism became so pervasive and powerful: early Christianity used Judaism as a foil by demonizing the Jews as the children of Satan. An adventurous and groundbreaking work of scholarship, the book is an exploration of how the followers of Jesus and the groups that subsequently became Christian turned against their own Jewish tradition. What is also remarkable about the book is that it is graceful and engaging.

The Origin of Satan begins, "In 1988, when my husband of twenty years died in a hiking accident, I became aware that, like many people who grieve, I was living in the presence of an invisible being—living, that is, with a vivid sense of someone who had died. During the following years I began to reflect on the ways that various religious traditions give shape to the invisible world, and how our imaginative perceptions of what is invisible relate to the ways we respond to the people around us, to events, and to the natural world." That Pagels, who had also lost a child a year before her husband's tragic accident, openly claims that the idea for the book emerged from her personal life is part of her popular appeal.

Dr. Pagels lives in Hollywood's vision of a professor's house in a college town. It is fall, the leaves are turning magnificently, and her handsome clapboard house seems to have been there forever. She is a little late for our meeting, so we wait in the car for her. We follow her into the house, and immediately a large dog bounds up, threatening to flatten all of us. Once the dog is taken care of and we settle in the living room, Pagels's teenaged daughter enters the room with a request to be taken to the mall. Soon after they work out a plan, her son David comes in and politely waits for his mother to address him. He's a sturdy, handsome, fair boy of eleven. "Mom, did you know that my book report was due today?" Pagels exclaims, "No!" She empathizes, and a collaborative discussion yields a quick solution. She returns to us as she was with her children: attentive and respectful. Witnessing the domestic part of Pagels's life gives dimension to the narrative that begins and also balances her Olympian intellectual side. It is good to see that her life is full again.

When asked how religion became her chosen field of study, she clasps her hands and says, "My parents had no use for religion. My father had given it up for Darwin, and my parents were freethinking Dutch rationalists. When I was an adolescent, to their horror I met some born-again and evangelical Christians, and I found a passion that was compelling and for a short time rather gratifying. The group said that I only belonged with born-again people, that I had nothing in common with other people like my friends and family. After a while I realized I didn't belong in this group, so I sadly left them and decided I would have to find God on my own.

"I didn't know why religion was so fascinating, since I had been taught a nine-teenth-century view that religion is obsolete: first there was magic, then religion, and now science. But I was amazed at the power of spiritual tradition. It didn't mat-ter much to me whether it was a Hopi dance, a Bar Mitzvah with a cantor singing in a language I didn't understand, or a Catholic church in France.

"I decided to go to graduate school to try to understand what was so com-pelling. Since I was so receptive to religious experience, I went to a nondenomi-national school as an inoculation against my susceptibility. I hoped that Harvard University wouldn't brainwash people." While she tells this in a deadpan manner, it is amusing to imagine Pagels "inoculating" herself with reason to protect her from spiritual rapture. "I mean, if you're filled with the drama of Moses receiving the Ten Commandments and suddenly you discover that there are four authors, what do you do with them? I found that rather liberating, actually.

"I was looking for the 'real Christianity' when I went to graduate school. At the first meeting with my adviser, he asked me, 'Why did you come here, anyway?' I mumbled something about finding the essence of Christianity. He looked at me severely and said, 'How do you know it *has* an essence?' And I thought, what a great question! That's why I went there: to be asked questions like that. It didn't shake me, because I had no traditional beliefs, just a lot of feeling. William James's *Varieties of Religious Experience* claims that the greatest component of religion is feeling." Jewish tradition says that angels are another name for feelings.

"I discovered that there was no early Christian world in the naive way I was looking at it; you know, there was no God handing down the Torah, and there was no direct transmission." I appreciate her sensitivity and ease in using language familiar to me. She continues, "I also discovered a gospel that identified itself as secret: the Gospel of Thomas. I was told it was blasphemy, heresy, but I had developed sympathy for heretics after being one of the few women in graduate school at Harvard."

> **G**nosticism is the doctrine of salvation by knowledge. Flourishing sometime before the Christian Era down to the fifth century, Gnosticism places the salvation of the soul in the quasi-intuitive knowledge of the mysteries of the universe and the magic formulae indicative of that knowledge. Gnostics were considered "people who knew," and their knowledge once constituted them a superior class of beings, whose present and future status was different from that of those who, for whatever reason, did not know.

"This particular gospel opened my heart to read that we should bring forth what is within us, and if we don't bring forth what is within, it will destroy us. I love this because I just know it's true; I don't have to believe it. It's not about faith, it's about recognition of some deep truth that is intuitively understood.

"I had never thought much about an intimate relationship with God. It was more about how one lives in the universe and the power of religious tradition. Christianity was like the cultural language I spoke that was most familiar for me. Of course, it could have been Buddhist or anything else, but Christianity was what I had to contend with. My research deepened my relationship to Christianity, but it also alienated me from a lot of the institutional structures. That frustration and alienation emerged in my work, and it spoke to people who had shared those experiences—the desire for an authentic spiritual connection and the disappointment in not finding social environments in which to share with other people and celebrate with them. The traditions have to be changed, and they always have been changed. We received it through millennia of transmissions, revision, transformation, elimination, suppression, and addition. It's always been part of a living tradition, or it wouldn't have survived, and we change it every time we receive and live it.

"When my husband died, my relationship to God became much more complicated. How does one live in a universe in which the randomness that my husband wrote about in *The Cosmic Code* seemed so amply demonstrated? It broke any connection I had with the view you find in Genesis: people who are good reap rewards, and people who are bad, like the people of Sodom and Gemorrah, have their towns destroyed. What we might think of as a natural event is taken to be divine punishment. Harold Kushner's book *When Bad Things Happen to Good People* buys into this idea unconsciously. The book is good; but the title is caught up in this paradox, which is deeply woven into the Bible.

"All that was totally shattered—whatever was left to shatter after the loss of our son. I didn't live in a universe that worked that way, and I couldn't maintain that connection to it. I thought of the gods of Greece, who were like the forces of wind, snow, rain, hail, sun. Sometimes they saved you and sometimes they killed you, and it didn't matter to them—that is what they do.

"When my son was diagnosed with an untreatable illness, I blamed myself. That's what mothers do, because we want a reason. We ask, 'Why me?' After his death—he was just six and a half—we adopted another child. We were beginning to think we could survive, and then suddenly my husband—such an amazing, wonderful man—died in a hiking accident. Job's story gives us an orderly universe. It would be nice to think that, but I didn't have a fantasy that, like Job, we were singled out by God," she says.

"It took a long time before I could think again. I began to wonder what difference does it make how we imagine the invisible world—whether as angels and demons or as Aphrodite and Zeus. That's when I started thinking about writing *The Origin of Satan*. I was trying to find the very practical and social difference that it makes by looking at what I called [to myself] the social history of Satan. Can the power of an invisible God prevail over the invisible forces of evil?" By making the Jews the children of the devil, the early Christians made Jews larger than life; fear and projection are parts of anti-Semitism.

"When I was dealing with so much pain and so much conflict in my life, the story of early Christianity, which involved so much pain and conflict, emerged. All this was suppressed in the Christian tradition and overlooked in scholarship, but I saw it because of what I was experiencing. What I was writing had little to do directly with loss of people you deeply love, but the writing came with a sense that it was dealing with what I had to look at. So much scholarship about early Christianity is apologetic.

"The work that I do in these texts is highly imagistic. It appeals to quite a number of women because it speaks to layers of experience that women tune into very well. Some men, too, of course. As women move into the place of spiritual leadership, they are making a difference in how religion is experienced—they shift hierarchy, balance, and expectations. Once, when I was very distressed about my son's illness, I was jogging around Central Park. I stopped at a big church next to the Guggenheim. I didn't go to church in those days, but there was a Eucharist being celebrated by a woman priest. I don't know why it made a difference, but the experience opened me up. I talked to her afterwards, and we became good friends. I joined the church because of what happened that day. Now I go to a local Episcopal church because my daughter sings in their choir and there are women priests. The sensibility is different, as you know.

"When I look at women like you who become rabbis, or priests in the Episcopal Church, I think, 'Why would you deal with that kind of structure and establishment as a woman?' But I know from myself that's what you have to deal with." That is what most individuals in this book share—the difficulty of being a woman in a patriarchal tradition. What they also share is unquenchable love for the spirit.

"Sometimes I think about the ministry for myself," she says, "but not too much, because I love the explorative aspect of my work. Maybe later in my life. I like the idea of participating in the lives of the people, where the parish matters to them. To do it well would mean to do it with great insight and compassion and presence. You also need a certain distance—you know, it's a skill.

"The other thing that distresses me is that Christianity requires belief in certain 'articles of faith'—and I just don't believe in those things very much. If I were an Episcopal priest, I would represent the church, and that would feel false to me. For example, the Christians claim that there is only one true religion. That's self-serving and dangerous. How did these people get the idea that there is one true religion—and they have it? It's not only weird, it's dangerous, and what I'm writing now is about these misperceptions. First identify it and show how it got there. That's what the book about Satan was.

"In Judaism you could follow this rabbi or that rabbi, but that's not the way Christianity has traditionally understood itself. That's what I find distressing." Pagels is referring to the commentaries, such as the Talmud. "My work has nothing to do with participation in dogma and much to do with the care of the human community. It has to do with how the tradition became the way it did, what about it I can be love, or not love at all. What I'm doing is more Jewish than Christian in the reinterpretation of text.

"An old friend was horrified with my book *The Origin of Satan* before it was published. 'You shouldn't write about these things, it stirs people up.' But I believe that an unconscious relationship is more powerful than a conscious one. He said, 'But isn't Christianity a religion of love?' I said, 'Yes, but it's also a religion of hate.' If people don't know that, then they don't know what they're dealing with. What Christianity has repressed is its own capacity for evil. Most seminaries, for example, don't deal with aggression, so it comes out in other ways." Testimonies accusing Catholic priests of child molestation may be a symptom of the suppressed aggression to which Pagels refers. "Animosity is part of human nature. In the origin of anti-Semitism, Christianity gave a moral interpretation to ordinary, human animosity, even made it seem morally right. It's not that I don't like you because you're different and smell bad; in 'Christian' terms, it's right not to like you, and may also seem right to destry you. Whether it's the Crusades or whatever, such views turn something that I care about into the service of violence."

Evil has been defined as the will to dominate. In the Pentateuch (the Five Books of Moses), the tribe of Amalek is the first to attack the Israelites as they left Egypt, and they attacked from behind, where the weakest were. The Torah despises nothing more than the will to dominate: this is the definition of evil. Therefore, God commands the Israelites to destroy this wicked people, but by the time the event was recorded, Amalek didn't exist. Jewish hatred of Amalek is as intense as early Christianity's hatred of Jews, but the difference is that a Jew was unable to persecute a descendant of the despised people.

Pagels says this about the direction of religion: "I don't see the institutions creating change. They're inefficient, and they're losing people. Different traditions have different strengths, and more and more we see sharing of traditions. The Buddhist tradition deals with the inarticulate; the Jewish tradition deals with the word, spoken and chanted and prayed. Many people are seeing that these traditions are repositories with different gifts and liabilities. Some call it cafeteria religion, but I don't mock it, because it's often part of a genuine exploration.

"When it comes to spiritual connection, I feel closest affinity with artists. Bill Viola, Dan Halperin, Sharon Olds, a Chinese choreographer—these people are working in another dimension. Their work is not institutional. They are close to their sensibility, and there is tremendous spiritual awareness.

"I'm working on the Gospel of Thomas now—an amazing work. It's an attempt to interpret Jesus of Nazareth through the language of Jewish mystical theology, and the theology has to do with the primordial life in the beginning of time. Here you will find words like these: 'I am the light that was before all things and is before all things. I am all things, all things come forth from Me, and all things extend to Me. Split a piece of wood and I am there; lift up a rock and you will find Me there.' It's about all things are made in the image of that light. The Gospel of Thomas is about the light hidden in everyone, the image of God hidden within each of us.

"The Gospel of John, now in the New Testament, challenged the teaching of the Gospel of Thomas, which sees Jesus as inclusive. John agrees that Jesus may be the divine light, but insists that he is the *only* light. John suggests that the rest of humankind is sinful, and that Jesus *alone* comes from God. He *is* God. This is the only Gospel that says Jesus is God. What I'm writing about now is how Christians developed this claim to truth and how the majority chose the Gospel of John over the Gospel of Thomas.

"I'm writing this in terms of my own personal exploration. I'm not interested only in history; I'm interested in how people try to make meaning out of this teaching. Adopting a child after losing my own—that's *constructing* meaning out of something that happened. It's the symbolic Jesus, not the historical Jesus, who interests me. That's what fascinates me: how human beings *make* meaning: myth and ritual make and create different realities."

Gay has been scouting the room for a place to pose Pagels. There is a table of photos with her late husband, Heinz, and their first son. Another table has more recent photos of her current family, including her husband, Kent, and her daughter, son, and stepchildren. Gay wants to move the photos onto one table. After considering this request, Pagels decides that Heinz wouldn't mind, but she's unsure about Kent, so she asks us to please not move the photos.

Dr. Beatrice Bruteau

If God is Mind, Beatrice Bruteau must be one of God's favorite children. Ever since a friend sent me "Gospel Zen," a chapter from Bruteau's audacious book, *What We Can Learn from the East,* which is a meditation on Buddhist practice to deepen Christian consciousness, I've wanted to meet Beatrice Bruteau. At seventy-two, this eclectic Christian has explored most major religions with the energy and enthusiasm of a precocious nine-year-old, thrilling to each new discovery that brings her closer to God.

With a special focus on Vedanta (contemplative Hinduism) and Catholic Christianity, she has created a vision of an inclusive spiritual reality and ways to transform consciousness.

Although she lives in North Carolina, she suggests that we meet in Cincinnati at a regional meeting of the Association of Contemplative Sisters, a group begun some twenty-five years ago for nuns of cloistered orders. Today it includes sisters working in the community as well as lay members such as Bruteau. The sisters are gracious and helpful with our plans to get there. They ask me to lead a Friday night Sabbath service, assuring me that they are familiar with the service and like the music very much. They will bring musical instruments, and will dance and sing. Having never led a service for such an enthusiastic congregation, I gratefully accept the invitation.

Someone is supposed to meet us at the airport, but our plane is early, and we don't see anyone who looks like a Sister Loretta. When the crowds thin, we notice an eighty-year-old woman in turquoise shorts and tee shirt, peering intently at us. She moves closer and, looking at both of us, she asks Gay, eight inches taller than I, "Rabbi Drucker?" "Sister Loretta?" we ask incredulously. This is what nuns and rabbis look like today, and we still fool each other.

Sister Loretta takes us to the Milford Jesuit Retreat Center, where the meeting is being held, and we join the group by playing "six degrees of separation" to demonstrate how we are all deeply interconnected. In small groups, we are to find people that we know in common. How can I possibly know anyone whom mostly sequestered Midwestern nuns would know? One of them asks if I know Debbie Friedman; she heard her music recently at a Seder that she attended. Who knew?

Over the weekend we will be renewed not only by the beautiful grounds of the retreat house, which light up at night with fireflies, but also by the spirit of sixty rare women of all ages. They are a community united by their commitment to live their lives as blessing, in return for the gift of life. What that feels like to me, as a stranger in their midst, is inclusion, generosity, and kindness. We meet a Carmelite nun, Jean Alice McGoff, who entered the Carmelite monastery fifty years ago with the intention to "live a life of prayer, reflection, and work, the way the founders had conceived it in the sixteenth century. I entered to feel the throb of the spirit. In 1962, Pope John XXIII opened the doors of cloisters in the Vatican Council. Local leaders understood that the enclosed and separate life needed change. God is a God of history, and we needed to have more contact with people, and the world needed more contact with a contemplative." One of the founders of the Association of Contemplative Sisters, McGoff says, "The planet has its own agenda, and this is the time for the rise in the feminine."

In the same order, we met Teresa Boersig, a generation younger than Jean Alice McGoff. Boersig, with the help of her community, edited, anonymously, the *People's Companion to the Breviary*, a two-volume, egalitarian work that serves not as a "companion" in most places but as the breviary itself. Two hundred thousand copies are in print. They began small. "In 1984 we had a young sister who was really into social justice and inclusive language. She left the monastery, but she had planted the seed. I thought, 'Let's just do it and begin by saying "God" whenever we see "Father."' I composed a little book and asked the community if we could print five hundred. They were reluctant, but they sold right away. Now we print ten thousand at a time, and they go all over the world. The book includes all traditions, psychology, women's issues, and ecology. We've also removed a lot of the anti-Semitism of the liturgy," she says. The *People's Companion to the Breviary* is a rich anthology of spiritual writings that would be useful to any spiritual leader.

Bruteau wants to write a book about the Jewish perspective on Jesus—"this wonderful man," as she calls him—and asks me to contribute an essay. "I want to get rabbis who will look at Jesus from their point of view. All we have is what others have written about him, and you have to discount part of it because you know that the literature is partly polemical. But you do get some sense of the man, what he's about, from these writings. I want to know how Jews understand him. Never mind what happened afterwards; you're not to think of that. There isn't anything like Christianity yet, unless you want to count the messianic movements within Judaism like the Essenes."

It's difficult for me to think about Jesus and forget about "what happened afterwards." While I understand the value of such a project that wants to do justice to a historical figure, and to the people and the tradition that produced him and therefore has first right to comment on him, I decline. Despite his brilliant prophetic teachings, I don't have enough curiosity about Jesus to do the research. In response to my hesitation, Bruteau says, "I don't claim to represent Christianity but Jesus, which is an entirely different proposition from my point of view." But it is Christianity's history that interests me, especially its recent attempt to reinterpret its early texts without using Jews as scapegoats. Her book came out last year, entitled *Jesus through Jewish Eyes*, and received positive reviews.

Although there is scarcely time in the schedule for the interview, when we do get to it, Bruteau starts talking, and the ideas rush in all directions. I ask that she begin at the beginning. "I was a kid mystic, in relation to the trees and sky. I swung and sang myself into an altered state of consciousness through thunderstorms, dancing under the full moon, looking at the stars, sitting under the plum tree with the petals falling, braiding grasses, sitting in the sunshine, or thrilling to the mysterious color of everything just before rain.

"I was an only child for eight years and spent a lot of time alone. My connection to nature had nothing to do with any kind of formal religion. My parents didn't belong to a church—they had been Southern Baptists and had left the church—and they weren't being anything except interested people. Both were well educated, and they taught me a lot at home. We had a separate room for a library, and we listened to classical music." One of the questions in this book is, Who becomes a spiritual leader? Are we called one by one, regardless of upbringing, or does it help to have religious parents? Many women in this book describe virtually secular childhoods.

"I was a very successful little kid, skipped a few grades, and in high school was very unsuccessful socially." Being a passionate woman of faith doesn't put one at the top of the list for party invitations, and all the more so when you are a child of faith. "Learning was the greatest joy, and I particularly liked math and science. I've forgotten most of the mathematics, but the interest in science has persisted. When I was about thirteen, I went to the library and discovered Plato. I opened the book at random, and it fell to a vision of heaven where a chariot with horses goes out beyond heaven and goes in the Ideas, following the world of the gods. I just marveled!"

Her words rush out breathlessly in a torrent, trying to keep pace with her thought. She talks intensely and passionately without a pause. She leans forward as she tells me about events occurring almost sixty years ago as if it were yesterday. "I insisted on being taken back to the library the next day to finish Phaedrus. Plato is still prominent in my private pantheon; I still read it and teach it." Bruteau has started a monastic nonresidential community and two seminars in North Carolina where these groups study with her weekly. "We include Platonism and neo-Platonism. The Christian mystics base themselves on Plato.

"When I was fourteen, I found Lin Yutang's *Wisdom of China and India*. Half of it was Hinduism, and half Buddhism. Later on I joined the Vedanta Society, and I still identify as a Vedantin and many of my ideas come from this tradition. This is where the sense of everything being divine comes from and the willingness to see the divine incarnation.

"The Hindus are very lavish with their willingness to recognize certain people as *avatars* ["descents"] of God into human form, and that piece of knowledge was a very big thing for me. By then, I couldn't stand high school any more, so in the middle of the tenth grade I decided I had to get out of there and doubled up my courses. I took correspondence courses from the University of Missouri in the summer, so I was sixteen when I entered the University of Kansas City [now a campus of the University of Missouri]. One of my favorite 'mystic' places there was the new science library in what had been Linda Hall's [Hallmark cards] home. I'd sit on the back porch with the long lawn before me and read these wonderful ideas about the world and about the human power to know the world.

"I became a humanist Unitarian, but that didn't last long because my appetite for the mystical was not fed by this experience. I certainly saw how various superstitions and myths fell short, but I had nothing in place of them to satisfy my craving for God. I had to find a way both to learn science and philosophy and to develop and deepen my love of God." A sister tells Beatrice that she has a fax, and she nods. While she is a member

---

Vedanta is a Hindu philosophy that all reality is a single principle, Brahman, and teaches that the believer's goal is to transcend the limitations of self-identity and realize his unity with Brahman.

of the Association of Contemplative Sisters, she is the busiest and most connected to the outside world this weekend. She is also the queen bee of this group,
which knows and respects her work. Few in the big world have heard of her eru-
dition and original work; her publishers are small and specialized.

At twenty, after she had entered the graduate department of mathematics at
the University of Pittsburgh, she accidentally encountered the life and words of Sri
Ramakrishna, a nineteenth-century guru, in Romain Rolland's *Prophets of New
India.* "This was what I was looking for! Ramakrishna showed me how to have
direct experience of God, and that's what I wanted, you see. Not dogmatism, creeds,
beliefs, but experience. Jewish renewal is on this track now. Some call yoga and religious tradition with multiple deities polytheism, but it's really just different paths to
the one God. The oldest sentence in the world is in Sanskrit: 'The reality is one;
people call it by various names.' God is infinite and finite, transcendent and immanent, formless and with form. This is metaphysics, and this is what I teach.

"From the Ramakrishna swamis [monks] in the Vedanta Society I learned to
meditate, and transferred from math to philosophy and completed my master's
degree. My dissertation was on the philosophy of mathematics. Plato was right,
you see—math is essential to understanding God." Jim Somerville, a former Jesuit
priest and Bruteau's husband of many years, comes over to announce that lunch
is being served. They edit a magazine, *The Roll*, a correspondence network of contemplatives from all traditions all over the world. They have no children.

"I moved to New York in 1950 and found an apartment next to the Vedanta
Society, where life is totalizing. Meditation three times a day, classes three times
a week, festivals, interviews with the Swami . . . it's a monastic life. This was
cloud nine, and a group of us were blissed out for years. People say this feeling
comes and goes, but for me it comes and stays. I'm turned on all the time." How
wild to hear this expression, the ecstatic language first used for sex and drugs,
coming from a senior citizen talking about God (who, it turned out, didn't know
the original meanings of the terms she was using!)

Ramakrishna's missionary to the United States, Swami Vivekananda, said,
'I'm not teaching you Vedanta to Hinduize you or even to get you to follow what
I myself do. I want you to be you. You must Americanize it.' We might add
Christianize it, and Judaize it. You can put it into any tradition, and it will work.
We studied the Christian mystics such as Meister Eckhardt, who intimated that
we are God in human form. Here is where I found support for my youthful

discovery that we must take away descriptions. Another thing that was formative about those early years was the music. In Pittsburgh, we math students listened to Bach and Vivaldi while working on our homework, and we attended performances of the great oratorios. In New York, we Vedantins would go to Episcopal churches every Sunday afternoon for vespers—and also to concerts, of course. Some of us wore out an LP set of the B Minor Mass by playing it every day!

"Later I took some classes in medieval philosophy at Columbia University, learning about Augustine, Anselm, Aquinas, Bonaventure, Duns Scotus. Then I enrolled at Fordham University, where I remained both as an employee and as a student until I finished my doctorate with a dissertation on Aurobindo Ghosh, a twentieth-century Hindu philosopher very much like Teilhard de Chardin. The Ramakrishna people had urged us to learn Catholic mysticism, so I was quite open to doing this. But I wasn't an easy convert. I considered that I was still doing Vedanta but in a European context rather than an Indian one. So I was selective about what I took aboard and what I set aside.

"I didn't delay over 'mortal sin.' Socrates taught me that there's no such thing as sin because if someone knew what he was doing was wrong he would not do it. They tried to convince me that there was hell. I called it superstition. What I did like was the Eucharist, and that became my focal point for years. This is where the Catholics gave you union with God regardless of whether you could jack up your consciousness; it was simply there."

Bruteau looked at the pluses of Catholicism as a nonbeliever. "You didn't need the perseverance, and you didn't have to be so well practiced in meditation that you could control your mind. Of course if you're in a state of 'mortal sin,' what mind are we talking about? But since I didn't believe in mortal sin, I simply thought, 'Imagine the idea that by taking a piece of ceremonial bread we will have the presence of God with us always. I gotta have that!' So I brushed the other stuff away and went for it. The first time I received Holy Communion, I felt the connection with a real person who was interested enough in me to come and be intimately present to me."

In her book *What We Can Learn from the East*, Bruteau makes it clear that the first thing we can learn is that religion is a matter of direct experience. Forget propositions in theology, belief, and authority. The question is, What is your practice? Not, What church do you go to? She says, "The point is that the approach to and the practice of the religion are adjusted to the person, not the person to the religion."

At Sinai, God spoke in seventy—that is, all—languages, and each of the two million people standing there heard God's special message to him and her. When God speaks to us personally, we shed the identification with finite characteristics that we call "me."

In considering her relationship to the feminine, Bruteau frowns for a moment in thought and says, "I learned this from my mother. She was very sensitive to how women were always getting the short end of things. She taught me not to play up to the male ego. When I was in high school, they wanted me to edit the newspaper and let the boy editor get the credit. The principal tried to persuade me that I had to learn to let the boy take the credit. I refused. I've always been on this track naturally, rather than something I focused on as an enterprise.

"Paleo-feminism may have characterized an early holistic worldview in which villages were built in circles and women were rejected for having strong magic because they produce life from their bodies. Then the masculine era comes afterwards, when there was warehousing of food, and an invitation to attack and steal what each group has. Men become prominent in this.

"Here is where the Genesis story turns the creator into a male and woman becomes man's helper. That's the flip-flop that maybe occurred when paternity was discovered. The masculine era, objective thinking, brings advantages, because now you can give an account of your ideas, and now you begin to get the mathematics of things.

"There were two faults in the way the women's movement began. First, women aping men in power will just lead us to be wicked and coarse. That will just double the world's trouble! The other mistake is to see the feminine as irrational, and therefore encourage everyone to cultivate the irrational in themselves. Rationality is always better than irrationality. So I proposed neo-feminism, which is again holistic, unified, synthetic, and cooperative, but includes analytic and reflective methods. It brings a feeling for wholeness. The analytic masculine period takes things apart to see how they work; the feminine period puts them back together again. It's synthetic, an organic approach.

"All my life people have said to me, 'You think like a man,' and I took it as a compliment. But the rational and the mystical go together; the way to the mystical is through the rational. I still use mathematics for metaphors. In this case, you approach along a certain line of thought, and that thought will lead you past all the finite forms to a 'singularity' that escapes the rule and transcends finite values."

Perhaps Bruteau has kept her youthful enthusiasm and hope because she has never had a pulpit. But how could she? Her imagination takes her beyond local community. Many women spiritual leaders who do congregational work love the shelter of a specific community. They work as nurturing mothers in a family to keep it stable and growing, and before ordination was permitted them, they worked behind the scenes as volunteers. Bruteau is not motherly and, more important, she works to break from exclusive community.

"We started the monastery to be a spiritual community with Vedanta ideas, Catholic liturgy, math, science, and philosophy. In the seventies, I became Episcopalian for political reasons. It's the same religion as Roman Catholicism, but the Episcopal Church ordains women and has open communion, meaning all demonimations are welcome to receive the sacrament. In our monastic community there is no common residence, but what makes us a monastery is the lifestyle and outlook of the group.

"Everything is part of your monastic practice. Your family is your monastic family, and you have to get along with these people, practice patience, forbearance, and all the virtues practiced in a residential monastery. It's a fellowship, and those of us within it have a special relationship to each other. It's an encouraging relationship that helps you with all your relationships, and certainly not one that cuts you off from others.

"I call it the Fellowship of the Holy Trinity. That's a familiar name, but it has a deep meaning, suggesting that the metaphysical problem of 'the One and the Many' has a resolution at the level of the Ground of Being, by considering that the Ground is of the nature of personhood and therefore must be interpersonal. Some people find this very appealing." Unless you're a Muslim or a Jew, I add silently. "The Ground of Being should itself be something like a community. The community is the place where we humans have to get our act together to form what Teilhard [de Chardin] called the hyper-personal, a new level of unity resulting from the interactions of the persons. The Fellowship celebrates community with common meals, meetings for study, song, and silent prayer. We teach meditation, philosophy, and up-to-the-minute scholarship in biblical studies and science.

"It takes five years to go through the formation program. The first year they study monasticism in general; the second, they learn to read the Bible for its instruction in mysticism and how to pray. The third year they study Plato, the fourth Hinduism and Buddhism, the fifth science and art, and then they make a final profession of commitment to this form of life." This is an ambitious, innovative curriculum for ten people.

I question how her syncretism might work with Jews. "You're right with the notion of Jesus being understood in one tradition as a prophet and in another as one teacher among many, not more important than other prophets. The real problem is probably not theological, but historical. I suggest that we leave the particulars aside and find the bridge. Death, wickedness—these are human issues. Let's try to find out what question each tradition focuses upon. I tell people to follow the tradition that attracts you. Be creative—you don't have to choose among them; you can make a combination. You can carve out your own space. We have to transcend these different paths, these social descriptions. We have to transcend our belief in finite identity. Mysticism—identity in terms of our relationship to the Ultimate—is the only way to free ourselves from the need to be better, truer; to supersede, to complete, to be the last or the best word. We don't have to describe ourselves this way. God transcends all description, and we are children of God.

"I began what was possible: a Roman Catholic monastery in an Episcopal church. Once everyone is gathered, then I can begin my subversive work. Everyone—you, Malka—should start a monastery! Let's start from scratch. Forget history. We have sense enough to sit and say, 'We are divine. We transcend all this.' It's okay if you want to follow your grandmother's tradition, but do it playfully. Remember that you are more than her history; you're much bigger than that. We all have to get back to feeding each other and to creating our own thing. We don't have to take bits and pieces out of the boring religions and put them together.

"Just because they said something thousands of years ago doesn't mean they had some advantage over us. The reverse is true!" Everything I've read about new yearnings for God, however, suggests that while people want religious experience and intimacy with God, they want it in traditional forms. Mega-churches attract thousands on Sunday mornings with cappuccino and soft rock God music, but their message is traditional. "Write new scripture, Malka! Don't be slavishly dependent on the past. If you can see into the heart of reality, walk. Let's collaborate on a generic Sabbath ritual so that people can experience its message of oneness." Okay, maybe it's not syncretism; maybe it's evolution. I'm still not interested in Jesus very much, or Vedanta, but I'm interested in Bruteau, who stands where all paths converge.

STARHAWK

Almost thirty years ago, Miriam Simos changed her name to Starhawk and began a new chapter in feminist spirituality. By resurrecting witchcraft, an ancient religion rooted in Goddess worship, the natural world, and reverence for ancestors, she would also offer a call for worldly spirituality. In Santa Fe, people give me knowing nods when I mention Starhawk's name. I'm eager to meet her, because I wonder what a Witch looks like. A warm, middle-aged woman greets us at the door of her communal home in San Francisco, dressed in a tie-dye tee shirt and jeans. What distinguishes her is the intensity of her eyes.

We sit in her bedroom, a little cramped, because a nursery co-op is happening in her living room with one of the house partners. She begins, "I'm a nice Jewish girl who grew up to be a Witch. My father was a Communist who died when I was five, and although my mother's real religion was psychology, she never lost her Jewish identity and her attachment to Judaism. We lived in Los Angeles, in an apartment upstairs from my Orthodox grandparents. I went to Hebrew High School and narrowly missed becoming a rabbi, but one day I realized that if I were a rabbi, I'd have to go to services all the time, and I always found it boring. The times when I felt that I was in the presence of the sacred has rarely been in the synagogue or studying holy books." Sadly, that is true almost everywhere. Abraham Joshua Heschel writes, "It is customary to blame secular science and antireligious philosophy for the eclipse of religion in modern society. It would be more honest to blame religion for its own defeats. Religion declined not because it was refuted, but because it became irrelevant, dull, oppressive, and insipid."

Starhawk explains, "I felt a lot more freedom in the Goddess tradition to be creative, to be spontaneous, and to create ritual. There's no reason why you couldn't have a Jewish ritual that involved dancing naked around the bonfire and plunging into the ocean, but doing that as a Witch seemed natural, and doing that as a Jew seemed strange.

"Witch" is the most unsanitized, politically challenging description of the followers of the Reclaiming movement. "Witch" invokes power that is potentially subversive, although modern Witches regard themselves as healers and channelers of positive energy. Wicca, or Wikka, taken from the British traditional Craft, is a religion. Many Witches feel that calling themselves such may be gratuitously off-putting and may turn others away from an earth-based spiritual practice. Others reclaim the name "Witch" proudly.

"I had first met Witches when I was at UCLA in 1968, when I did an anthropology project on witchcraft and was fascinated by the idea of the Goddess. It was tremendously empowering to think about divinity in female form and to think about a religion that said sexuality was sacred and nature was sacred. This fit the real experiences I've had in life.

"I joined a women's consciousness-raising group. Some of the women were athletic and loved to backpack and hike, and I'd always wanted to do that stuff and hadn't done much of it—my mother wasn't a real nature-oriented person. I went off on a long bicycle trip for a summer, and it became a spiritual journey for me to be in contact with nature. And that was when it really came to me that spiritual work was core to my life.

"It must have been 1973 or '74. Women were just starting to explore spirituality as part of feminism and were starting to look at why we had only male images of God. I moved up to San Francisco and found there were women who followed witchcraft in the New Reformed Orthodox Order of the Golden Dawn. The first ritual was with a beautiful group of two hundred people in a public park. They had a great ritual, beautiful costumes, and a huge basket of rose-shaped cookies. I was amazed by the organization, community, and connection. I felt high for days afterward."

While the intention of Jewish gatherings is also to create a liminal moment that connects people to one another in community, what Starhawk witnessed rarely takes place in mainstream religions. Because religion is dangerous, fear keeps churches and synagogues from allowing religious experience.

"There are tried and true techniques for shifting consciousness that are thousands of years old—drumming and rhythm, chanting and repetition, rhyme, music, song. These are the things that help us move into a state where the interconnectedness of everything is corporeal and in the foreground. In our culture, we're made wary of shifting into a deeper, more intimate place, and there is often a reluctance to go there with strangers.

"Yesterday we had a Summer Solstice at the beach, and suddenly I see a hundred naked people running into the ocean for purification. And I see one of my goddess-daughters, who was born when her family lived in this house, go in as naturally as I went to temple for the High Holidays in September. It's amazing to think how quickly a tradition can spring up that feels thousands of years old. The ritual we began twenty years ago stuck because it works. It has power. We did lots of things, and some have taken root. Our chants have evolved from what we've made up through the years.

"Reclaiming, which is what we call our movement, began in 1980. We wanted to model a flow of power, so a few of us began teaching and started a newsletter. Things grew slowly, and we became involved in direct action around nuclear issues, AIDS, and Central American issues. We joined the blockade at Diablo Canyon nuclear power plant, and that was life transforming for Reclaiming. We'd come back from working together with people and being in a trusting group. We'd be in jail together and use that time to educate.

"I've tried to have the growth of Reclaiming not center around me but to center around the work. Let people bring their creativity and take on responsibility for organizing and taking on roles of teaching and leadership. From the very beginning I never wanted to be a guru. I've always wanted to be working with equal companions. Part of the problem is that our whole culture centers around celebrities, and it's hard on a practical level to buck that trend. But if you don't, it can eat you alive. You carry people's projections about you, and it's like wading through a fog of sticky spider webs. Adulation is like eating sugar candy—it's present, but there's no substance there. It's not like having somebody who genuinely loves you.

"It's vital for women to be in positions of leadership in spirituality. Unless women are out there and visible, it creates the idea in people's minds that women are inferior in every dimension. At the same time, there are many men who are involved in the Goddess movement. We encourage their presence in roles of teaching and leadership. There was a time when we worried that the men would take over, but we learned that it's not true. Men who are comfortable with themselves are comfortable with strong women in positions of leadership.

> "If we are nurtured and inspired by a tradition, we can worry less about who our ancestors are, and start to think of ourselves as the ancestors of the future, taking on responsibility for the lives and well-being of the children of that culture, and for creating the world we want all the children to grow up in."
> —Starhawk, *The Spiral Dance*

"The Goddess religion provides another vision for religions like Judaism and Christianity. It shows that women can be spiritual leaders and religion can be built around female images of beauty. In the pagan world, women rested against rocks and let the sun warm and celebrate their vulvas. We're the radical edge. Women pushing for more of a role within their religions seem moderate by comparison. I don't think anyone in the Goddess movement would want to see everyone become a Witch. But I do think that understanding the earth is something sacred, and that the whole web of life is to be cherished, protected, and loved.

"My practice has evolved in two directions. As the Reclaiming movement has grown I've become comfortable with large groups. In the seventies we'd have maybe five or ten people in the room for a ritual. My practice today centers more on spending time by myself in nature, simply observing what's going on around me, rather than internal meditation. I live out in the country most of the time now. I listen to the birds and try to figure out what they're saying to each other. I grow food as part of my practice, and I take walks to know the land and its ecology.

"I talked for years about nature's secret, and now I'm finally getting to know it in intimate relationship. I'm co-owner of a large ranch. It's a great community with people who share common values and who get together to work on real-life things like a volunteer fire department. It's a community that exists, and I don't have to organize it.

"When I first began writing and teaching, my biggest struggle was the inner voice that said, 'Who's going to listen to this? Who cares about this?' Now after years of learning to get that voice to shut up, it's more a question of 'What am I really called to work on right now?' When I'm in the country and rejuvenating myself, I feel almost selfish about it. Shouldn't I be suffering more?" It's a Jewish joke, and we laugh. "How can I be enjoying life so much?" she asks. "How do I empower other people and not just drop the ball?"

When I ask Starhawk for suggestions of women to meet, she mentions Luisah Teish; Z Budapest, founder of the first feminist coven, and other women in the Goddess movement, and then she talks about Rabbi Laura Geller. "Laura was driving my mother to some conference—they didn't know each other before—and my mother spent the whole

Reclaiming organizes public rituals for the eight Sabbats: the winter and summer solstices, the spring and fall equinoxes, Halloween (also called Samhain), Brigid (also called Imbolc or Candlemas, February 2), May Day (also called Beltane), and Lammas (also called Lughnasad, August 1); publishes a quarterly magazine; offers classes and workshops focusing on modern feminist spirituality and traditional teachings; and maintains a web page (www.reclaiming.org). The Reclaiming community includes people who identify with the Reclaiming Tradition of witchcraft. Some just attend rituals occasionally; others practice the tradition in their own covens, in circles, or as solitaries. Community members often participate in political actions directed toward nonviolence, social justice, and a healthy planet.

drive agonizing about me. 'My daughter's a Witch, and I always wished she'd become a rabbi.' That sort of thing.

"'What's her name?' Laura asked. When my mother told her, she pulled the car over to the side, stopped, and said, 'Bertha, are you trying to tell me your daughter is Starhawk?'

"'Yes, that's what I've been telling you.'

"Laura looked at her and said, 'Bertha, leave your daughter alone. She's doing a great service to Judaism. She's famous.' My mother called me afterwards, hurt because I never told her that I was famous. 'Would you believe it if I told you?' I asked." Starhawk shakes her head and laughs.

"I'm deeply Jewish at my core being, and it affects everything I do. What I took from my Jewish education is the sense of this world being the center of religion. It's about paying attention to what's going on around you in this life, not about the afterlife." This sounds like her current practice. "It's about the real relationships you have, being active in the world. Justice is core to religious being. For me, that's translated directly into my approach in Goddess religion. Unfortunately, social consciousness isn't as universal in Judaism as I once thought it was.

The *Shema* is the first prayer a Jewish child learns and the last words a Jew says.

"When my mother died in 1992, having my practice helped. She'd been sick for three years and was really suffering. It was tragic to see that; yet, the moment she died, there was this wonderful relief, peace, and joy that filled the room. Death is not the end, and death is nothing to be afraid of." Three years later, Starhawk wrote *The Pagan Book of Living and Dying*. In it she describes saying the *Shema* with her mother: "As we recited the words together, I felt a profound sense of grief. Here was the prayer that, as a child, I had said every night before I went to sleep, the prayer that was on the lips of martyrs when they died, the prayer that the victims of the Holocaust murmured as they went to the gas chambers, the prayer said by all of my ancestors for thousands of years. In saying it together with my mother as she died, I felt connected to all of them. And yet it was not a prayer that I could believe in."

After wrestling with whether there should be a core statement of Pagan belief, Starhawk decided that when you are dying, you aren't creative. It's not the time to come up with a new ritual or prayer. Her book, dedicated to her mother, is her effort to create a ritual in which she and others could believe.

On October 30, 1999, two thousand people of all ages, colors, family units, genders, and beliefs gather at Herbst pavilion in San Francisco to mark the Witches' Halloween and the twentieth anniversary of the Spiral Dance ritual created by Starhawk. The immense, high-ceilinged space faces the water; it was once a military installation, last used in World War II. Wet, salty fragrance mingles with musk, incense, and other aromatic evocations of a more idealistic and hopeful time. Some of the multitude are devoted Witches; others come to be warmed by the fellowship.

Bowers of flowers, incense, candles, altars to the four elements, and altars for departed loved ones turn a cold pavilion into sacred space. The altars to the dead are not somber. They glow with the cheer of photographs taken at a happy moment to remember a life. Their woven arches with leafy boughs, food, and photos create a meeting place for life and death. People kneel, stand in front of altars, chant, or sing. There is no one way to pray here. Very little is for sale, admission is on a sliding scale, and the mood is inclusive, mellow, and playful.

A nine-year-old girl tells me seriously, "I like it here. It's fun, and the people are nice—nicer than what you'd find outside this room. And some of the people are wise." This is a tempting path.

The Spiral Dance ritual, as with all rituals, attempts to bring heaven to Earth, the transcendent to the ordinary. Here it takes the form of reclaiming gentleness, simplicity, quiet, warmth, and generosity. This is witchcraft, new thought ideas, and the sixties, reclaimed for the sake of heaven. San Francisco is the perfect city, because this is where the sixties began.

Starhawk is not easy to find during the preparation for the Halloween because she walks her talk; it all comes together without someone directing and leading. She wanders around, and people ask her questions; she encourages and offers presence. At eight in the evening the show begins: two giant figures on stilts, representing the masculine and the feminine, stride into the center of a circle ringed with participants. Chanting follows as trapeze artists dance the song of Earth overhead. Names of new babies are celebrated, and those who have died in the last year are also named, reminiscent of the Jewish practice of reading names for the Mourner's Prayer.

This is not boring, and neither was the great Temple in Jerusalem. Three thousand years ago, the people experienced God with fire on the altar; incense to mask the animal smells, and drums, horns, and cymbals. Some say there were elephants. Starhawk's celebration may be more traditional than anything we find inside synagogues and churches today. Let's have a little more of that compelling, primordial, old-time religion that fits the time in which we live.

3

Law

As you walk, you cut open and create that riverbed into which the stream of your descendants shall enter and flow.

NIKOS KAZANTZAKIS

WOMEN WHO HAVE CHOSEN TO UPHOLD THE HISTORIC PRACTICES AND BELIEFS of a traditional faith path, including those that have only recently admitted women into the clergy, may have the easiest time of it. They serve with the power of the establishment behind them because they are lovers of their respective traditions and do not wish to innovate. As loyal and devout members of a long-rooted family, they are secure and strong with the legacy of inherited knowledge.

On the other hand, it is in the traditional institutions that women find the most resistance to their authority, because no matter how conservative their outlook, women are still women: they look and behave differently from men, and they interpret the world from their experience. God as Creator takes on new meaning when a woman imagines God from the perspective of having a body that can bear life. In Hebrew and Arabic, the word for compassion derives from the same root as the word for womb, and one of God's names is Compassion. Cosmic creation looks different when we imagine God's womb opening to give birth to the world. The paradigm shift, however, is without gender: when a woman is a leader, both men and women experience religion in a new way.

Episcopal priest Katherine Campbell and Deacon Bettye Reynolds serve a congregation of single-parent children in a South Sacramento housing project where most male priests are unwilling to serve. Reynelda James, an Episcopal Native American, lives on ancestral land in the Paiute reservation near Reno, Nevada, where she serves as an elder who teaches, organizes, advises, and consoles.

Because of the blessing from Father Peter McCall, Maryanne Lacy became a faith healer, practicing the laying on of hands in a mainstream Roman Catholic church. Mother Ammachi is an Indian Hindu who transcends the boundaries of language and culture by bringing a unique ministry of physical embrace that its followers describe as the experience of unconditional, divine love. Devoted Muslim Connie Yaqub, a native daughter of America's heartland, is married to a Palestinian Muslim and is the mother of two daughters. She teaches about Islam in Albuquerque schools to dispel prejudice and to be an advocate for Islam and Palestinian rights.

Joan Halifax Roshi, head of the Upaya Zen Center in Santa Fe, represents the growing trend of women priests in the American Buddhist community. Finally, author and lecturer Sister Jose Hobday, a Native American Franciscan nun, brings her ministry to truck stops and prisons in Gallup, New Mexico, the poorest diocese in the United States.

THE REVEREND CATHERINE CAMPBELL
AND DEACON BETTYE REYNOLDS

The Reverend Catherine Campbell and Deacon Bettye Reynolds are Episcopal ministers in South Sacramento, sixty miles and a planet away from the high-steepled Grace Cathedral where the Reverend Dr. Lauren Artress presides. Their pulpit is the common open field of a housing project of 125 four-unit homes. Single mothers who speak only Spanish head 90 percent of the families. The congregation consists of twenty to thirty children. Each Saturday night, Campbell and Reynolds come to bring ceremony, drama, art, music, and hope to children who are rarely read to, listened to, or held. Perhaps most important of all, when a child takes Communion, she tastes the sweetness of being cared about by two really nice women who love God.

Deacon Bettye drives us to the service. We are staying in her house for the weekend with Reynelda James, a Paiute elder, thanks to Bettye, who arranged the whole weekend for us. The modest tract house is so welcoming and homey that it feels like a slumber party. Portraits of Jesus abound, verses from Scripture decorate the walls, as well as a Jewish prayer for peace.

Wearing her collar and a deadpan expression, as if she is accustomed to strangers as houseguests, Deacon Bettye settles us into bedrooms that look like a cozy bed-and-breakfast. When we're ready to leave, she puts a portable Communion kit in the trunk of her car, along with cookies and juice for the children. Bettye is a little like Lucille Ball, seemingly dizzy but in the end pulling everything together. As we get into the car, a fifteen-year-old girl slides in next to me. Deacon Bettye is keeping an eye on her over the weekend, I learn later, because the girl has a six-month-old child, and she's a child herself.

For much of the weekend, Deacon Bettye won't be around because she assists not only at the Saturday night service but also on Sunday morning, at 8:00 and 9:30, at another church. At 12:30 she works with Catherine Campbell at an Anglo service, and in the afternoon she leads drumming and services at Four

Winds, a Native American worship center, a ministry of the Episcopal diocese of northern California. A widow in her sixties, she works seven days a week as an unpaid deacon.

She pulls up to a cluster of faded yellow stucco four-unit buildings. At 6:00 P.M. it is at least ninety degrees and deadly still, except for Reverend Campbell's flock. They are sitting on the ground, working quietly and seriously with colored paper and markers to make masks for a play they will perform for their parents. Bettye joins Catherine Campbell with the children. Although she is almost twice Catherine's age, they are good friends with deep respect for each other. As deacon to the priest, she cautiously squats down with the kids and tries to speak a little Spanish. A nine-year-old girl holds up her mask and announces that it is a woman "who is pregnant and who will never get skinny again." With seven younger siblings, she has never seen her mother not pregnant.

This is not a coveted pulpit. When Campbell came to the community, she says as she cuts out a mask, "We began in a local church here, and the kids were really excited and drawn to it. Suddenly we have twenty-five kids coming on a Saturday or Sunday night, lots of ten- and eleven-year-old boys. The Anglo congregation spread a rumor that the kids were going to break all the windows and destroy the building. So they said we needed two English-speaking adults for every ten kids to escort them out if they caused trouble.

"A Latino worship community isn't like a regular English Sunday worship service. The kids run around, and there is little parental control of kids. So we said, 'Thank you very much, and good-bye. We don't want those conditions.'" Looking around, she says, "It's working pretty well here. We have two houses that

offer a place to worship when the weather is bad. From May to October we have our services outside."

There are few trees for shelter in the dry, dusty field, and only six chairs for the adults. I sit next to Reynelda James, who observes, "These two women work hard with their community." A boy of about six or seven arrives on a bike with the seat up to his armpits. He's cool and respected. Although he never lets go of the bike during the service, he soaks in every word as if it is, indeed, God's word.

The children's play and the service are bilingual for the mothers. The children pass out the service booklets, "El Divino Salvador," a liturgy that Rev. Catherine Campbell created for the children. One of the few adult men in the housing project is working on his car during the service, and occasionally engine noise overpowers the prayer. After the play, Campbell tells the parents, in Spanish, that the day before, three synagogues were firebombed in Sacramento, and she asks everyone to pray for the congregations. After the children take Communion with Rev. Catherine Campbell assisted by Deacon Bettye, they end the service with an exuberant "Yea God!"—a new translation for "Hallelujah."

Catherine, a gentle-faced, grave woman in her thirties, invites us to dinner at a family barbecue restaurant nearby and insists on treating us, even though it is we who have asked for the interview. Born and brought up in Mexico, she says, "I always wanted to do Hispanic ministry. My father was an architect in Mexico City. I'm Anglo in blood, but culturally I'm very Mexican. When I was fourteen, I volunteered at a children's clinic in Monterrey for the poorest of the poor; 50 percent of the children died there. It was a sad little place; yet, the atmosphere was spiritually enhancing because volunteer doctors, nurses, and helpers ran the clinic. I got to know God in a wonderful, mysterious way even in the midst of death. I gave shots, primary care, because they didn't have enough volunteers. I felt called by God to serve the poor, and I kept this feeling in my heart. At the time, there were no women priests, so I never thought about becoming one. I thought about going into medicine.

"My mother had a severe stroke when she was fifty, and we moved to the States. I ended up taking care of both my parents, because my father was ill, too. I was in college pre-med, but it wasn't the easiest thing to take care of two sick parents and go to medical school. So I got a chemistry degree instead because I thought that maybe through medicinal chemistry I could save the world with a drug, maybe, to eliminate cancer. All I knew was that I was called by God to save people.

"Then my father got so sick I had to leave graduate school. We were in Houston. My parents died within six weeks of each other. I had to wait a year before I knew what to do. I did a chaplaincy program at the county hospital, and then I knew that I would become a priest. I went to Virginia Theological Seminary because it had more focus on Hispanic ministries than any other. While I was in school, I started a Salvadoran congregation, and we grew to a hundred and twenty in the two years I was there. We started from nothing and blossomed into a really good strong congregation. That's what I'm proudest of in my twelve years in the ministry.

"Because most of the religion is passed on maternally, I don't have a problem with male parishioners. They are very accepting, and I think it's because of their relationship to women and the religion. Most of the resistance to women doesn't come from the congregation; it comes from male clergy. When I started the process for ordination in Texas, the bishop said a woman couldn't have a Hispanic ministry. Many women give up, but I'm known for my tenacity. Now there are twenty-two Hispanic Episcopal churches in Los Angeles, and most are led by women because the men don't want them.

"There is a lot of prejudice towards Hispanics and Hispanic ministry in the Episcopal Church in the United States. I'm the Hispanic missionary for the whole diocese, and I'm supposed to promote and expand Hispanic ministry throughout northern California. But the reality is that most congregations are like the one that we left, willing to boot us out because of their fear of the Latino population. California is very, very difficult." She shakes her head. Deacon Bettye, listening intently, nods. "In Virginia, people acknowledged their racism, so we could talk about it. Here there is no conversation because there is no recognition that this is a problem.

"Most Hispanics are either Catholic or Pentecostal. Many come to us because their marriage situation is ambiguous. They're either not married, weren't married in the church, or they're living with somebody who has a wife somewhere else. They feel excluded from the Roman Catholic Church. Our church is also more family-oriented, and they get to know the clergy much better than at a Roman Catholic church.

"I don't quibble whether they become Episcopalian. The kids here come from different backgrounds and some have no religion at all. Giving them a faith stamps them with a moral ground and offers them a way to learn that God loves them just as they are. I do pastoral care and life-cycle events for these families, too.

"I don't work that much, around forty to sixty hours a week, not too bad. I'd like more to do, to really get a congregation going here. I love the one-on-one with the people. Like these kids. To see them blossom is wonderful. They get no attention anywhere; they're marginal in school. If you ask them what they think about their future, they have no expectation. When I was growing up, I expected to go to college and do something with my life."

Sunday afternoon we join Deacon Bettye at Four Winds Native American Episcopal Church, where she serves as spiritual leader. She is the oldest, whitest, and least indigenous or hip person in the room. But I hadn't seen her drum or chant yet. A dozen people

prepare for the service by putting a large drum in the center of the room and sprinkling tobacco on it in a traditional pattern. Six, including Bettye, sit around the drum and begin slow, emphatic drumming. No one is a full-blooded Indian, but most have Native American ancestry. An hour of drumming precedes the service.

Bettye's drumming looks as if she is praying, immersed and in connection. The zany Lucy resemblance comes up again as she starts the drumming. Tidy auburn hair that frames her grandmotherly face bounces to the beat of the drum; her arms blur as she pounds the taut skin of the drum. Drumming fills the room and everyone in it until there is nothing but sound. Next to Bettye a young man with long, black hair straddles his year-old son between his legs. The baby's hand rests on the drum as his father pounds away, inches away from his little fingers absorbing the sound. The drummers slow down and stop; the room fills with silence.

The families arriving for the 5:00 P.M. service are mostly Anglo. Two blond-haired boys, eight and ten, dressed in clean collared shirts, look happier than most children I've seen in worship settings. We turn in four directions and ask God to be in the middle of everything. After the children drum a sweet Native American children's song, the adult drummers sing a song of blessing for the children. We settle into a circle around the drum for the rest of the service, which is a standard Episcopal service with prayer, homily, and Communion. Bettye's teaching is about how much she loves Jesus and that everyone can believe in Him as well as in their own tradition.

The Jewish people share with Native Americans an ancient, inherited tradition that struggles to transmit its wisdom from generation to generation. We tell a story about a grandmother who takes her granddaughter to the edge of a dense forest. Taking the child's hand, the grandmother says, "A long time ago, when my great-grandmother was a little girl, her grandmother took her to this forest. They went to a special place, lit a fire, and said a prayer. When my great-grandmother grew up, she took her granddaughter to the place where her grandmother had taken her and lit a fire, but she no longer remembered the prayer. When the little girl grew up she took her granddaughter to the special place but no longer remembered how to light the fire." Grandmother smiled at the little girl. "I don't know the prayer, I don't know how to light the fire, and I no longer remember the place. But come, let's go and search for the place together."

Many of us today, regardless of background, search together for the sacred. By gathering people of mixed ages and backgrounds, the Four Winds Church demonstrates that an ethnic community can define itself not only by blood but also by heart. That is why Anglos follow Native Americans into the forest; they feel their hearts fill with the rhythm of the drumbeat.

It's a long day, but Bettye squeezes in the interview, which begins with asking how she came to be a deacon. "I had been widowed for some years, and I had been doing a few things such as visiting the sick and shut-ins at the church. I worked with the ECW, the Episcopal Church Women. My former pastor one day suggested that with the work that I was doing, I should consider the diaconate. I think the priest saw beyond what I was doing, saw I could do more. Once I began the path, it was the only path for me. I went to a school for deacons in 1988.

"I became a deacon because I didn't feel called to be a priest. A lot of the priest's work is doing research and being in a room alone, and that's not my thing. I want to work with people, listen to them. I saw my mother do that. She was the repository for half the town's secrets, because she would listen. Listening skills may be more important than counseling skills. My mother, like Catherine, wanted to go to medical school but couldn't because her mother died. That had a lot to do with our becoming friends.

"I deal a lot with death—it's a great challenge not to see death as the enemy to be fought, because my nature is to fix things. I take someone's hand and help them out of life as well as into life. The ministry of presence is more important than anything I could say or do. It helps people to feel that God is a friend.

"When I was in the school for deacons I was sure I wanted to be a hospital chaplain. Then I met a couple in our church who were going to be married there, and he was Native American. He asked me to sponsor him for confirmation, and I suggested that he wear one of his festival shirts. He did, and it was gorgeous. The bishop talked to him and me and said that maybe we could start a Native American group that would welcome all who came. It would help those who were searching for their backgrounds to find answers and to recapture traditions. That was the beginning.

"I started a food closet and a clothes closet. Everybody knows where to discard, and I take everything because I know who needs them. It's like a puzzle, putting the pieces together. A church that only ministers to itself dies if it doesn't reach out into the community.

"What I've learned is how close cultures are to each other. That's my job, to keep looking for similarities. The rhythms of the Native music are similar to my Celtic background. Why do we fight over the color of skin or a different way of doing things? A lot of people say you can't be both Native American and Christian, but you can. Sometimes a Native American will come to a service and say, 'Don't give me this God stuff,' and then he'll suddenly see a connection between the Creator and God. That just sends my heart skyrocketing. Women are better at this because we're more flexible, because of the nature of our lives, learn to bend, adjust, adapt in ways that men don't have to do.

"A young friend in the Native community said to me that I was her elder, and it shocked me, but I was so pleased. Elders in the Native community are those who have earned their place by the things they've done. I don't think of myself that way." Bettye was widowed young and brought up her children alone. At the service she told the group bad news about a daughter with a recurring cancer.

As we are leaving, Bettye says, "You've done something wonderful by coming here." She is not speaking for herself as much as for the people she serves. By coming to witness an important part of their lives, we helped them remember that each one is made in the image of God. Because poor people, especially non-Anglos, are often unseen and ignored in our society, our presence was medicine to them. Seeing the kindness of Catherine and Bettye and the trust given to them by men as well as women in their communities strengthened us, too. Deacon Bettye may have known that good would come of it when she strongly encouraged us to come to Sacramento and planned a full, smooth schedule for us.

She is unassuming and almost shy, bearing a humility that borders on low self-esteem. She doesn't feel that she knows something others don't know, and she doesn't proffer advice or suggestion of any kind. What she does know is that her presence makes a difference.

REYNELDA JAMES

Reynelda James, an elder in the Paiute tribe in Nixon, Nevada, is a deep, steady, and quiet spirit whose eyes listen. She brings us a candle wrapped in leaves that she bought on the road from Reno to Sacramento because it was so "neat"—a playful, surprising word from an elder. It makes her more approachable. She also gives us a bunch of fragrant blue-green sage branches tied with colored ribbons, and water from Pyramid Lake, the crystalline sacred lake of her people. Her tribe dips sage into the pure, cleansing water that provides life to the people. We meet Reynelda at Deacon Bettye Reynolds's home. On Sunday afternoon at the Four Winds Native American Episcopal Church, Reynelda meets a man about to take an initiation journey and blesses him with the sage dipped in lake water. Waving the pungent bundle in four directions, she chants and speaks in a low, deliberate, and hypnotically rhythmic voice. There is a single focus in the room.

At Bettye's house afterward, I asked about the blessing she offered the young man. Reynelda says, "There are no special words with the blessing: It comes from the heart when you bless someone with a prayer of healing and cleansing. I speak in the language of my people, and the blessing is from head to toe. I've also said the blessing at gatherings in church and for the annual gathering of Native American women. Each tribe has a way of using the elements to teach the love we have for Jesus." While most of us know only one path, Native Americans are the sages of blended traditions.

"I was born November 8, 1932, and was raised by my grandparents. My grandparents are full-blooded Paiute Indians, and my grandmother was born here in Nixon. She took me on lots of walks, and we did a lot of the prayerful things. She used an eagle feather for healing, because the eagle is sacred to us as a messenger to the Creator. She also used sage. She took me to the lake and she took me to church, always by foot. We'd begin to walk, and as we passed other houses, people would gather, and by the time we got there, we were a whole congregation.

"My grandmother was an elder. People came to her, and I watched what she did but didn't ask questions. One thing she did, and we do it even now, is the draining of blood to relieve pressure."

When asked what it takes to be an elder, Reynelda laughs and says, "Gray hair. Usually it's someone at least in their sixties. There are lots of Paiute elders, and they are very respected women. An elder is someone who has lived a full life, who knows a lot because she's lived through hardships. Some people have experience and use it; others just let it fly away. Elders teach the Native ways, yet many of them are Christian. The women were the mentors, and they were the ones who took care of the grandchildren. Men are elders, too, but I look to the women because they taught me a lot. The elders are all gentle, and they've lived hard lives, raising their families on hardly anything."

How is gentleness taught? "Just watching, watching. Many times with my grandmother there was silence when we walked in the bushes. She was also brave. Once we were crossing the river to visit a woman on the other side of the river. It was Marble Bluff, where the river is high. My grandmother had a long stick, and the river was flowing to the lake. She had the stick on one side of her, and she had me against her, against the water flow. I knew that she would get me across—it was kind of scary—but she was strong and she was faithful. It was faith that took us across that river. I trusted her.

"Once we were in church singing 'Onward Christian Soldiers,' and I looked up at my grandmother and she was just singing, but I never forgot how she looked. When I see the elders at the senior center, gentle women, I see my grandmother. They speak in Paiute, and I feel a love for them because this language is like a spirit that was given to us. They laugh a lot, too.

"I was sent to Stewart Indian Boarding School, and it was a good experience, although we didn't learn that much because we studied half the day and worked half the day. I worked as a governess when I was fifteen for Mimi and Marty Kronberg, and we stayed friends until their last days. They were Polish Jews. Every time Mimi's mother came to visit, she brought me cosmetics from Helena Rubinstein, where she worked. I really enjoyed the gifts because I was young and couldn't afford things like that.

"My husband and I left the reservation because of his work with the state, but we always helped his father farm on weekends. We always wanted to return to the reservation, our homeland, and after we raised our children in Carson, we moved back in 1982. We live along the Truckee River, and from the east side there is no access to the river or lake except through the reservation.

"I still go to St. Mary's, where I was baptized. The church was always meaningful to me. But the thing I remember, and what I always see, is the picture they showed us of Jesus: blue-eyed and blonde. Until I became really involved with the Natives at the boarding school, I couldn't get rid of that picture." Her pain and anger echo that expressed by Bishop Kelly. "Then I saw a picture of a brown Apache Christ. It took me a long time to see Christ as an Indian because of my early education. This was an overwhelming discovery. I felt that I had been deceived.

"I learned to keep the church separate from the home. At home I learned the blessing with sage and water. The elders in our community didn't believe it belonged in the church, but now we've brought these things together. We were made in his image, so God created us brown, red, yellow, like the colored ribbons I gave you." And the candle she gave us is the light that God shines on all the colors.

"I perform services at St. Mary's in the morning when we don't have a priest. And I've recently entered a calling process because I've prayed to know if I've been called to preach. I don't know if I'm wise enough or if I can do it, but I have a lot of encouragement from our little congregation. It's the community that decides whether I should be a preacher. Four of us are doing this: a young man who feels called to be a priest, two women who want to be deacons, and me. I want to be a preacher. The hardest thing in my life has been to learn what God wants of me in the church. I don't know what my decision is about this, but it will come from my heart. I've thought of calling my bishop, because I need to talk with someone to see if I can do it." She laughs and shrugs. "I guess I'm modest.

"One time I remember going to church, and my little brothers and sisters were sick. I was a child, too. When I came home I had them kneel down and I gave them bread and water. I've always had a sense I could do this. When my stepfather died, I was depressed. I went to talk to the bishop and told him I wanted to be a nun. And he said I shouldn't do this if I was looking for a refuge from hurt, and he was right. I wanted a place for comfort. Now it's different, because I want to help people."

It's difficult to imagine that she could be any busier serving her community. A typical day might begin with bathing and feeding her aged aunt, who is afflicted with Alzheimer's and lives with her. After Reynelda takes her to daycare, she visits one of her children or grandchildren and then stops at the parish hall to see what needs to be done in the community. "I receive a lot of telephone calls from women all over the state. When they're troubled, I pray with them over the phone, with prayers from my heart. And many come to the house. A grandmother's house is where everyone gathers. I always have a pot cooking for whoever comes."

At a Saturday evening Episcopal service in an open field near a mainly Hispanic housing project, Reynelda and I sit next to each other while we watch Rev. Catherine Campbell and Deacon Bettye Reynolds preside over twenty mostly attentive children and a few mothers. She says, "It must be hard to want to do something in your heart that you're not allowed to do." What prompts these words is unclear. I ask her if she feels that she's been able to do what her heart wants as the other two women have. She answers, "Not yet."

She explains, "Eight years ago I felt that we needed a support group for women who have alcoholic spouses. A few, especially the men, said it would never work; our community is too small, and there would never be confidentiality. Women don't have formal positions of authority in my tribe. So I put the idea away. But I kept thinking, 'How can I do this?' I went to St. Mary's, our local church, and called on three women. One was a social worker, one a Head Start director, and the youngest was traditional and practiced our Native ways. They liked the idea, and we decided to have a gathering of Episcopal Native American women of all ages, teenagers, elders, and single mothers. We found a woman of the Crow nation in Montana, and she told her story of going from being an alcoholic to the chairperson of her nation. She came home one morning, and her oldest child said that she had given the two youngest the last bit of dry bread. It was an awakening for her. She heard God tell her to put away the alcohol and become a loving mother to her children.

"Women came from far away, and the conference was successful. The elders spoke to the young women, told them to stay in school and take leadership roles in their communities. This began a women's group that gathers every couple of years. It's a time for learning, sharing, listening, and singing. We all get good things to take back to our communities. When many more women from my own Paiute community take part in our women's group, and when all the women from other neighboring tribes begin to join us, that's when I'll feel that I've fulfilled what I want to do.

"My four children feel that I've instilled the spirit in them, and I hope they will teach their own children. Not so many young people attend church, because they're too busy. Maybe they'll go to a powwow, but I don't see how they're going to become leaders in the church. But they work with the community and keep our reservation going. You never know when someone will emerge as a leader."

MARYANNE LACY

It is noontime on a Tuesday in Dobbs Ferry, New York, and the main sanctuary of the century-old Sacred Heart Roman Catholic Church is nearly full. Folk-rock hymns sung by a young woman soften and warm the great room for half an hour before the service. Father Peter McCall and Maryanne Lacy sit near the altar until the service begins with Lacy standing up and saying, "Praise the Lord!" She asks for a moment of silent adoration, followed by an invitation to newcomers to raise their hands for a blessing: "Loving Lord God, we are gathered here today in the holy and wonderful and glorious name of Jesus Christ of Nazareth. We pray that everything we say and do today will bring us God's unconditional, personal, intimate, caring, and sweet love. And we thank and praise you and give you great honor and glory. Amen." She welcomes and introduces Gay and me by name. Many eyes turn to the rabbi being blessed in the name of Jesus, and I give a regal wave.

During the service, Maryanne sings a lilting, melodic song with unrecognizable words and melody. She says later that it is glossolalia, or tongues, "a charismatic gift of the Holy Spirit. After Jesus ascended to heaven and the apostles were waiting and scared, the Holy Spirit came upon them, and tongues of fire entered them. They began speaking in different languages, and studies say that speaking in tongues is a combination of ancient languages. It comes out in different ways. Sometimes I sing in praise, and it sounds different if I'm praying over people. I can't carry a tune," she says earnestly. "If you asked me to sing 'When Irish Eyes Are Smiling,' I couldn't do it. Only under the power of the Holy Spirit can I do it. It's completely spontaneous."

After Father Peter's intelligent homily about tolerance of all peoples, Maryanne stands in front of the congregation, eyes closed and still, and says, "I feel a fragility in the room." Despite the drama of her healing ministry, this isn't shtick to arouse the people. She means it, and it is such sincerity that makes her credible. Does a priest offer his feelings like this? She invites those who wish healing to come forward. An elderly woman waiting her turn speaks to me. "I was born Jewish. My parents came from Russia. I married a Catholic, and we had a Catholic home." She closes her eyes in concentration, and I am reminded of the Dalai Lama's observation that the Jews are a very spiritual people.

Six teams of four ministers, trained by Lacy and McCall, stand ready to facilitate the healing. Seventy-five people stand in line, waiting their turn to come up to Maryanne and Peter to tell them what is hurting. Each stands in front of Father Peter, who takes anointing oil mixed with beeswax from his ring and rubs it into the forehead of the suffering person. Placing her hands on the person, Maryanne asks God to help him or her, and then she chants in tongues. Postures visibly relax, and most people allow the gentle pressure of her hands on their chest to push them backward, where they are supported by the team that slowly places them on the floor. They remain there until, at their own pace, they are ready to get up and return to their seats.

Maryanne has a two o'clock appointment with us, and it is now three minutes to two. While I'm deciding whether to interrupt her, she comes over to me with an outstretched hand and the bluest eyes I've ever seen. She's on top of it; Father Peter and the teams will carry on without her. "Rabbi Drucker," she says, firmly grasping my hand. Following her into another immense room, this one empty and unheated, we set up for the interview. I want to know what it feels like to heal someone.

"When I pray with a person, I feel relief. The hands of our people in the ministry feel the healing power coming through them. It's hot, usually, and sometimes there is a vibrating energy. A lot of people come here regularly for healing, every week. When you have a life-threatening illness like cancer, healing is an ongoing process. Years ago we'd see people on a one-on-one in our office, and we'd have a few services a year. When the numbers grew bigger, we couldn't see people individually anymore, so we started the Tuesday noon service.

"When someone tells me that they have a broken hand, I feel it in *my* hand," she says. "Each week it's different. I felt brokenness today in the room. Maybe the very cold weather today was making people feel fragile. Sometimes I feel aggression or anger. People don't only come for physical healing. Somebody may be going through a divorce, or they want healing for a family member." I had learned about Maryanne Lacy from a friend whose son had leukemia. Although he didn't survive, my friend said that Lacy had been a wonderful presence for her family.

My stepsister has cancer, and the chemotherapy and radiation aren't working. Maryanne says gently, "It may be too late to expect a cure." She takes my hand and begins to pray: "Heavenly Father, in the name of Jesus, we ask blessings for Malka's sister, and we ask you to heal her. Let Malka use her gift to bring Gale healing, love, and peace." My eyes are closed, filled with tears, and I feel heat coming through her hands. Father Peter anoints me with the olive oil wax; it is fragrant, and his touch feels like a massage. Catholicism, with its frequent reference to Jesus, is confusing and challenging; yet, these two speak a language I understand.

"The more the disease takes over the body, the person's will to live gets diminished," Maryanne says. "The thing to do is to get a person to healing prayer as soon as they know. The first thing they have to decide is to choose life, that life is worth living. Your sister may have made a decision, conscious or unconscious, to die. Then the fear of pain, of dying, makes people sicker. It's almost like an evil entity that takes over.

"There's a little girl of ten whose had leukemia since she was two, and now she's in total remission, thank God. The unusual thing about it is that she was given a bone marrow transplant, and since she's been getting a healing prayer, the doctors say that the donor cells are being overpowered by her own cells. The doctors have scared the mother because they say that if her cells are taking over, they may become cancerous again. They want to start her on chemo, but the mother wants to think this healing could be a miracle. She wants to wait as long as there is no cancer."

Lacy was born in 1936 into an Irish Catholic family in Brooklyn. Her mother died when she was two. She and her five siblings were put in foster homes. "I suffered terribly, married young, and had five children right away. I didn't understand anything except that I was miserable. After the fifth child, I fell into a serious depression, which was the best thing that ever happened to me because it made me helpless. Then I found the Catholic Charismatic Renewal movement. They prayed over me, and I literally and immediately fell in love with God. I couldn't believe that this was going on in a Catholic church. I wept and wept and felt all this love touching my wounds. I was so starved for love that only God could fill me.

"I began to attend a prayer meeting in a private home with twelve people. One night the weather was terrible, and although I hate to drive in the rain, I felt I had to go. When I arrived, no one was there except the leader and one woman in great distress. She had come in desperation because she had an obstruction in her throat and the doctors wanted to operate. She coughed constantly but didn't want the operation. She hoped prayer would help her.

"My self-confidence was still low in those days, but that night there were just three of us, so I wasn't insecure. As we began to pray I felt an engulfing, loving, peaceful presence, and with my hands on her head, I began to ask God's blessing on the woman. I felt my hands gently touch her throat without any effort or power of my own. In a few minutes she said, with surprise and awe, that the growth was gone. It was confirmed later that, indeed, it had disappeared. This was how God showed me my new set of plans. The group was Catholic. Although I still went to church every Sunday, it had no meaning for me.

"Father Peter and I met on a bus going to a Ruth Carter Stapleton

Maryanne Lacy's best friend, business partner, and spiritual spouse, Father Peter McCall, died in March 2001. Many wondered whether she could continue the work without his support and courage in bringing her into the church. After months of mourning, she returned to the work that they had begun, and once again the ministry offers healing services in Dobbs Ferry, New York.

healing service in 1978. He started coming to the prayer group, and then we started working together. We made house calls to people with depression, cancer, everything." She smiles at McCall, who wanders in and out during the interview. "When I look back on my early life, it's almost like observing somebody else. I can't even believe that I'm doing what I'm doing because I was very shy. My closest friends say they can't believe that I'm the same person.

"When I had breast cancer, Father Peter asked me why I wanted to be healed. 'Because people need me.' He said no. 'Because I'm a good person.' He said no. I thought a long time, and then I knew. I wanted healing because God loves me. Now you might think, 'So God loves me and I'm still not cured. Does it mean God doesn't love me?' Well, even if the person eventually dies, as long as they know God loves them, their mission was accomplished." Whatever else we understand about faith healing, this is psychologically healthy. When serious illness befalls us, our minds race to find the reason: "I've been working too hard." "My parents were cruel." "It's the divorce that caused it."

Forget about it. It doesn't mean that we've fallen from grace because something in our lives went wrong. There is no answer to the plaintive "Why me?" Know that you are a child of God and that God isn't punishing you. Lacy explains, "Healing means that we learn that God loves us. We make the connection. Unfortunately, lots of people are in pain and don't know God; they don't understand the depth, height, and width of God's love for them personally. Everyone dies sooner or later, and there are different ways to die.

"In the Catholic religion, people have been taught to offer up their suffering, to be passive rather than to be participants in their healing. This is a whole new concept for people who come to us—they don't know that they can participate in their healing. They think God sends the sickness, so they're willing to go along with it if it will purify them of their sins of their past life, and it's just not right. They need to be taught how to participate through healing prayer. I give talks on nutrition, exercise, and alternative medicine. We do centering prayer, teaching patience, so it's a holistic approach to healing, not just magic and laying on of hands. Healing is work!"

Asked about the difference between her work and Father Peter's, she says, "I have no desire to be a woman priest. I'm sort of easy going and I wouldn't want to learn all the rituals and do the different things required of a priest. It would drive me crazy. I'm just too spontaneous. I do know nuns who have a desire to be priests, and it's really hard if you have a calling. I'm probably one of the few women in the Catholic Church who have been given a voice because I work with a priest, so I have to be grateful that I've been given this role. I wouldn't be able to do it if I weren't working with a priest.

"You saw the way I pray with people and the way Father Peter prays. He just anoints them. I comfort them, and the women who work with us do the same thing. Women are more intuitive, and they understand people more. It takes more from you, and the challenge is to have the strength to do this work. It's burnout all the time. You're giving all your energy." Clergy work is to comfort the afflicted. That is an energy offering, too, but what Lacy does in being a channel for healing requires a large piece of herself, and for that she must prepare.

"I'm sort of flighty, and if I weren't doing this I'd be doing all kinds of things. I love movies, but I don't have cable or I'd be watching all the old classics. I discipline myself to prepare for services by reading and by prayer. I enter into an inner quiet; I commune with God and feel the love and unity. This is what feeds me. It's what I love best, because it has brought me into a closer relationship with God. The day of and the day after the service, I'm so in tune with God everything flows. I'll make all the lights when I'm driving, the elevator opens as soon as I get there, people will call who I haven't heard from in a long time."

Maryanne offhandedly speaks of the Hebrew Bible's God of wrath and the New Testament's God/Jesus of love. A friend of hers is listening in on the interview and sees my shoulders rise towards my ears. A hard-boiled newspaperman, he became a believer after his leg was saved from amputation, as a result of a serious accident, by Lacy's healing prayer. He takes me aside while she is being photographed and says, "Look, Maryanne is a natural. She doesn't know the books; she knows the heart." I stop taking it personally and finish the interview in attunement with her.

Lacy continues, "I think I'm a model for many women; some of the female ministers imitate me. At first I thought it was strange, but I know imitation is a great compliment. I hope that women discover that there are possibilities for them. If I can do it, anyone can do it."

Anyone may learn to emulate Lacy's warmth and eye contact, and a few may learn ways to be a messenger of love. Whether anyone can sing in tongues and melt tumors by touch is another story.

MOTHER AMMACHI

Although every woman in this book is unique, Mother Ammachi is different from them all. She is less of a mortal than I've ever seen, which may be another way of saying that she is more like the Divine. The spirit is sovereign for all these women, but I cannot imagine Ammachi ever kicking back and kibbitzing with friends, as I can with all the others. She is more physically immanent in her ministry than anyone that I have ever heard of, let alone encountered. She is also transcendent.

At the entrance to the light and airy barnlike building of the Mother Ammachi Center in northern California, hundreds of people remove their shoes mellowly and, carrying a gift such as a flower, go into a space filled with talking, walking, and meditating beings. There is also an hours-long line of kneeling petitioners waiting their turn with Mother.

The morning *darshan* begins with low, soft chanting in preparation for Mother Ammachi's entrance. A greatly amplified male voice chants "Ah Ma" over and over, a hypnotic sighing mantra that begins a fifteen-minute meditation. It ends with the cry of a horn toned like a conch shell and hundreds of tinkling bells, along with chanting devotees in bright-colored robes and scarves who announce Mother's presence in the ashram. All heads turn in her direction as she takes the seat from which she will not move for as long as ten hours.

I ask a friendly volunteer how I can find the publicist with whom we made our arrangements. After she graciously helps us, she explains why she is here. "I was at a friend's house and saw a picture of Ammachi on the refrigerator. I wasn't seeking anything, but I went to a *darshan* with her. That was seven years ago. I've even followed Ammachi to India."

The large gift shop sells a variety of Ammachi products, such as four-by-six photographs

Darshan is the beholding of a deity, person, or object as part of Hindu worship.

of her sweet, smiling face, gold-plated pendants with her image, amulets of silk taken from a sari worn by her, and books by and about her. A biographical sketch of her life in her book *For My Children* explains, "Amma is unique. To our knowledge, no being like her has ever come down so near to us, blessing us in such a personal and affectionate way. She may place her finger on your forehead and apply sandalwood paste at the place of the third eye of inner vision. This has the effect of awakening your spiritual energy as well as soothing, cooling, and rejuvenating the body's nervous system and vital energies."

Born in 1953 to a peasant family in a remote village along the southwest coast of India, she soon became a prodigy. At six months she was walking and talking. At five she began composing songs in praise of Lord Krishna that were full of love and poignant with longing for the Beloved. Despite her precocity, Ammachi left school at eight to take over the household duties her sick mother couldn't perform. Ammachi, the darkest and therefore the most inferior of her siblings, was made the servant girl. She lived in a cowshed, her mother frequently beat her, and yet she smiled all the time because her life was rich with rapture for Krishna.

Her spiritual ecstasies became known in her community, and the village elders respected the child who sang to Krishna in a trancelike state and who constantly demonstrated compassion and sacrifice for others. When she was twenty-two, her life of devotion expanded beyond her village. At a neighbor's Krishna celebration, the people there asked her to perform a miracle, and she retorted, "I am here not to perform miracles but to remove your desire for them."

One day she heard a voice within her say, "You have not been born to enjoy bliss and peace for yourself, but rather to give comfort and solace to suffering humanity." From that day on, Ammachi devoted herself to the welfare of all human beings. She refused her family's attempts to arrange a marriage, and eventually her parents realized that she was not destined for a worldly life. She performed a miracle to assure her people of her gift—she turned water into a sugary substance—and all came to know her as a manifestation of Krishna.

Several times a week, she sat dressed as Krishna under a banyan tree with her devotees drawing close to her divine being. Various extraordinary traits now marked her: unconditional love, complete peace, an unusual tender fragrance surrounding her, and a power to heal physical and emotional problems. People described receiving a blessing of energy and opening when they were in her presence. Some spoke of feeling that they were enveloped in the compassion that is her essence.

As her reputation grew, so did her enemies, who accused her of being a threat to rational thought. When they sent police to arrest her, the police were enthralled by the young woman. When they tried to have her killed, her would-be assassin threw down his knife. It was at this point that she began to receive people one by one into her lap as a mother comforts a child. She has no bodyguards, and thousands come close enough to kill each day. Amma says that invisible forces of light protect her.

As stories of her miracles spread in the early 1980s, Westerners came to be healed, and several stayed to help her mission. In 1985 they built an ashram that now houses three hundred residents and up to a thousand guests. In 1987 she made her first trip to the West, where she touched, literally and figuratively, thousands of people. They say that she will never turn a person away.

It is my turn to meet Mother Ammachi. I have wiped my face with a

tissue handed to me a few minutes earlier by a person who also told me not to touch Mother but to allow her to embrace me. She touches some on the forehead, listens and talks, and with others she barely says a word. I bring her a chrysanthemum and feel nervous. I don't know whether I'm worried that nothing will happen or that something will. Despite my work, my default is not faith and trust. I struggle with skepticism and, worse, cynicism. In addition, I don't like being touched by a stranger, so this is difficult for me.

An assistant takes the flower, and I scoot up to Amma on my knees. Up close, she seems small, a little plump, and not charismatic, at least to me. Her unassuming bearing is actually evidence of her power: nothing visible draws people to her. The air around her is complicated and heavy, bearing the scent of the hundreds whom Mother Ammachi has already embraced. It is my turn. Barely glancing at me, she gestures me to lean toward her. Firmly putting her arms around me, she pulls me to her right side, says something repetitive and incomprehensible in my left ear for fifteen seconds, and releases me. An assistant moves me on, and I have no time to ask someone to translate what she said to me.

I didn't have a transcendent experience, but I have no question of her authenticity and power. The throngs at the ashram are nice, intelligent, down-to-earth people who practice cooperation and helpfulness as well as meditation. We talk to our liaison and find out that Amma won't let us interview her. He himself hasn't had access to her since she arrived yesterday. He suggests that we send him a series of questions that he will ask for us, and he introduces us to the leader of the center and one of her early supporters.

Swamiji Paramatmananda works in a separate building that houses offices and a small prayer room. Waiting in the anteroom, I pick up a pamphlet, "Being with Ammachi." Ammachi's formal name is Amma Mata Amritanandamayi; she represents India's Vedantic tradition by "emanating knowledge of the ultimate reality, love of the divine, and selfless service to others." Ammachi transcends not only gender and personality but also religion. She's a natural who would have found God no matter where she had been born.

Swamiji, a handsome, affable man in his fifties with beautiful brown eyes,

ushers us into his office, smiling. I confess my disappointment in not meeting
Ammachi. I want to know what the experience of the embrace might feel like.
He is sympathetic and assures me that I am not the first person to miss the
moment. He says, "Amma radiates a motherly presence, and when I am with her,
I feel like her child." It doesn't matter that in reality she is younger than he.
"And," he goes on, "I don't think that feeling is different whether you're a man
or woman."

I'm curious about how he, a Westerner, came to be Swamiji. He says about
his family, "We were Reform Jews in Chicago, and my family didn't believe in
God. Being Jewish was a cultural thing. When my father died when I was
twelve, I started changing and woke up to the world. By the time I was a teenager, I started to wonder about what was real. I read a book about an Indian saint
that answered all my questions. So, in my twenties, I decided to become a
monk. First I went to Japan to practice in a Zen monastery, but it was too aus-
tere for me.

"I went to India after that and lived there for thirty years. Amma asked me
to look after this center, and I've been here for the past ten years. Her work is
unique; just because we all can hug doesn't mean that we all can embrace.
What's inside Mother is the vision of universal oneness.

"I met her when I was very sick; I was almost dead. Someone took me to
her. She was living in her family house, completely unknown. I didn't understand her at all. She was just a teenaged girl, but there was something different
about her, because I'd heard she was curing all kinds of sickness. She put her
hands out to me, but I was a monk and was not about to take her hands in mine.
I hesitated, but she kept her hands out. I'd brought a bag of peanuts for her and
put them in her hands. She laughed, took them, and again put out her hands.
So I hesitatingly put out my hands, and she took them and pulled me into a little temple she had on her property. She put her fingers between my eyes, and
my mind became completely still.

"She told me that I was sick because God wanted me to finish my cycle of
birth and death now. If I persisted in surrendering to God's will, this would be
my last birth. Or she could remove the sickness, but it would mean that I would
have to take another birth, at least one more. She asked me what I wanted to do,
and I said, 'Do what is good for me, Mother.' She put her hand on my stomach.

I hadn't eaten anything but milk for two months. She closed her eyes and said that I'd be better but I would never be well.

"She said, 'I'll make you better enough so that you don't have to lay down all the time and have someone looking after you, but you'll still suffer the rest of your life. Use it as your spiritual practice.' The next day I ate normally, and the next night Amma gave a *darshan*. The temple was very small, and when she called me, I stood outside. She came to the door, and her form grew brighter and brighter. I couldn't see anything. The brilliance eclipsed everything, the temple and Amma herself. Then it grew into a star point, and Amma was smiling at me. I felt she had entered me. She felt it too and said that I was lucky that my Mother had blessed me like that. After that," he says, "I could never leave her. I've never met anyone like her. She doesn't change. She's divine. I've never even read about any personality who is like her. Just looking at her is like a thousand words." I tell him that I'd like to communicate with her directly. He tells us about a woman who wanted to write Ammachi's biography and followed her to India to spend six months chronicling her life, but she never got an interview with her. Swamiji also suggests e-mail. I didn't receive a reply.

Swamiji tells us about his initiation of getting his priestly white robe. "I was very excited, finally felt worthy of it, and it seemed like the greatest day of my life. Amma introduced him to the monks by saying, 'Neilu [his nickname] is a Jew.' He shakes with laughter. "I'm about to be ordained as a priest, I've been an orthodox Hindu for twenty years, and she calls me a Jew! She meant it as the greatest accolade. She thinks that Jews are Brahmins." The Dalai Lama has said that Jews are a very spiritual people, because most of his Western devotees are Jewish. Swamiji is one of our shining stars in search of spirit.

When we get to the airport, I imagine what it would feel like if I hugged everyone in the terminal. I cannot imagine myself doing it; I don't have that much love. You have to be a saint, a *tzadik* [Jewish holy person], or a guru—a being so God-like that you behave like God by embracing everyone as beloved members of your family. Amma demonstrates what

By 2002 Mother Ammachi has hugged 21,000,000 people.

it looks like to love your neighbor as yourself: embrace the stranger as your child. Her life is a lesson in loving that transcends language, culture, and belief.

God may be the source of the love we give one another, and some people are better at it than others. Mother Ammachi is the Olympic champion of loving, and there is nothing the world needs more than boundless, unconditional love. For some, it may be the first time they've ever received it.

CONNIE BIWER YAQUB

Although Connie Yaqub, an American Muslim living in Albuquerque, New Mexico, is a much-sought-after participant in interfaith dialogues and a prominent Islamic spokesperson in local schools, she is surprised that I'd like to interview her. "I'm really not important enough to call a spiritual leader," she says, when I explain that Albuquerque rabbi Lynne Gottlieb has suggested that I call her. When asked for recommendations of other women, however, she cannot come up with any. We talk about Nahid Angha's work and the sacredness of study in Islam, and she reconsiders. "Well, if you think teachers are leaders," she says, "then I guess you could call me a leader, because Americans don't know enough about Islam." Especially in New Mexico. The opportunity for her to reach many Americans through our book convinces her to participate.

As a first-grade teacher in Albuquerque who encountered widespread ignorance about Islam among students and teachers, Yaqub has become a one-woman cultural and religious outreach organization to educate her non-Muslim neighbors. A blonde, blue-eyed, fifth-generation Iowan, she has created a guide for the schools to help them understand Muslim children's religious practices.

She writes, "During Ramadan, students who are fasting may find it difficult to watch others eat and therefore may prefer to go to the library rather than the cafeteria at lunch. Fasting students may find it a bit harder to concentrate and may have a difficult time doing strenuous exercise in physical education. At all times of the year, some Muslim children will not recite the Pledge of Allegiance or sing songs about the flag. This has nothing to do with patriotism; it has to do with prohibitions against paying homage to symbols. Please be aware that decorations, cards, and parties commemorating holidays, especially those with a religious connotation (even if secular symbols are used, such as Santa Claus or the Easter Bunny), may make your Muslim students feel uncomfortable." Here is a good, unifying project on which Jews, Muslims, and all other non-Christians can work together.

We visit Connie Yaqub in the suburban home she shares with her Israeli Palestinian husband, their two daughters, and her mother-in-law. Although the exterior of the house is identical to others on the street, Yaqub's long dress and covered arms immediately identify her family as different from its neighbors. When she goes out of the house, she covers her hair, too. Some women cover their faces and hands as well. She welcomes us warmly, eager to give me a respectable and authentic vision of Islam. Before we leave, she hands me her guidelines, a suggested reading list for adults and children, and a stack of recent issues of *Aramco World*, a handsome, glossy magazine published by the oil company Saudi Aramco. It isn't sold, but one can request a copy.

Yaqub is part of the growing trend of Anglo women becoming leaders in non-Western religions. Born and brought up in Iowa, she says, "I was a Catholic, went to Catholic school, was raised by nuns, and all my friends were Catholic. Being Catholic was my identity, not being a Midwesterner. I was so sheltered that I didn't know about prostitution until I was grown.

"I met my husband in graduate school at the University of Wisconsin. He was the boy from Baghdad!" His family was from Iraq originally but had moved to Palestine and lived there for generations. In 1948, when they lost their home, they came to the United States. "We met while watching the news in the dorm; both of us were interested in the happenings of the world. What attracted me, though, was that he was just the finest person I'd ever met. It was all over his face. I'd never met a Muslim before, but I did some reading right away to see if this would be compatible with me remaining a Christian. I had become Lutheran in college.

"My parents came to visit, and my husband asked them for their blessings to be married. My parents decided he was a great fellow, and they were touched that he'd asked their permission to marry me. My parents didn't have a problem with my getting married to him, but there were some fears because of the way Muslims are so negatively portrayed in the media. My husband assured them that he'd take care of me and wouldn't take another wife. My mother has really taken to this ecumenical idea, and she's spoken about Islam a couple of times in her church.

Islam accepts Abraham, Moses, and Jesus as prophets but considers that Christianity's Trinitarian belief is contrary to monotheism.

"We married in 1984, two months after we met. We had a small wedding, about ten people, at the mosque in Madison, Wisconsin. Islam doesn't require that men marry Muslim women, but women must marry Muslims. This comes from the idea of raising the kids Muslim, and since the father is Muslim, then probably the children will follow.

"After we married, we returned to Iowa, but my husband decided that the Midwest was a difficult place to be a person of color, so we moved to Albuquerque." Hispanics and Native Americans outnumber Anglos in New Mexico. "I converted about three years ago. I had embraced parts of Islam over the years. When my sister-in-law came here after the Gulf War in 1990 as a refugee, she said, 'Connie, you're basically Muslim; you just have to say the words that make you a Muslim. Why don't you just do it?' But I still wasn't ready. I wanted to make sure it wasn't just because of my husband; it had to be genuine for me.

"That year I fasted with my husband and children during Ramadan, which is very special, without food or water from before sunrise to after sunset. It was the final thing I needed to put me more in touch with my spirituality and made me more focused about Islam. I knew it was the right time to become Muslim." For Connie, Islam fulfills spiritual, social, and intellectual needs. It is her organizing principle, her identity, her passion, and her work. While she is self-effacing, she speaks of her adopted tradition without hesitation or shyness.

"Ours is a Muslim home, and there are certain phrases that we say that remind me that I'm Muslim. 'As Salaam Aleikum' (Peace be upon you) is our greeting, and we're required to say it if a Muslim comes into the house. We also say 'Allah Subhana Wa Tala' (God who is highly glorified and honored) whenever we want God's blessing. If I put bread in the oven and I want it to turn out right, I say the blessing, and if I'm afraid I'll lock my keys in the car, I say it before I close the car door. And we say 'Inshallah' (if God wills it). So instead of saying, 'I'll do this tomorrow,' you say, 'I'll do this if God wills it.'

"Saying these things many times throughout the day is a good reminder of God's blessing in our lives," she explains. This reminds me of another path to consciousness and gratitude. Whenever my grandmother spoke of the future, she would say something like, "When you have children of your own, God willing, you'll understand." If she spoke of something negative, she would say, "If it rains, God forbid, we'll go inside." I always thought of it as superstition. Connie gives me a new way to understand it.

"Islam is a simple religion, and that's appealing. It isn't like Christianity, with the idea that Jesus was both human and divine, and that there are three parts to one God. I always had trouble with this, even as a person of faith. Islam considers the messages of Judaism and Christianity the same as ours. We have the same prophets and messengers. It's a religion of justice and peace.

"It's also respectful of the intellect. We study the Qur'an as required practice. I'm required to say prayers in Arabic; we have six-year-olds who speak Urdu and Arabic. There are illiterate Muslims who can recite the Qur'an! Muslims respect education and personal excellence. Hopefully it's for the benefit of God.

"Since the Sabbath is on Friday and my teenage daughters have school, we really celebrate the Sabbath on Saturday. We go as a family every Saturday to a study class for women at the mosque. The imam [spiritual leader] leads it, and my husband is a translator.

"My husband and I speak about faith all the time with the children. He's a professor of philosophy and is a wise person who believes in the power of rationality. We've always raised the children to try to do things because they are right, not because we say so, not even because God says so. God says so because it's right.

"A year and a half ago, I met Rabbi Lynne Gottlieb, who created a dialogue between Palestinians and Jews who want to change the way things are in Israel. I went to the first meeting and was touched by how genuine everyone was." Rabbi Gottlieb is a leader in interfaith dialogues and a critic of Israeli policies regarding the Palestinians. Yaqub says, "I'm a member of the Arab-American Antidiscrimination Committee, which is a national organization looking out for the rights of Arabs and promoting positive images of Arabs. Many of the people in Lynne's group are also in the Peace with Iraq movement. I made several friends in Lynne's congregation, and together we want to educate ourselves about the current situation in Palestine." She never refers to Israel. "It's been wonderful knowing Lynne and being there for her congregation. She's a wonderful spokesperson for justice, and she's very brave."

As Sufi leader Dr. Nahid Angha points out, Islam and Judaism are closer to each other theologically than Christianity, and dialogues between Jews and Muslims discussing the realm of religion and spirit could do great good. Yaqub is providing an important service by teaching children about the fastest-growing religion in the world: we live in the global village, and it is imperative to know our neighbors. As of this date, Judaism and Islam both have six million American followers. Yaqub has a larger agenda, however. She wants to tell the non-Muslim world the truth, as she understands it, about the Middle East.

"After the Iraq war, all the sanctions were kept in place. The purpose was to get Iraq out of Kuwait. There aren't weapons of mass destruction there; the country has been destroyed, and the economy has been destroyed. The sanctions have destroyed the people. My husband's sister and her husband are physicians in Iraq and they nearly lost a grandchild because they didn't have medicine. How they've been treated is so unfair! It's anti-Muslim and anti-Arab.

"I know many Palestinians in the States. There are stories of loss, injustices, and of families being separated that have gone on for generations. I've been very touched and heartened to know that Lynne and her friends in the Jewish community are committed to changing things."

When asked why she called the land of Israel Palestine, she answered, "I always say Palestine because if I say that my mother-in-law is from Israel, I'm robbing her of her identity. If you look on a map, yes, you have the country called Israel, but then within it you have these pockets called Palestine. Instead of having one chunk over here called Palestine and another chunk called Israel, you have little pockets of people all over.

"The Palestinians can't have power. The two-state solution in which both states have adequate economic opportunities and adequate security is probably the best way. Arabs and Jews have coexisted for thousands of years, and I would hope that it could be possible." I agree about this and say so. She replies, "It can't be possible, though, without acknowledging that there are inadequacies and injustice. We have to question what was done in 1948 and figure out a way to change it."

I ask Connie what it is like to be a Muslim woman. It's one thing to be born into a culture where women's rights are nonexistent, I say, but it's something else when you're born into a democratic, egalitarian society. She quickly replies, "It's not a problem. We're non-Shi'ite, and we believe that women can get the same permission to lead as men—they can apply the law, interpret decisions, and be independent scholars. They can even be muftis, the heads of scholars. This is like being a bishop. The only thing they can't do is lead prayer in the presence of men. But leading prayer is not such a big deal in Islam, the way study and scholarship is.

"Despite what is seen in the movies or on the news, women are actually held in very high regard in Islam. Since the beginning, Muslim women have been able to have their own property, and they've basically had equal status with men, long before other countries. We can be in business, law, and medicine. And women are teaching in new Islamic schools here in America. There are so many opportunities for women.

"Women are supposed to cover their hair and limbs for modesty, not because women are subservient and should be treated like property. Men are supposed to be modest, too, and not go around bare-chested. We remove issues of gender so that we can interact as human beings and not be concerned about each other from a sexual standpoint. It protects our humanity. Some American converts say to me, 'You should cover your face and wear gloves,' but that's not the teaching of Islam. Some say that you can't even talk to men! This is not mainstream thinking.

"I teach first grade in the Rio Rancho public school, and I'm in a position where I can influence children. I don't talk to them about Palestine, but I teach them about prejudice and hate and justice. They know I wear a scarf, and they know I wear funny clothes, but they don't know why. When they ask, I tell them. I try to introduce them to other religions so they know something about their neighbors. I hope that I'm teaching them to be better citizens and more tolerant of others.

"I work closely with newly arrived families and show them how things work here. We have people in our mosque from countries in North Africa, Southeast Asia, all over the States, rich and poor. And we all come together to pray, and it's wonderful. I never felt this coming together in the Catholic or Lutheran churches. At the same time, it's very difficult to manage these various folks. Our imam doesn't even speak English!

"Because of the way I dress, people can spot me a mile away and know that I am a person of faith. If I were still a Lutheran or a Catholic, they wouldn't know what my degree of spirituality is. But now people talk to me about prayer. Since I've started wearing the *hijab* [head covering], Christians and Jews have shared with me that they are also people of faith.

"We have about three thousand Muslims in Albuquerque, and it's a community that helps if you're sick or in need. That's our culture: It's our duty to care for one another." How can it not be everybody's culture? "We help immigrants, and we look out for each other. My mother-in-law has friends here, but if my mother were living with us, I don't know if my American friends would call her.

"The reason I don't consider myself a teacher within the Muslim community in Albuquerque is because I don't have the spiritual knowledge yet to teach. I'm a new convert, I don't know enough Arabic, and I don't know enough about Islam. I do outreach, because I have a lot of contacts with non-Muslims, more than most Muslim women here. I'm eager to dialogue and to be an activist with people who want to know about Islam."

Connie Yaqub is modest. She is a spiritual leader of her chosen religion because of her mission to teach Islam sympathetically. She also believes that she is fighting for justice when she speaks out against the occupations of Palestine and Iraq. Whether this will help the cause of peace remains to be seen.

JOAN HALIFAX ROSHI

Joan Halifax Roshi represents a new trend in American Buddhism: the growing presence of women priests leading Zen centers all over the country. As author Diana Eck notes in *A New Religious America*, feminist perspective is bringing an egalitarian, nonhierarchical style to the traditionally rigorous and formal practice of Zen Buddhism. Roshi Joan, as her students affectionately call her, is founder and head teacher of the Upaya Zen Center in Santa Fe, New Mexico, where classes and residential retreats draw Western Buddhists and meditators from all over the world. Ordained by two leading Buddhists, Thich Nhat Hanh and Bernard Glassman Tetsugen Roshi, Halifax has practiced an engaged Buddhism for the past thirty years that reflects both tradition and unique vision.

Internationally known as a writer and speaker, she has woven her passion for social activism into a spiritual life of compassionate action. Through the Upaya Prison Project she has taught meditation to inmates; visiting men on death row, she has knelt on the floor to speak and listen through the food port in the middle of the cell's steel door. The project On Being with Dying, which works with dying people and caregivers, is intended "to inspire a gentle revolution in dying," Halifax says. The dying have taught her how fearlessness and freedom are always possible.

Joan is among the fortunate who can look good with a shaved head. Besides conferring priestly status, it has additional meaning in a society where many people undergo chemotherapy. My friends with cancer report the staring eyes of the curious—or worse, the ones that look away. Like the Danes who wore Stars of David during the Holocaust to express solidarity with the Jews, Halifax in her practice includes herself with people with cancer by making baldness acceptable.

Designer eyeglasses that disappear into her nearly flawless face, brilliant blue eyes, and good teeth exposed by her frequent laugh suggest California, where Joan lived and taught for a decade as founder of the Ojai Foundation and School. Even in full priestly regalia, Joan Halifax Roshi still looks like a member of her generation, a 1960s flower child who has spent the past forty years of her life looking more deeply for her life's work than her patrician southern roots would have predicted.

She describes her Florida childhood as rich and sweet despite, at four, contracting a virus in her eye muscles that left her blind for two years. Instead of forming friendships and learning physical skills, she developed a deep internal life, lying in her parents' bed as she listened to her sister and her friends playing outside. She says, "Because I was not physically normal, I invented a world inside of myself to compensate for loneliness and disability. My family hired a black woman, whose mother had been a slave, to take care of me, and that woman, Lilla, had a great influence on me. She was pretty, very religious and spiritual, and seemed to love me as her own child. Although she had no education, she was wise and knew something about freedom that I needed to understand. When I was a child I thought that Lilla was one of my relatives. Looking back I realize she was my closest relation.

"When I became aware that there was racial prejudice in my community, and not only in relation to blacks but to Jews, too, it was frightening. Because we lived in a restricted community, I grew up with a certain sense of protection—and narrowness—but it wasn't hatred. At the same time, I received love and compassion from Lilla, a woman that society was protecting me from!

"When I went to Sophie Newcomb College at Tulane University in New Orleans in 1960, I immediately got involved in the civil rights movement, and it led me to what I wanted to do with my life: I wanted to work for social justice with people outside the mainstream culture. I left Newcomb a year early, because I found the environment oppressive, and went to New York.

"It was 1963, and I worked for Alan Lomax, an anthropologist and folklorist who was studying song and dance cross-culturally. I sat in a laboratory at Columbia University listening to the music of the world, and it was an incredible experience learning how complex the issue of culture is. I came to see that Western culture was destroying many cultures, and that this included the destruction of the natural world. I was charged up politically, and so was everyone around me between the civil rights and anti-Vietnam war movements. Lomax, his friends and associates gave me a huge dose of what social concern looks like among highly motivated people."

Joan also learned that there are drawbacks to everything. "Even though the civil rights movement was strongly influenced by Quakers, I found myself in the same social atmosphere I'd been brought up in—there were good guys and bad guys. I needed another way to see things. I had begun to read about meditation and ways of living with faith and compassion. There were no classes then, so I began practicing meditation on my own. I also knew that I needed to do more than sit in a lab or put flowers on bayoneted guns at the Pentagon.

"I went to Paris in 1968 and was again in the midst of demonstrations and police. Many of the people I was working with there had done work in Africa, and I felt Lilla's presence strong in me. I drove across the Sahara to live with the Dogon people in Mali and witnessed a rite of passage that occurs once every fifty-three to sixty years—it's a seven-year period of ritual. The oldest Dogon women, the ones who were alive during the previous ritual, stepped forward into roles of leadership, and men dressed as women. The world turned into its opposite.

"I was blown away! This wasn't a rite of passage for an individual but for an entire culture. I thought about my own culture and realized that we had no rites that marked change. How can individuals, families, and culture be renewed without rituals to encourage maturity? My culture's horizon seemed small. And I thought of my own life. What did I know of my ancestors, their prayers, their work, and their stories? The social, cultural, psychological, and spiritual aspect has been deeply neglected in our culture.

"Agricultural societies are tied to the natural world through seasons of planting, growing, and harvesting. What do we have? The Super Bowl, the Emmys, and the Oscars! I watch the Super Bowl and the Oscars, too, but it's not enough." She sees my surprise at picturing her in front of a television cheering for the Broncos. "I'm not going to pretend that my so-called monastic authorization separates me from the culture. I need to know the world I live in—how else can I relate to the people?"

Having someone's trust is key to the work that she does, and it takes priority over the boundaries of a monastic life. "I can't be concerned about what a priest 'looks' like," she says. "For example, I have needed the cooperation of the correctional officers in the prison, for obvious reasons. I have to have a good relationship with them. When I shaved my head, they wouldn't deal with me, so I grew a little hair back. If I need hair to gain trust, no problem. Some traditional teachers might disapprove, and I've been criticized. Critics are less important than the work I do in the penitentiary.

"Can I be in a personal relationship? In the Japanese School of Buddhism you can have family, but I've chosen the vow of celibacy. I'm sixty, I've never been great at relationships, and I'm not interested in investing the time any more. It's just easier not to be in one, and I have another kind of life at this point. It's not as if I've deprived myself; I've just had enough of it. I need solitude and quiet."

Joan still likes to have a good time. After the formal dedication of a new temple at Upaya, she threw a salsa party with a red-hot band. "A lot of people think it means giving your whole life to the practice, which you do, but that doesn't mean sitting twenty-four hours a day. I cook and sew; I live a very domestic life here," she says, spreading her arms. "This beautiful robe is made from pieces of cloth from garments of people I know with catastrophic illnesses or who have died. Here's Rick Fields [author of *Chop Wood, Carry Water*]" and, pointing to her back, "my mother and my father. I sewed them together into a robe to remind me of impermanence, how precious this life is and that I should use it well. I'm in a continuum that includes my biological and spiritual ancestors.

"Being a monk makes it easier for me to live my life. I'm a monk with or without hair who cooks, cleans, and takes walks with her women friends. I'm a part-time hermit. I walk up the mountain in the woods every few days to gain the autonomy that comes with quiet. It's one of the critical things that women need, which isn't acknowledged in our culture. I wouldn't encourage everyone to live my life, but I would encourage people to have more solitude. It's a way to understand your life, whether you're a Jew, Christian, Buddhist, or Hindu."

Besides solitude, I ask what else it takes for her to do her work. She clasps her hands and thinks for a moment. "You really have to have the right constitution. You have to have a pretty big heart to be with the suffering, and you have to have worked through your own suffering." Suffering is a word that comes up often in Buddhism as a natural condition and a whetstone for perfecting character. By being awake to our lives, through the practice of meditation, we find a way beyond suffering. Joan's life has carried its share of both physical and emotional suffering. Both physical and emotional breakdowns have been active parts of her life; yet, she calls them "extraordinary gifts."

"Because I was down and out—not just once, but a number of times, complete failure, completely lost, completely flattened—and I managed to pull myself up, I am a lot stronger for getting back on my feet. I've also been privately and publicly humiliated. As a woman I've been attacked for my gifts and my edges, by not only men who were scared of me, but by my sisters as well."

Sometimes the work is difficult, especially when her students want her to be their guru. "I'm wary of the relationship because I've suffered through the negative and positive transference dynamic that happens to a teacher." She pauses and rubs her smooth head. "That's why it works best for me as a teacher to look on relationships with people as learning relationships. I learn from those who study with me, and I can teach only by example. I'm not interested in devotion or adoration, and that's why I prefer to work with mature people rather than younger students. The people who study with me are more like colleagues."

Although many of Roshi's followers are middle-aged, some still become entranced. It may come from a never-ending desire to find the answer outside ourselves, to look to someone who "knows" and who will tell us who we really are and how we should live. The charismatic figures in this book all have faithful, passionate women followers; it can be a serious temptation for them to use devotees for their own needs and purposes.

Anyone as respected, revered, and adored as Roshi Joan naturally has her share of detractors. At times she has lost friendship and support from some of her students. In a recent crisis at Upaya, she had to reorganize the center. The episode had its costs. Those who left the center carried bitterness and feelings of spiritual betrayal. Perhaps betrayal in both directions goes with the territory of stellar spiritual success. Whenever I mentioned the name of any celebrity in this book, I became a magnet for rumors about her dark side. When I see how much good they accomplish, I admire these larger-than-life women, but when I heard about Roshi Joan I didn't want to be in her shoes. That doesn't mean, however, that she isn't up to the challenge of being a teacher.

She sees being a woman as having a lot to do with it. "Women have more room for failure than men; little is expected of us. We're often marginalized, so we can do deep, dark, strange things. The social expectation is to marry and have children, but if you don't conform to that expectation, you can have a hell of a lot of fun as an outsider. That's why women are agents of change."

We invite Joan for dinner. We talk about our work, our similarity of styles, and the way that all paths lead to the same place. After we've had a little wine, she observes, "You know, we're less alike than we appear." It's true. Buddhism and

Judaism are not the same, and Joan and I are not the same; that's why we interest each other. She invites me to do a *dharma* talk (a teaching about practice), and since I've only seen one of hers, I ask that we do it together. She suggests that we talk about compassion.

The new temple reflects Joan Halifax Roshi's taste in its excellence, beauty, and drama. It is exquisite, maybe the most beautiful one in America in its blending of Japanese and Santa Fe architecture and natural materials. Light and wood prevail in the sacred space. Her style of Buddhism reminds me of high-church Episcopal in its ritual. Before we enter together, a conch shell is blown and a cymbal is struck; temple officiants sit in special places near the Roshi. I sit next to Roshi Joan in the center of the room, surrounded on three sides by roughly seventy-five devotees.

For a week I've worried about what to say about compassion and how I'm going to be able to sit for an hour cross-legged on the floor. When I'm thinking, I pace. How can I think in the lotus position? I whisper my worry to Joan. Flashing me a smile with a hint of mischief, she says, "You're not supposed to think!" I wish I understood this. Maybe it's got something to do with the faith required to allow the free fall of letting it be.

Joan is wearing a rich, ornate fabric made into a kimono. She introduces me warmly as a teacher representing another wisdom path, and connects us as two women doing new things in our ancient traditions. Pointing to her clothes, she tells us the country of origin for each: the wisdom of China, Japan, and India rest upon her. Apparel is often a question for women clergy. I'm in slacks and a sweater.

Into well-amplified cordless microphones we ponder the question of unconditional compassion. We never disagree, and we frequently laugh because we're having a great time. Her words connect to my parables and legends, and they amplify her message. Inspiring to each other, we're delighted that the collaboration worked so well, and those assembled seem to enjoy the synergy as much as we do.

We leave the temple first to greet devo-

A Buddhist term literally translated as "that which sustains or upholds," *dharma* is the body of cosmic rituals by which all things exist. *Dharma* talk is a term commonly used for the instruction of these rituals.

tees, the way rabbis and ministers receive congregants at the end of a service. Many stop to tell me that they're Jewish and they're glad I was there. Perhaps my presence made the Buddha "kosher," or perhaps they found the Jewish correspondences to Buddhism useful. Dharma or Torah, they are paths to the same place. That is what I hope most people took from our encounter.

Later, Roshi Joan came again for dinner, and it turned out to be the night before Gay and I planned to euthanize Harriet, our schnauzer friend who had been with us for almost fourteen years. It was a sad time, but we tried to put it aside.

Harriet lay in the bedroom, withdrawn and sleeping. Toward the end of the evening, she came slowly into the living room, looking at us through eyes clouded by cataracts. My feelings of helplessness and heavy-heartedness returned. Roshi Joan said gently, "I think she'd really like it if you picked her up and put her in your lap."

I'd stopped doing that with her weeks ago because she seemed so miserably uncomfortable. Nothing we did seemed to make her calm, so we let her sleep, which she was doing most of the time. Now I lifted her gingerly and put her on the couch next to me, her head in my lap. Joan murmured, "Good. Look at her, how relaxed she is." At last Harriet seemed comfortable. I whispered in her ear, "It's going to be all right, girl." Joan stopped me with, "Malka, the truth is she's going to die."

I thought that I had understood her work about compassion with the dying, but what she demonstrated requires witness. By taking me into the place I feared, the sacred space around the dying, she freed me to help Harriet with her fear. At first her words stung me, but what I learned in that moment was the importance of being present to the truth that death is inevitable. To deny it for both of us takes my authentic self away from Harriet. Until we put her down the next day, I kept her close to me and sensed that she was no longer afraid, because she wasn't alone. The Twenty-third Psalm offers the same assurance.

Sister Jose Hobday

At the University of Creation Spirituality in Oakland, California, each classroom is named for a sage. Sojourner Truth and Abraham Joshua Heschel flank Sister Jose Hobday, the only living person with a room named after her. A Franciscan nun of Seneca, Iroquois, and Seminole descent, Hobday writes and teaches about how to live because she is an expert. Not only was she fortunate to grow up in two wisdom paths, she also had unusually helpful parents. Mingled with her adventurous and sensuous spirit, these elements combined to create a joyful, audacious, and free woman recognized widely as a sage.

Setting up a meeting with her takes months; she is lecturing and teaching, traveling 75,000 miles a year, cut back from 150,000 as a concession to her seventy-two years. When she is home in Gallup, New Mexico, she is still difficult to reach because she doesn't have a telephone messaging system. Via a letter, she tells me to call her before seven in the morning or late at night. During the day she returns calls or looks after needy parishioners. Gallup is the poorest diocese in America.

Her stationery is bordered with these words: "This is the fast that pleases me, to break the unjust fetters, to let the oppressed go free, to share your bread with the hungry and shelter the homeless poor. If you do away with the yoke, the clenched fist, the wicked word, if you give your bread to the hungry and relief to the oppressed, your light will rise in the darkness. Isaiah 58." In her letter she tells us that we can do the interview in Albuquerque, where she is giving a workshop on spiritual growth to Native American Catholics.

Despite being a nun and an elder, she is the most revolutionary voice in this book. She lives on eight thousand dollars a year and apologizes

Founded in 1996, the University of Creation Spirituality seeks to integrate the wisdom of Western spirituality and global indigenous cultures with the emerging scientific understanding of the universe and the passionate creativity of art.

for its being too much. Her book *Simple Living* asserts that spareness is the path to joy and freedom and gives suggestions on how to get there. After our interview, she will throw away my letter to her, airily explaining that she keeps nothing unnecessary. She tells everybody that simplicity is what they want, and after spending a couple of buoyant, joyful hours with her, I'm convinced.

In her drab hotel room near the airport, she is the light. While her statuesque carriage and strong-featured face evoke an Edward Curtis portrait, she looks far more cheerful. Possessing the ardent voice of a young woman, she is immediately approachable and playful, and within minutes we are old friends. An ascetic and celibate life has not made her naive; she is, by choice, innocent and amazed at everyday things. Like the beginner's mind of Buddhism, she delights in the wonder of new experience. Eros surrounds her because she lives a life that ebbs and flows with the giving and receiving of love; she has the glow of a well-loved woman who loves God.

Jose offers us water. "I drink a lot of water; I keep it by the bedside; I just like to keep moist. I try to drink fifteen to twenty glasses a day in New Mexico, because I feel so good when I do." After a sip she says, "I live in the poorest part of town, close to the tracks. It's a simple little house without grass in the front or back. Everyone knows where I live.

"I don't have a Sister living with me, because many people don't want to live the way I live. They couldn't stand this little, dinky town of Gallup, New Mexico, where nothing goes on—but things do go on. You have to look for them. I'm a jail chaplain, a hospital chaplain, and a truck stop chaplain. Those poor guys are away from home on the holidays, and sometimes the weather is bad, so I offer to take them to church services or whatever. I feed a lot of people, so I make soups to have available when people off the reservations stop in to see me. Presence is a big word with me, because if you don't do anything else in life, if you just stay awake and alert and available to people, your life is very worthwhile.

"I've been after the priests because we've gotten away from our strict vow of poverty. The Franciscans never lived a life of joyless poverty—joy is at the heart of what we've always done—but we're in a consumer society, and as we've lifted up poor kids we've lifted our own standard of living." She sighs. "I don't want to live middle-class, and too many of us in the orders are doing exactly that.

"They think I'm a nut because of my passion for living with the poor and identifying with them. 'You do it,' they tell me. 'You're different.' No one else wants that ministry. But they're wrong! Young people don't want to join comfortable communities. They want adventure, risk, and they want to be with people who live that life."

As illustration she tells the following story. "I don't have a credit card. Did you ever try to rent a car without a credit card? It's so much fun to resort to all your abilities and not have it easy! I had to go to Canada, so I went to Hertz and asked to rent a car with a fifty-dollar deposit. 'Are you crazy?' the clerk asked. 'No, I'm just asking. You're Hertz, supposed to be the best. I'll go over to Avis. Maybe they can take a risk. Maybe they have an adventuresome spirit. You clearly don't have it here.' The manager overheard us and asked what was going on. I explained that my flight was canceled, there was no other one today, and I had to talk to two thousand educators tonight. 'I've got to rent a car and get over this border!'

"He said, 'Well, do you have a lot of ID?' I told him I had tons—passport, driver's license, everything, and I have only fifty dollars in cash. I'll be back in one day, but he had to trust. 'I don't have a credit card; all I have is integrity.' Men can't stand not meeting a challenge, so he told the clerk, 'I think we can give her a car.'

"When I got to the place everyone was crazy, worrying whether I'd get there because they knew the flight was canceled. They paid me double for my extra effort. I told them about Hertz and that I needed a fifty-dollar basket of fruit to give the manager. The next day I drove back to New York. I went over a bridge and I was the millionth person over the bridge and I won three hundred dollars in cash! I saw the man at Hertz, and he asked how it went. I told him I'd won three hundred dollars, and he was shocked.

"Then I told him that I'd been at a conference of Sisters who had given him a gift. I went to the back of the car and brought in the most gorgeous basket. His face—it was just great! He started to cry and said, 'I don't know how people live on faith like that.'"

Born in Texas to a Native American mother and a Southern Baptist father, Jose Hobday calls herself a "student of life and a missionary-at-large." With her multiple master's degrees in theology, literature, and architecture and space engineering, learning is a key part of her practice and faith path, and nothing is off limits. A glimpse of her childhood may give a clue to her expansive essence.

"My mother had long, gorgeous black hair," she begins. "When my parents were married for two weeks, my father came home and told Mother that women with bobbed hair—it was the twenties—looked like plucked chickens. He said, 'If my wife ever did that . . . ' She didn't say a thing. The next day he came home from work, and my mother greeted him at the door with her hair cut to her neck. He said, 'How could you? You know how much I love your hair!' He cried and cried. She said, 'John, I am not my hair. I'll always consult you and appreciate what you think, but don't you ever tell me what you will do if your wife does so and so.'

"'But I loved your hair!' She told him that he could get it at the beauty parlor. In our dining room we had a big, red velvet box with my mother's hair in it. When my dad died, I buried him with it. It filled the coffin. People asked what it was but Mother wouldn't tell the story to anyone but us."

She says, "My parents weren't hampered by traditional understandings. If a revival came through town, we'd go and learn from it, and it was very exciting entertainment. But we didn't laugh at the holy rollers and back bench jumpers because it was serious to them."

She describes her first mystical experience. "I was nine years old. I ran home to tell my mother something but couldn't find her. I threw open the door to the bathroom, and there was my mother standing in the tub ready to dry off. I'd seen my mother in a nightgown or slip but never naked. She had beautiful bronze skin, and hair that came to the back of her knees. The sun was coming in on her.

"I was scared to death because I'd marched in on her naked, and I was so attracted that I couldn't move. My feet froze right to the floor. I wasn't going to leave; I was going to see everything I could see. I knew I should get out of the bathroom. I looked at my mother, and I don't know what she saw, but she said, 'Come here, Jo, and I'll show you how wonderful it is to be a woman.' And my mother took my right hand and let me feel her whole body, her breasts, buttocks, pelvic hair, thighs . . . My! I still tingle when I think of it. I still feel my mother's body. She said, 'Always love being a woman, Jo. That's who you are. All right, honey, now you go out, and next time, knock.'

"That was the only reprimand I got. I went into my tiny bedroom closet to hold on to the transcendence that I experienced when I touched my mother. I didn't know that it was ecstasy, but it woke me up. Now I knew that the world is full of wonderful mysteries.

"I thought I was marriage-oriented, but in my senior year of college, a priest suggested that I become a Sister. I thought it was the most abnormal way in the world to live. But I decided to at least check it out to see if I liked it. I wrote 103 Franciscan religious communities and asked them questions. Some responded by saying that I clearly had no vocation to religious life—I was too proud. I asked questions like 'Do you consider your habit practical and hygienic?' I also wanted to know if they worked with men, because I grew up with men and I didn't want to be with only women. The only one that answered every question with 'yes' was the community I joined in Milwaukee.

"I was determined to give it a year, and get it over with so I could get on with my life. Convent life turned out to be the best thing I'd ever done! We ran our own lives; we didn't have men telling us what to do or doing our finances. It was so marvelous to have a life that gave time for reflection, prayer, and serving others. Our habits were simple. I could drive easily in them. We worked in schools, some of them for the mentally retarded and orphaned. Rosemary Kennedy [John F. Kennedy's sister] was one of our students. We were puked on and did the work no one else wanted to do.

"I thought the vow of celibacy would exclude intimate relationships with anybody, and it took me ten years to realize I gave up nothing. Everything, everything good has multiplied and multiplied in my life.

"Sometimes somebody says to me that I might have it all wrong: that God and all this religious 'stuff' is just a snow job; Jesus is a hoax." She cackles, her eyes blazing. "My life is so much better for the way I've lived, and if it's all a joke, I'll go into eternity laughing my head off. But if it's not, watch out!"

She tells us about her friendship with the Dalai Lama. "In 1998, we were both invited to an international dialogue between Christians and Buddhists in Chicago. Before he came over he told the organizers, 'I'm tired of these men, I'd like to speak with an American woman, especially a Native American. I need another point of view!' They gave him ten names, and he chose me to come to the conference. We hit it off immediately. He's a wonderful, spiritual, down-to-earth humorous man.

"He asked me, 'You know the difference between our religions?' And I said, 'Yes. Three words. Act on it.' He laughed and said that was exactly the difference, and he felt influenced by us to get out of the monasteries and to become active.

Americans are the 'can do' people, so when Tibetan monks come to America, they do compassionate service in the community.

"We have to learn from each other like this. When I was in the Holy Land, they let me spend the night in the chapel with the Chagall windows of the twelve tribes. I had to see the sun come up on those windows! It was a vision, an eternal experience—when the sun shines through all the colors and images in the glass, it imprints on your being and soaks into you. I'm Catholic, but I can't be contained in only Catholicism. I need to be happy in my own spirit.

"I worry about when the Dalai Lama is gone, because he's a right balance, like all holy people. They don't look saintly; they're just so good! I don't like people who are trying to be perfect. They drive me crazy. We're here to be good, not perfect, and trying to be perfect keeps us from being good. It makes us self-centered, self-absorbed, and we don't see the needs and gifts and talents around us." Lauren Artress makes the same point when she says that anything worth doing is worth doing poorly.

"Everybody is your teacher," she says. "When you're standing in the supermarket line, learn. We're supposed to be learning and expanding our vitality, our imagination, and that leads to prayer, mysticism, and ecstasy in everyday life. When my parents asked, 'What happened today?' woe to the child who said, 'Nothin'.'"

I ask her if she'll speak to my community. "About what? I've never spoken to a Jewish group before." I say, "About how to live." "Oh, I know how to do that. I've been asked that question many times."

How does she receive an honorarium? "I charge my expenses, and if they want to offer anything more, they do. I never set a fee. This time I asked for seventy-five dollars for gas and food. They had four times as many people as they thought they would, so they offered me five hundred dollars, but I don't expect that. When I go to a little parish, I always give the money back if I don't need it. I never have any money in the bank.

"I need money when I see a man sitting on the curb holding his head. I stop and ask what's the matter. 'My teeth are killing me!' he says. "I take him to a dentist and then I find the money. I need money for art supplies, musical instruments, and then I find the children, and then I find them a teacher. These kids will never get off drugs if they don't have exciting things that are making their lives go 'round." New Mexico is one of the poorest states, and with Native Americans and Hispanics, one of the highest minority populations.

"I have no interest in being a priest, because you'd just be dressed like a man following rules written by men. I like the freedom of going around the country criticizing the Catholic system. I say to bishops, 'You still don't know that God is a woman?'" She throws back her head and laughs. "If I don't see girls on the altar, I complain. My mother said that institutions move a hundred times more slowly than the people do, so I stick with the people."

4

Wilderness

Human history has been written by a white hand, a male hand, from the dominating social class. The perspective of the defeated in history is different. Attempts have been made to wipe from their minds the memories of their struggles. This is to deprive them of a source of energy or an historical will to rebellion.

GUSTAV NEIBUHR

GOD MAY LOVE THESE WOMEN THE MOST BECAUSE OF WHAT THEY HAVE ENDURED to be spiritual leaders. Their struggle may be so great that an outsider cannot imagine why they do not give up. The truth is, they can't, because they love the work too much. Gender is not their only problem: besides being women, they may be lesbian, black, Asian, or ordained from unconventional seminaries. Whatever the reason, theirs is always an uphill struggle, and ironically they are often the most gifted. Despite the obstacles, these women manage to achieve far more than many with more advantages.

The name of this section takes its inspiration from the Book of Numbers, the fourth book of Moses, known in Hebrew as *Bamidbar*, which means "in the

Wilderness." The journey through the forbidding Sinai Desert is a terrifying, physical, emotional, and spiritual challenge. By the end of the forty-year journey, however, the sojourning Hebrews will bless all that they went through, because it will make them who they are. It is the same with the women in this section. Rejection has not embittered or discouraged them; rather, they have become more sensitive, empathic people with a toughness that comes from surviving. "That which does not kill us makes us stronger," wrote Nietzsche. These women exemplify his words.

After a nearly fatal accident at sixty-two, the Reverend Diane Winley sacrificed a successful career in New York as a powerful health care advocate for the poor to become the minister of a weary, dying congregation of elderly blacks and Koreans at the Good Shepherd Presbyterian Church in Manhattan, where she works to bring a revitalization to the community in body, mind, and spirit. Leading healing services as a seminary student at Riverside Church had shifted her interest from the politics of health care to the ministry of healing.

Ma Jaya grew up a poor Jewish kid from the streets of Brooklyn, New York. Married at fifteen and living in a cold-water flat in Brooklyn with her husband and three children, one evening while in the bathtub she had a vision of Jesus. From this first mystical experience, her odyssey led her to become founder and head of Kashi Ashram in Jupiter, Florida, which provides a haven for homeless people with AIDS. The transformation of Joyce Green into Ma Jaya Sati Bhagavati is a story that is cosmic and tragic and paradoxical—but her awakening into the "religion of kindness" has made a difference in the lives of thousands of people, many of them outcasts from modern society.

No one has made a greater contribution to modern Jewish music and liturgy than composer and singer Debbie Friedman. Her vision of Jewish healing and wholeness is a wonderful example of *tikkun olam*—the healing of the world. Her success has not depended upon support by Jewish institutions but was achieved by her phenomenal popularity in the liberal Jewish community. Methodist minister Sandy Gess is a lesbian who has created a small interfaith community in Oakland, California, for all who believe in the importance of bringing forth the wisdom of the feminine.

Janice Mirikitani spent her infancy in an Arkansas internment camp for Japanese Americans in World War II. This experience, coupled with childhood sexual abuse from a member of her family, informs her leadership as Director of Programs at Glide Memorial Methodist Church, where thousands who are poor in body and spirit are helped daily. She reaches out to countless others through her books of prose and poetry, including *Love Works* and *Watch Out! We're Talking*.

THE REVEREND DIANE WINLEY

The Reverend Diane Winley works hard to engage the assembled people who are sitting in the cold, cavernous sanctuary at Good Shepherd Presbyterian Church on the Upper West Side of Manhattan. But no "Amen! Sister!" comes from this small congregation of fifteen black and Korean senior citizens. That they are here is evidence of their devotion to God, but that is the limit of their expression. It seems a shame that more people aren't getting the benefit of her intelligent and meticulous service, and I feel for her in this one-hundred-year-old high-ceilinged church built to hold hundreds of parishioners. The service concludes with the congregation leaving the pews to join hands to form a healing circle. We turn to one another and ask for specific blessing in the coming week. A white-haired black man and I bless each other with wishes for good health.

After a hearty potluck fellowship with at least thirty people who suddenly appear, we interview Rev. Diane Winley in her office which also serves as a storage room. She looks around and past the clutter. "I've been here eight months. The church has been without a permanent pastor for four years, and much has eroded. The challenge now is to build a congregation here. One has to minister to the people while getting a plan for fund raising so we can tutor our young people—the education system is horrible—and so we can have a decent choir. I'm starting midday services, which will focus on healing prayer and meditation, touch, stress relief, and to get people, with music and prayer, to feel a wholeness of body, mind, and spirit. You have to have good music; you can't make it without that."

New to the ministry after a long, successful career as a health care advocate for the poor, Diane Winley is at a disadvantage because she is black, not young, and understated, in a time when congregants shop for the best show. When I remark about the size and nature of her congregation, the pastor sighs. "It's been a lot harder as a woman to do this work. One is not offered a thriving church; one is offered something that is dead or dying. The clergy and leadership are still

181

male-dominated. It's very difficult to minister where you don't get response, especially when you grew up in a Christian home with Baptist and Pentecostal roots, as I did.

"We were part of a community of black people who shared and cared for each other. We didn't know that we were poor because we always had something to eat. My parents worked in the factory; it was a company town. We lived in—I hate to say it, it's such a horrible town—Waterbury, Connecticut; it was segregated when I was growing up in the fifties and sixties. Race relations are still not great. The *New York Times* recently described it as a place where intermarriage is between a Catholic and a Protestant.

"My family was very politically aware and culturally sensitive, so I grew up hating segregation and hate. There were still lynchings when I was growing up; the last lynching was in New Jersey in 1949. Social justice and concern for the poor were my priorities when I went to the University of Connecticut. I saw how the antipoverty programs in the sixties took my father out of the factory to get a GED [graduate equivalency degree]. Ultimately he headed the antipoverty program in Waterbury. He'd still be firing furnaces if it weren't for this program. And my mother went on to train as a practical nurse. I am also an example of someone who benefited by the opportunities the government offered."

Perhaps only a woman of faith has the strength to keep working and hoping in a place like this—or perhaps what it takes is someone who knows how to keep the big picture. She has been at this church less than a year and it takes time to build community. The Reverend Winley is a pastor today because she could no longer hear tragic story after story and be helpless to do anything about it. When she began her advocacy, she worked with New York City mayor Ed Koch and saw the fruit of her insistent efforts. But in the years that followed, the work grew frustrating. Every year services diminished, hospitals serving the poor closed, and facilities deteriorated. Winley became discouraged and disillusioned. A near-fatal car accident was her wake-up call.

Feeling her spirit awaken, she turned to God and asked for an answer. It came, giving her a better way to serve than cajoling and fighting with the mayor. "I began to feel there was a call on my life, that I was in relationship with God. I spent a lot of time crying, feeling joyful mostly that God was wooing me back. That was in 1985, and I went to New York Theological Seminary.

"At first I hoped that this was a call to the cloister, where I could just spend time in prayer and contemplation, but that didn't happen. My call is to continue to struggle for fairness, but struggle in a different way." Winley pauses a moment, perhaps reflecting on the difficulty of the task we call living; her eyes fill. "I still struggle against the systems of oppression, but no longer with anger and hate; now I struggle with love. I have to do it this way, to find ways for forgiveness and help others to the place of forgiveness.

"I feel my calling very deeply, both the joy and pain, and the struggle is very difficult. But this is God's world, and all I have to do is my best. We don't know how things will end or what our work means, but I do know it is the work, the road, to live holy, to reach others.

"Sometimes I yearn for the black church, but right out of the seminary I went to Riverside Church." It was in a *New York Times* article about the emerging presence of healing services that featured Reverend Winley that I first learned about her. "It was the first time I had worshipped in other than a black church. The first Sunday we passed the peace, and you had to turn around to shake someone's hand, pass the peace, and mean it. I turned around to someone who was white, the one I'd struggled against all my life. That was the beginning of my understanding that this was part of my calling, a ministry with diverse people.

"I still am and remain a member of the board of directors of the New York City Health and Hospitals Corporation, but now I'm deeply concerned with personal health, and that has brought me into a broad range of healing ministries, including energy healing and the laying on of hands. That is very real for me from my Pentecostal roots, but I never expected to find it at Riverside Church. They have a Wellness Center directed by the Reverend Fanny Erickson, who through her own experience of being miraculously healed brought it to this very liberal Protestant church [United Church of Christ]. I participated in her Sunday healing services.

"When I talk about laying on of hands and prayer, I'm not talking so much about miraculous

In addition to her work at Good Shepherd Presbyterian Church, Reverend Diane Winley is now the chaplain at Hunter College in New York City.

healing as I am trying to involve people in their own healing, trying to help them see that there is within themselves the element of healing. We can be the medicine of support for each other. Recently I had a second consultation for a mammogram, and when I came out of there, I was in such a state of anxiety that I would have loved to have someone lay their hands on me and say, 'Pray.'

"My goal is to lead people into a deeper level of spirituality, because it is in that state that the healing takes place. This is one of God's major gifts, and we need it so much at this time. Maybe that is why we have people like Larry Dossey and Herbert Benson talking about this. Oprah has them on her show and I think it's a miracle. God is saying, 'Yes, this is available. We all can do it.' We all have a healing gift. It's not necessary to have a spiritual practice to be healed, but it helps. Both the healer and the patient need a practice.

"My being a woman led me to care about the poor and sick and has generated in me this nurturing. Maybe my calling to have love in my heart for people different from me is also part of my being a woman. I've always been a mediator, someone who could work with people across age, race, and class. Women learn to do this to survive.

"I think of the nameless mothers of the church—women who have been on the front line but who couldn't be elders or deacons or trustees or pastors, but who loved us as teenagers and who encouraged us even as adults. And I think of the pioneers in leadership, the first to be ministers or rabbis. The first time I received Communion from a woman was quite an experience.

"Women spiritual leaders need a sisterhood. We need to be in dialogue, particularly across religious beliefs. I've worked that way in social justice projects, and I like to work that way in the faith-based community as well. We can both nurture and critique each other in ways that no one else can do. We can share the troubles of our respective callings. Suzan Johnson Cook is the best known of the women pastors around here, and she started with nothing. She's got a tremendous gift. I think, as women move up we'll be tested like male pastors, with money and sex and power. But if we stay true to where we are, women will make a difference. We're important now because this is a healing time."

Some pulpit leaders have so much ego that they think they are generating the light. And then there is Reverend Winley, humble and excellent in her calling, with just enough ego to believe that she is a vital servant of God. When I ask about her personal life, she tells me that her husband is a minister, too—they met in the seminary—and that he has grown children. She asks if I have children, and how they feel about my ministry. "They say that it's not such a big deal," I tell her, "because Mom has always been a rabbi." She laughs, claps her hands, and says, "Wonderful! Wonderful!"

MA JAYA SATI BHAGAVATI

That Ma Jaya is gutsy and powerful should be no surprise to anyone who knows her childhood. Born in 1940 into an impoverished Jewish family in Brooklyn, Joyce Green grew up with street people under the boardwalk, taking care of herself from young adolescence. How she became Ma Jaya Sati Bhagavati, head of Kashi Ashram, an interfaith spiritual community in central Florida, is a story that could shake anyone's disbelief.

In 1973, she was living in the Red Hook section of Brooklyn with Sal, her "beautiful Italian stud" whom she married at fifteen, and their three children. Weighing about 275 pounds and having failed at many diets, she heard from a friend about Jack LaLanne's health club, where they taught a five-minute yoga breathing exercise for weight loss. Ma learned it easily and reasoned, "Why not do it for hours and lose lots of weight?"

Locking herself for extended periods of time in the bathroom, the only quiet place in the house for meditation, one day she found that she wasn't alone. While she was sitting in the bathtub, practicing her new-found yogic breathing, Christ came to her. She told him that she was a Jew and that he must have the wrong address. But Christ answered her, saying, "Teach all ways, for all ways are mine." She told very few what had happened to her, because she "wasn't looking to become a saint, a teacher, a holy person, and least of all, a freak."

But she had been called. Visionary appearances of two esteemed gurus, Swami Nityananda and Neem Karoli Baba, led her to Hinduism, which she saw as embracing all religions. She began to teach in her living room, divorced her husband, and in 1976 left with a group of students to start an ashram in Sebastian, Florida. By now her students called her Ma Jaya, an endearing Sanskrit name for "holy woman."

Today the ashram is an eighty-acre woodland paradise that is home to two hundred people devoted to bringing forth Ma's ministry of loving service. While Ma initially established Kashi for people seeking God, spiritual enlightenment, and a life of service, it gradually became a refuge for sexually abused children and

Kashi Ashram embraces the sacred practices of many traditions. "Kashi" means "city of light" and is the ancient name for
the holy city of Benares in India. The essence of the teaching
is based upon loving-kindness, compassion, and a commitment to the Truth through service to humanity.

for dying people with no one to care for them. The ashram received its first AIDS case in 1982, and word spread throughout the gay community that Kashi Ashram was a place that turned no one away.

The ashram became blessed with the children of its residents. Because the public schools refused to take children from the ashram because of racial tension in the local community, Ma started the River School in 1979, the only known school in the country established to support racial diversity. In time, the school became respected for its academic curriculum and its spiritual training from nursery school through high school. Today, ninety percent of the one hundred students come from neighboring communities.

We knew Ma because she had performed the wedding of our friends, the celebrated gay writer Paul Monette and his lover, Winston Wilde. Paul was dying of AIDS. He asked her to be the key speaker at his memorial service, attended by hundreds of friends, including leaders of many religions, because he told her, "You're the only one who won't 'make it nice.' Talk about your people who are dying."

When we set up our appointment with Ma, the ashram staff invites us to stay overnight. After settling into a spacious guest suite with a hot tub and meditation porch, we are eager to see Ma.

Ma, however, isn't ready to see us yet. She is painting in her room, which overlooks a large pond in the center of the ashram. Rimmed by shrines honoring many religions, the pond stands for the Ganges, India's sacred river. It is a manifestation of the Divine Mother, who purifies anyone who touches Her waters. The pond holds the ashes of thousands of lives ended by AIDS.

As we stroll around the pond waiting for Ma, we pass a redwood Ten Commandments with a Star of David, a stone Buddha, a screened meditation cottage with several Hindu gods, and a shrine to the Virgin Mary that contains the words Ma heard when Jesus called her. The setting would be tranquil were it not for mega-decibel rock music blasting from Ma's room.

We visit the River House, a residence for people with HIV/AIDS and other life-challenging illnesses. As with every inch of Kashi Ashram, the house is impeccably clean, with each bedroom personalized by its occupant. In the living room, which feels like a weekend house with games, magazines, and a television, we meet an attractive, energetic man wanting to tell his story. Gary says, "Before I came here, my kidneys had shut down and my nurse practitioner in the hospital said I was going to die. Ma told her to send me here, and two days later I was conscious again.

"I had no concept of a spiritual life. My life was in shambles, I was separated from my wife, I hadn't seen my children in a long time, and I was seventy-five pounds lighter than I am now. Through the kindness, compassion, and spiritual guidance of Ma and everyone who works here, slowly I began to heal. I gained weight, and my son loves to come here to visit. I'm happier than I've ever been. What happens here is more than physical healing; it's also spiritual and emotional healing.

"I'm not a Hindu, but I have a firm belief in God, and I try to give back what was given to me. We go to nursing homes and bring brownies and music. The homes we go to are on the bottom of the ladder. No one visits them, but because of Ma, we're allowed to go in there and bring them love and kindness. Ma is very present and accessible. She has some back problems now, but she still comes by the River House once a week."

The afternoon grows late, and we need light to photograph and videotape the interview. Ma still isn't ready for us, however, so we walk to the Sebastian River via a three-hundred-foot boardwalk, each plank bearing the name of someone who has died of AIDS. Built in 1994, it is a bridge that connects the living to the dead. The boardwalk leads to the river's edge, where we see a fisherman floating downstream in a rowboat. This Winslow Homer scene vanishes when we return to the boardwalk.

When we get to the main building, we find Bina, our contact, who is responsible for keeping track of us. She has bad news. Ma's back is giving her a lot of pain. She cannot talk much and doesn't want her picture taken. We have come fifteen hundred miles to see her. Bina offers us photographs from Ma's press kit. I look around the room. Mother Kali is the most prominent deity; she is Ma's patron goddess. Kali is not the Virgin Mary. Bloody claws and fanglike teeth exposed in a fierce grimace reveal the power of the one who destroys ego and tears away everything that stands in the way of knowing. Besides Kali, photographs of

Ma over the past twenty-five years fill the room. Why can't we photograph her? Is it that she really feels bad, or is she offering me the opportunity to face my ego and its desire to "get" the interview?

Bina hints that if we go with the flow, Ma may relent and let us photograph. The *darshan* that evening begins at 7:30, and we will meet some time before that. At 6:45, Bina escorts us into Ma's richly adorned private chambers, where we find her in a long brocade gown, a traditional Indian *pujabe,* regally sitting in full lotus position on a velvet-upholstered bench. Four people dressed in white sit nearby on the floor. Two chairs are set up for us in front of Ma. On the back of her left hand is a red-looped ribbon tattoo in memory of the dying and the dead AIDS victims. Her guru's name is tattooed on her other hand. A glimpse of her ankle reveals a tattooed anklet of skulls. While tattooing is part of Hindu culture, Ma's rough and tough persona is at home with skin symbols, too.

She shakes her head and waves away the video camera. "I don't want to let you girls down, but this isn't vanity," she says. "One day I'll show you what my back looks like—you won't believe it. There's nothing holding up my spine but scars. I was beaten, and everything got infected. But I forgave, because that's what you do when you live in the streets," she says. "I can't have anything that's going to show my pain. I have people out there in the streets, and I don't want them saying, 'Ma, what's the matter?'" She looks the same to me, except that her hair is different. Instead of being long, curly, and black, it is platinum blonde and about two inches long.

"I have *great* pictures of me. Why don't you use one of them?" Gay explains that the photograph is her art, her impression and expression of Ma, and that is what our collaboration is about. Without her portrait, she cannot be in the book. We agree, however, not to point the video camera at Ma; we will use it only for recording the spoken interview. In the end, she will allow Gay a few minutes to take her portrait, but no one will be satisfied with it. (Fortunately, Gay had another opportunity a year later, and Ma had no problem being photographed. That time her hair was its usual color.)

A red dot on her forehead (called a *tilak*), her trademark huge gold hoop earrings, and a huge gold BROOKLYN necklace add to the room's pageantry. Pointing to the necklace, she says, "This part of me should never die. A black lady who raised me under the boardwalk told me, 'Never forget your roots, no matter how far or how high you go.'"

In preparation for the interview, we sent her a copy of our earlier collabora-tive work. "I saw your book about Holocaust rescuers, about where they hid the Jews. You know I lost my whole family? I have nobody left, just three cousins." Ma sighs. Her only religious experience as a child was watching her grandmother light Shabbos candles on an orange crate. Only Joycey was allowed to be present for the Friday night ritual.

"You know Zalman?" she asks. I do; in the guesthouse I noticed a photo of the great rabbi/magician, Reb Zalman Schachter-Shalomi. Her face softens at the mention of his name. "Zalman is the most profoundly religious man; he loves God and accepts everyone. He sat on the couch with me and looked at all my children ravished by the disease. Someone asked, 'Where was God in the Holocaust?' He said, 'Where was God? God was inside everyone who was crying, and God was crying, too.' When I told him I was asked to speak in Germany and I didn't want to go, he said, 'Why wouldn't you take your God where it is most needed?' Zalman and his wife, Eve, came here after their wedding to spend the traditional seven days after the ceremony. We had forty-two rabbis here!

"When Zalman comes to me and says, 'We're having Shabbat. I want you to come,' I tell him to get real. I don't want the pain. When I was very young I was terribly beaten by a rabbi screaming out the name of God. But I went, and we sat at the table with the rabbi staring into my eyes. I felt lost for a moment. I'm Ma. I touch. I am not touched. This is too personal. Reb Zalman handed me a beautiful shawl that he had made especially for me in Israel. I wanted to cry, but I stopped myself. He placed the shawl around my shoulders and head and showed me how to light the candles. Me, Ma, who holds the dying babies, the junkies, the prostitutes, and the crack addicts. Me, who always holds—I was now being held. In that moment he gave me everything that I was and will be. He gave me back my Judaism that I really never lost, Shabbos, and my ancestors from Russia. I touch his feet. This man has the Mother. This is a man," she says softly. Even Ma resists surrender.

She calls herself a maverick Hindu. "I have students and devotees from India come here and say I shouldn't do gay weddings. They say it's against their religion. I say, 'I'm your guru. What's your religion?' God doesn't know gender." Ma has been a hero in the gay and lesbian community for years, because she says, "I'm more comfortable with gays and lesbians. I just love how they love. I'm outra-geous, but they're more outrageous than me."

Ma's history with gays began in her teens as a newlywed. She and her husband became friends with Millie and Jimmy, a handsome couple next door. One day, when Jimmy was coming out of the shared shower in the hall, Ma saw that he had "the biggest, highest, fullest breasts that I have ever seen on a woman, let alone a man." She screamed "Freak!" and ran into her apartment. She continued to be abusive and rejecting until Jimmy hit her after she called Millie a whore. When she awakened in the hospital with a broken eardrum, Jimmy was in her room. As Ma contemplated throwing a vase of flowers at her, Jimmy said that she was so sorry. She had never hit anyone before. Ma remembers, "The room was filled with their friends in all kinds of dress. I didn't know who was a man or a woman, and I didn't care. They were human beings who had come to see me. I was ashamed of my words. That was my first lesson in not judging anyone.

"I'm a mother of a lot of gay, dead children, a woman with an open wound. In 1982 a young man, twenty-four years old from San Francisco, heard about the ashram as a haven for gays. He was burning up with a fever; I saw marks on his face, and I saw death. I took him to the emergency room, where they kept him for two hours. The next thing I know they've shipped him back to San Francisco, where he died alone. He left me a note on a paper napkin: 'Please Ma, pick up the torch, carry it, never put it down.' He was the first AIDS case in Florida. I've never forgiven myself for letting him go.

"No other group, besides the Jews in the Holocaust, have been so persecuted. You cannot be the Mother for the straight community and not be the Mother for the gay community; you cannot single out a white baby to care for and not care for the black baby. You have to be Mother to all. I'm talking about the power to give milk to a young boy who has only been fed poison. I went to Washington for the AIDS quilt, and I'm talking to a group of gay kids. I say, 'If God wanted you to be straight, he would have made you straight.' Five hundred kids stood up, tears streaming down their faces."

She describes the River School's spiritual

> **"U**se the breath to lose the fear of death. If you can quiet the mind, the body relaxes, and you can feel the relief that the heart needs to feel by watching the breath and being in the moment. Toward the end you can feel little deaths like a death of each moment. You can get lost in its wonderment. The breath is the secret of a pleasant death and a focused life."
> —Ma Jaya

curriculum. "Every child begins to serve at five. We take them to the 'grandmas and grandpas'; that's what we call the nursing homes. When they're seven, they go to the River House and to Mary's House, where the babies with AIDS live. When they are ten, I take them with me to watch me wash and prepare bodies for death. When someone dies, I call the children to sing at the celebration of death." She pauses and says, "There is only one religion and that religion is kindness."

I ask about her relationship to the feminine, and she explodes. "How can you ask me about what being a woman has to do with my work? Are you a nut?" She punches her chest and proclaims, "I AM THE MOTHER! The Mother of mothers! We have the breasts, and we can have children. Mother Kali has breasts. It's not just women who have breasts. My male teachers, my gurus had breasts— breasts that you could see and touch!"

Much of what this book is about is how the appearance of the messenger has an impact on the message. That Mother has come to earth in the form of a New York mouth makes for instructional paradox. It's also comic, an often underrated path to awakening. Ma and Mother will slip in and out throughout our visit.

"When I go into the streets in the darkest of nights looking for my children, it's not a man that my children want. I hold the boys right between my breasts, and they get the Mother. They had mothers who threw them out because they were gay. I give them unconditional Mother. A man cannot do that unless he has the Mother, unless he says, 'I am as much woman as I am man.'"

More calmly, she says, "There are other women who are doing what I'm doing. Jean Houston [see pp. 257–265] is my dearest, most wonderful friend. She is a woman's woman. She sees this emerging woman, the power within every one of us that must grow and spread. Only if we act together, alone we're nothing."

When my first child was born, the wonder of him destroyed my atheism. I became a rabbi because I fell in love with the world through my baby. Is there room to speak that language in a patriarchal tradition? I doubt that the Jewish sages understood how childbirth unveils God.

"You want to know how much I love you?" she says. Given her reaction to my last question, I'm surprised.

"I'm going to shock the shit out of you. I'm going to take you to a place where I'm going to trust you. Very few people are invited into my private space where my altar honors the dead. I think maybe I took seven people there. You can't bring your camera; it's a teeny little room." The three of us enter her living quarters. We pass a wall of audiocassettes that she waves at and says, "That's my drug." Apart from a banco with hundreds of grinning plaster skulls (a reminder to contemplate the temporality of all things), the room is cozy and warm. We crowd into a space that was once a closet. Niches and shelves hold the ashes of hundreds within urns, shells, and a Godiva chocolate box. Disarming photographs rest near the containers. Beautiful children, some near death, some deliciously healthy; young mothers; and gorgeous boys and young men who shared disease and abandonment. The concentration of so many lives lost feels suffocating. I cough and burst into tears. Ma says quietly, "Many ask if they can be close to me, so I made my death room. This is where I stay in the morning. I look in the pond and I look around me."

As we return to where we first met Ma, the room affectionately known as the Ganesh room, we hear ecstatic singing accompanied by drums and tambourines coming from the main room. It's a half hour past the time the *darshan* is supposed to begin, but no one seems to care. Ma orders Gay to shut off the video camera. "I have something to give, you and I don't want it recorded." She leans forward until her face is six inches from mine. "Do you feel heat from my eye?" she asks me. I'm not sure, but I nod, not wanting to incur wrath or dismissal. Several times during the interview she had told me that my questions were boring.

"It's a gift I have," she says, about her intuition. "You have pain you shouldn't have. You have so much happiness now, but the pain is mauling you." She is not the first person to tell me to get over it. She speaks about the injustices done to her and speaks with humility about the difficulty and necessity of forgiving. She turns to Gay and tells her that her privileged childhood hasn't done her much good; it has taught her very little. "My life on the streets was better than yours," she concludes.

The music grows louder. We enter the main room, where two hundred people are waiting mellowly in varieties of cross-legged sitting positions. Ma sits on a grand bench, and I sit in a chair near her. The children sit in front of her. "*Namaste!*" Ma shouts. "What's with you? Did you expect me to come out in a wheelchair? Get real! I'm going to be okay!" She turns to me. "Tonight I have two

---

Namaste is a Sanskrit word meaning "I bow to the divine within you."

wonderful women with us, and one happens to be a gay rabbi. I've been looking for one for years!"

Everyone laughs like crazy. She orders me to look and to stop writing. "Give
us a little prayer, Rabbi. Make sure it's Jewish; don't do something universal. I'll
do that; you do Jewish." I recite a prayer for peace in Hebrew and offer thanks for
the blessing of being at Kashi Ashram. Satisfied, Ma begins her teaching in a new
voice. Her Brooklyn accent shifts to deep and slow Mother as she describes the
world as a dream.

I almost fall asleep until she begins to speak to a young couple. They are
Indian, and the woman lives in the ashram. Ma asks if they are sleeping together, if he is married. He whispers yes. Is he still living with his wife? Not one body
moves in the room. The couple both nod, eyes downcast. "You know better!" she
screams at the woman. To the blushing man she points and says, "You may not
use her as an object. Go away until you leave your wife!"

After the *darshan*, we return to our cottage to find a sumptuous vegetarian
dinner waiting for us in the kitchen. The young woman that Ma has chastised is
talking on the phone to her mother in India. It sounds as if the mother agrees
with Ma. Kashi Ashram is a homey place that feels like an ideal spiritual community. I wouldn't mind staying a while, but early the next morning we leave this
sacred place built by the visionary, generous, ferocious, funny, and, above all,
greatly loving Ma.

DEBBIE FRIEDMAN

In the liberal Jewish world, Debbie Friedman is known by her first name alone, a level of fame given to only a few performers. While there are many talented singers and composers of contemporary Jewish music, no one has made a greater contribution than she has in setting old prayers to new lyrics and in creating new songs that have become a regular part of the prayer service. Three thousand years ago, the Levites sang the Psalms in the Great Temple in Jerusalem. Traditional Jews still chant almost the entire service, including Scripture. Judaism has always relied upon song to open and connect the heart to the Divine. That Debbie's music has become part of the canon in a tradition that takes music so seriously is further testimony of her accomplishment.

Called the High Priestess of Jewish healing, the Jewish Joan Baez, and the Pied Piper of Jewish summer camps, her songs are attuned to this generation's ear. Her music teaches the Hebrew alphabet, introduces overlooked women in the Bible, and gives fresh meaning to old holidays. She writes songs for life-cycle events and is a pioneer in the healing service. For many Jews, hers is the first music to move them to clap, sing, and cry. Her songs are so well known that many know her music without knowing its author; yet, she has filled Carnegie Hall for the past several years with adoring fans on their feet singing with her. Not definable by denomination, she may be starting her own: Ecstatic Judaism. At fifty-two, Debbie is enjoying the harvest of three decades of brilliant songwriting and performing. Yet, the price for being a woman and breaking new ground has been high. "Being a woman really gets in the way," she says. "Had I not been a woman, I would have gotten in the door much earlier, and there wouldn't have been so much resistance. The underlying, unconscious political barrier has been going on for all these years. I can't say that I'm a militant feminist, but I know people who were militant on my behalf. But things have mellowed some, and in the last ten to fifteen years the music has taken on a life of its own.

"If the world has softened, it's because it has absorbed some of the feminine attributes or aspects of gentleness and inclusiveness. The level of women's sensitivity and the way we relate to each other has affected the world. For example, people in the Reform movement didn't talk about feelings. It wasn't part of the vocabulary, and my music was about feelings, because women are about feelings. In that way, I've helped pave the way a little for women in Judaism. Women are the vessels for the transformation of liturgy and spirituality. It's like music. You have notes on paper but no sound until someone sings them. Women are singing the music I've written. That's my gift. I give it away because that's what I'm here to do.

"My hope is not just for women," Debbie says. "It's across the board. I want men to develop the feminine in themselves and to move out of imprisonment. I want women to do this, too, and women have a special role at this time. Some are putting themselves on the line.

"Look at you, Malka, what you're doing. You've been totally pushing the envelope. We all have to stand at the sea, like Miriam and her sisters, and get our toes wet. We're up to our knees, but we haven't made the decision to cross yet. Some have crossed and come back and have crossed the river time and again. And there is a whole bunch waiting for us to come back and get them. They're too frightened to do it themselves; too much risk is involved.

"Women's voices are very strong now, and they are singing more loudly in the metaphoric sense. Men don't have permission to sing; they have permission to scream and yell. No one has helped them to cultivate their sensitivity and their feeling selves."

Singing is a way to develop the tender part in us. From the beginning of her career, Debbie has invited audiences to participate by singing certain songs with her. Now people know her work so well that the only songs they won't sing with her are new ones or ones she asks them not to sing, because she wants to sing to them by herself.

Debbie says, "Cantors complain that people are not singing traditional *nusah* [melodies] because of me, but every culture has its own melodies—Syrians, Yemenites, Algerians. They are all different and all authentic. What I'd like is to create a *nusah* reflective of our culture." Eastern European music in its haunting, weeping, minor key was, until recently, the standard liturgical music of Jewish services. Debbie's music sings a new song. It's bluesey, folksy, sexy, sometimes funny, and, most of all, contemporary. People of all ages sing it because they like it.

Although thousands of children adore her, Debbie does not have children. Given that she travels close to half the year with concerts, she might have found motherhood an impossible conflict. As we speak, Farfel, Debbie's dog, nudges her, and when she doesn't get her attention, she begins to bark, like a two-year-old objecting to her mother talking to anyone else.

When asked why people should sing, Debbie answers, "Because the world was created for love. If we sang our liturgy during our daily lives, we wouldn't need to go to a synagogue to find God's love. Singing prayer would be such a natural part of our existence that we would live it all the time. Prayer would help our pain and increase our joy. What happens when we sing is that it touches every cell in our bodies, and every cell vibrates when we sing. We open ourselves to let the air in and out.

"Listen to this. After the Oklahoma bombing I went to do a benefit for the citizens of Oklahoma City. My piano player and I did a sound check, and I began to play 'Oklahoma.' One by one each person stood up and started singing. Soon everyone was singing loudly, and tears fell everywhere. At that moment, everyone remembered that there was more than a bombing that connected them." Maybe it doesn't matter what you sing.

Debbie says, "I bring my whole life experience to my work, including growing up in Utica [New York] with my father, the butcher, my mother, and siblings. I remember the big, long table on Shabbos and the wine all around the table. Bubbe (Yiddish for "grandmother") cooking upstairs and we're cooking downstairs; I remember the smells. My father couldn't stand his mother because he was a misogynist, and because of this he was intolerable. My two sisters and I became invisible with his voice and the violence of his hands. I don't want to embarrass anyone, but my father's abuse and the alienation and isolation of having lived in that situation has influenced me. It's made me want to go into communities and make things better. For a little while, I can make a home with those people. We can sing peacefully and make beautiful sounds together. There is no yelling and screaming, and I can be a part of that joy that was missing from my home."

While mainstream Jewish leadership in the late 1980s didn't think the AIDS epidemic had to do with their community, Debbie began her ministry of healing by creating a ritual for people with AIDS. What distinguishes her service is an authenticity that can come only from one who has asked to be healed herself. Besides the childhood she describes, she has other wounds to heal.

Fifteen years ago she took a medication that practically killed her. She says, "I can't run, but at least now I can walk. When I couldn't walk and when I couldn't run, when I couldn't get up from the table without spasms . . . those were the times when I felt totally helpless and hopeless. When I saw someone with cerebral palsy or heard of a child who had died, it freed me to talk about living and dying and illness. I believe that when we are aware of each others' fragility we have the capacity to lift one another from despair to places of hope.

"When I was in Tucson a few years ago for High Holidays, I needed both rabbis to help me up the steps. Afterwards, someone told me how important that was for the older members of the congregation to see. I could consider myself damaged because I needed help, but for somebody else, I was an example."

Debbie says, "Even before I got sick, before the healing services, my work was the same. I've always wanted to bring people together, to feel closeness, and to create community. Each of us is hurting, and everyone knows that. Everyone wants to find a safe place. When we come together, we heal each other. This is what a leader can do."

Called affectionately—and not always affectionately—the "diva," Debbie is like any performer, interested in herself. If that were her only focus, however, she wouldn't be in this book. Whatever else she may be, she is a healer. Her pain has given her music its emotional depth; her song reaches into even the most isolated soul, as the following letter she shows me describes: "Dear Debbie, We have a two-year-old child and none of his limbs move. The baby boy is going to die and the only thing he can do is blink his eyes. When he hears your music, sometimes he twitches and there is movement." Her eyes glance at mine with quiet amazement. "Nobody in the world gets gifts like this all the time like I do. I don't need the big picture, because this little picture is great!

"The issue of healing is the bottom line of prayer, and the bottom line of being a Jew is to engage in *tikkun olam*, the healing of the world. You can't repair the world unless you repair yourself. It's not that you have to be totally intact, but you have to know how to look at yourself honestly and commit to your own healing.

"When I teach seminary students, I want them to draw a line between their lives and the lives of the people in their community. They need to be separate. When rabbis and cantors stand before a congregation, they sometimes become objects of transference, and they become who those congregants need them to be. While spiritual leaders need to be open they also need to keep their private lives private. I'm open on the stage, but nobody knows the details of my life.

"I once went to a conference, and there was a rabbi wearing a turban because she was getting chemotherapy. She was dying, and on this Shabbos she got up to talk at length about her illness in gross details, and how she was almost dead. Anybody who was there with his or her own pain, like a divorce, didn't matter. You can't do that. You need to make room for everybody; you can't use the community to feed yourself." This is another reason, besides her talent, why Debbie has so many loving fans. She knows her boundaries.

When asked what in the past twenty-five years has made her most proud, she responds, "Last night during the concert I almost cried when everyone was singing the healing *MiSheberach*." This is one of Debbie's best-known songs. "When people of all ages, every walk of life, stand up and sing from the *kishkes* [Yiddish for 'guts'], I feel that I've done my work and this is my dream." At this moment Farfel's friend Romeo breaks into canine song, and Debbie isn't surprised. There are no boundaries of communication for her.

Debbie and I have led High Holiday services in Santa Fe. We have a great time because the congregation gets right into it with us: they sing from the heart, they clap and bounce, and macho men weep. People who haven't been in a synagogue for years go out snapping their fingers. While many love the experience, a few complain that it is too "feminist." Debbie and I do the same traditional service as any male rabbi and cantor, however, it feels different.

Debbie says, "There are millions who sing better than I, who play guitar better. But I know that I am totally present, and I come to people with love; the only people I don't love are the people who won't let me love them." Debbie's eyes and voice can show a vulnerability that draws people near. Each person in a gathering of thousands feels her love. While other famous women spiritual leaders also have followers, Debbie's people are more passionate, like groupies in love with a glamorous star.

"Whenever I work with my Jewish comrades, they're so surprised that I'm not arrogant and impossible to work with. That's my reputation. Both men and women say this. People don't like me who don't even know me." She shrugs. Her gift is great and she will be remembered, and that may compensate for the pain. I don't imagine that it is easy to be Deborah Lynne Friedman.

This much I know: Debbie puts God's words upon our hearts, and people hear those words in a woman's voice. Debbie is singing the anthem of the women spiritual leaders. Two generations are now familiar with her songs that give Judaism a fresh sound and a new way to imagine God.

THE REVEREND SANDY GESS

While everyone in this book has put a woman's imprint on her work, the most intentionally feminist, such as Starhawk and Luisah Teish, have made a complete break from traditional patriarchal religions. Those leaders who have chosen to remain in mainstream congregations may be feminists, but it is not the focus of their ministry. Methodist minister Reverend Sandy Gess has taken the most difficult path in her attempt to enrich congregational Christianity with deminism. In 1994 she began Weave of Faith: a Christian Feminist Worshipping Community.

In her early fifties, Sandy offers us tea and cookies in her warm, Craftsman-style cottage that she shares with her long-time partner and their child in Oakland, California. Lacey, a German shepherd, wanders in and out of the living room. "I am a visible example that something has changed in the church," she begins.

Just as Mary Poppins looked harmless and therefore could do outrageous things, the fact that the Reverend Sandy Gess looks more like a minister's wife than an alchemist is to her advantage.

"I was raised in the evangelical United Brethren Church; they wanted to save my soul but only if I stayed in my place. When I was in high school I left to join the Methodist church, because it was into social action and offered a good mix of emotion and reason. I learned how to be engaged in religion in a different way. I did feel called, but because I was a woman I didn't go into the ministry right away. I worked where women worked in the church, in education. There were female ministers in the seventies, but they were marginal. A male friend of mine was in the Methodist seminary, and he

Weave of Faith is what the Christian feminist movement calls a Women Church, in which women, children, and men find empowerment to affect their individual lives and communities. Interfaith and intergenerational, it is a welcoming worshipping community that draws from Judeo-Christian traditions while it honors and brings forth the special spiritual gifts of the feminine. Weave of Faith seeks to be an inclusive church, creating a supportive environment for spiritual nurturing and reflection.

introduced me to his women colleagues. I was the first woman to come out of the congregation and go into the ministry following the seminary's three-year program. My church in Fullerton supported me, and I was ordained in 1974.

"I began in mainstream congregations, but there was concern about the church losing weddings, which were a moneymaker for the church. As a minister I had authority to perform them, but they were afraid that people wanted a man. The other problem was that people needed lots of reassurance that there was a long tradition of Methodist women ministers. I left the pastorate after several years.

"Ten years ago I wanted to get back into ministry again, and I wanted to find something that was more feminist. I couldn't find it anywhere. I found a few other women who also wanted this, so we started meeting on a monthly basis. Since I'd participated in a women's house church years before, and it had imploded because of so many perspectives, traditions, and agendas, I insisted that we meet and design what we really wanted to do. We met for eight months before we came up with a statement of purpose, and we found a place to have services instead of meeting in homes. We wanted to be very public and to welcome everyone.

"Three of us started this: two lay people and me. I could be a lay leader of this church, but I think it's important that I'm ordained because it gives authority when somebody who knows what she's doing and is recognized by the mainstream leads the liturgy. Once I was ordained, I was amazed at how people would open up to me because I had "Reverend" in front of my name. They didn't know my thoughts or beliefs, but just because I was a minister it created a dynamic that was unique and precious.

"While I am ordained, I really try to be in the background as much as possible. At Communion I put on a stole, but I'll still be wearing this," she says, pointing to her slacks and shirt. "When I go guest preaching in Sunday morning services, I do put on all the vestments. It's the tradition, and it creates an aura that people welcome." She laughs and says, "Isn't it ironic that people have trouble seeing women in a robe but not men? A robe is basically a dress! I also have Communion each Sunday, the breaking of bread, because it is important to witness women doing this."

The first woman ordained in Methodism was Anna Howard Shaw in 1890, but she wasn't received into the Conference, the "club." She was a traveling evangelist and worked for the suffrage movement.

When I became a rabbi, family and old friends still treated me as Malka, but there was a change when the conversation turned to things invisible—the things we live for but cannot see, like love and faith. Now they shared these places with me with new intimacy. When I entered the seminary, my stepmother asked, "Malka, you've decided to commit yourself to being a good person. I understand that. But will it make you behave differently in the world?" My answer was yes, being a rabbi would give me permission and authority to be a model of loving-kindness. What I found out along the way is that I always had that opportunity and obligation.

Sandy says, "The first church we approached didn't accept us at all. They asked, 'Is this that "Sophia" stuff? You're not worshipping God. You're worshipping some goddess.' We found the Lake Merritt Church, who had a clergywoman as a primary minister, and she was quite enthusiastic about renting the space to us. I'm a member of the church and so is my partner, but I'm no longer a member of the Methodist Conference, because I cannot serve as a minister in the Methodist Church and be in a same-sex relationship. It's basically 'don't ask, don't tell' with ministers, although many gays and lesbians serve the church. Many colleagues ask me to consider getting back into the Conference because there is much I could do, but I'm too out. It's a political, public statement that I am not a member.

"I also like my independence, which I wouldn't have in the Methodist church. I'm into pioneering. When I was in the seminary, there was much talk about how women can bring more to the church with our different process and ways of seeing things, but the church structure contributes to silencing and squashing. The gratification of my path outweighs the frustrations. When I began in the ministry, I saw that Jesus' model of ministering to the outcast is what we all should be doing, as opposed to going to an institution and having it easy. Now I feel that I'm ministering to people who aren't outcasts but people who don't get their needs satisfied somewhere else. We get calls from women who have left their tradition and are participating in the Goddess tradition. They miss the community, and so they think they might be able to find something with us."

While it is true that a pastor's work is to

"Sophia," meaning "wisdom" in Greek, is the word used by Christian feminists to describe the feminine nature of God or Christ.

comfort the afflicted, what about afflicting the comfortable? If Sandy Gess were to lead a service celebrating the feminine in Atherton, a wealthy suburb not far from working-class Oakland, she would be offering a different but no less necessary ministry in awakening consciousness. Of course, the likelihood of her being chosen as consecrated leader of a wealthy establishment congregation is remote.

"I have no difficulty with being a lesbian and being a religious leader, nor do I have a problem with my connection to God. Because I view myself as created in God's image and it's a wonderment, anything that would exclude me is only a social construct. As for the Bible, we are people of the Book, so we have to deal with the text. Many verses are taken out of context to condemn or limit people. A lot of the Old Testament was written specifically for the priests and there is no prohibition against lesbianism in Scripture.

"As a Christian I know that Jesus had nothing to say about homosexuality— and besides, don't we pick and choose what is the text of authority for us? Only six biblical passages condemn homosexuality. But if we include the New Testament, two hundred passages condemn different heterosexual behaviors. This doesn't mean that God doesn't love heterosexuals any less; they just need more supervision." She looks questioningly at me, making sure that I get the joke.

"We struggle to bring insight and spirituality into Judeo-Christian traditions. I really respect the differences between the faiths; we get information from our Jewish members, but we can only go so far out of respect for Judaism. Same with Catholicism. Our services are participatory and nonhierarchical. We've brought together women from various religious traditions and to work through our differences and commonalities. There may be differences of opinion, mostly differences from traditions, and we share our experiences grounded from these traditions. We're following in the long line of Christians who borrowed from other traditions to make it real and meaningful to ourselves.

"I'm not what you call Christomonistic, where Christ is the one God. Christ is a model for us, a brother, and an aspect of Divinity that came to show us how humans could be more divine. I want to be Christian partly because that is our tradition that we are dealing with. For some, Jesus has given us the Christ; for others, he is just Jesus, a man. I'm not here to proselytize a new face in the traditional way or to say you have to accept Jesus as your savior. But I do think the tenets of Christianity are worth operating on. I want people to find Christianity, the lost Christianity that once included women.

"When I pray, I talk to the Divine Spirit of the universe within and without. I have a continuing conversation with that divine person, being he/she. It's not anthropomorphic, but since developing this community, sometimes a feminine image will come up that comforts me. In fact, whenever I have a vision these days of the Divine, it's primarily the feminine.

"We cannot assume that anyone knows, including feminists, who we are worshipping when we use the name of God as *Ruah* [spirit], or Sophia [wisdom], or *El Shaddai* [God the Mighty Breasted One]. We do a lot of teaching, but our first principle is to be a community. We want to be a support to the people who come, and to show that we can be God's presence in the world to each other—not just on Sunday evening twice a month, but in our lives. A year ago, one of the members went through postpartum depression. People started to call her to go for a walk, share their own experience, and help her with finding day care and a therapist."

Pastoral counseling is available to members, and anyone who attends services is a member. Weave of Faith depends upon donations given during the offerings at the service. Sandy says, "Some of us struggle economically, and some are fine. There is an equality that we try to model, and we experience commonality as women. The men who come are open to the feminine in themselves, or they want to know a gentler, more loving God."

While Sandy puts in about thirty hours a week helping the community, she is not paid. She works as a reference librarian and has a partner with a good income. Sandy says, "Women involved with Women Church have to find other work to support themselves. I'd like to see if we can get enough funding for more publications and special events, but the important thing is just to do it and make it possible to do it.

"Our services empower lots of people to participate from various traditions. Because what we do is more on the edge and experimental, male colleagues say, 'Gosh, I never looked at God this way before.' We offer a living model of how to find new theological insights and talk about women's issues. I hear from all kinds of ministers all over the country who have found us through our web site." Gess designed the web site for the Graduate Theological Union's Center for Women and Religion, and it was from their link that I found Weave of Faith. The experiment is difficult, however, when you are unpaid and have a child. The Weave of Faith web site is rarely updated.

Founded in 1970, the Center for Women and Religion is an interfaith and multicultural organization that promotes justice for women in religious institutions. It also provides a critical pedagogy for ministerial leadership skills, women-oriented resources, and academic programs, particularly in the areas of women's spirituality, women's ways of knowing and teaching, and women's culture and health.

"Look what we do for kids in our group," Sandy says. "We include them in the church in a way mainline denominations can't conceive. Go to Sunday school, they're told, and stay there. When you can add to the offering, you can join us. Our kids take part in every aspect of the service; they are even involved with the Communion table: baking bread, carrying the elements, and blessing the Eucharistic meal."

We attend the biweekly service at Lake Merritt Church, this one devoted to celebrating women mystics. The back of the program explains that: "A mystic is one who directly experiences God. Mysticism, a term associated with the Greek mysteries, is a universal religious phenomenon common to Christianity, Judaism, and Islam. They have in common an attempt to know the inner reality, which is associated with the Divine."

Twenty-five people fill a small part of the large sanctuary in the modern and beautiful church. In the program, Gess has written the text celebrating Hildegard of Bingen, Clare of Assisi, Hadewijch of Antwerp, Mechthild of Magdeburg, and Julian of Norwich. Otherwise, the service is lay-run.

People bring items that represent spirit or a religious tradition, and they create an altar that includes fifty rainbow-colored, twisted Hanukkah candles in sand that are lit by each participant to welcome the Divine. That Weave of Faith has found a new way to use Jewish ritual candles is not surprising. Every year they celebrate Purim, hold a Passover Seder, and mark Yom HaShoah, Holocaust Remembrance Day. While I don't participate in the Communion that is open to all, I help build the altar. After a fifteen-minute meditation, the leader invites us to choose a picture or saying that the minister has collected for altar offerings. I sort through only the text pieces because I cannot imagine the Divine visually. While Plato tempts me with "Geometry existed before Creation," it is Teresa of Ávila's words that I understand: "Enter into yourself."

They echo God's words to Abram, the son of a wealthy idol maker, when God orders, "*Lech Lecha!* Go to yourself!" He is to leave everything—money, recognition, and power—and enter into a new consciousness that will lead him to a promised place beyond human imagination. Did the saint know this text? I place her words on the altar, delighted to employ Teresa's help in building heaven in Oakland.

It's an easygoing, lengthy service that runs with the minister behind the scenes. The music reflects the vision of pluralism and feminism, with Taize chants and a lyric from Judy Fjell's "Dinner Party." Immanent and homey, the evening's service is pleasant and satisfies an enthusiastic community. Fire, mystery, and eros are absent. If God has seventy faces, then this is the milk-and-cookies face.

In a note thanking us for attending the service, Sandy apologizes for it not being "tighter." She explains that what she is trying to do is empower others by giving them the responsibility of preparation and presiding. She also writes, "Your project is important to me because you are giving voice to the breadth of women's spiritual experience, which is profound and subtle, life-enhancing and life-changing. It is a force in our communities that has not been acknowledged. The possibilities for your returning and our learning from each other are also of great interest to me.

"When you said that you had attended church service with three hundred people, I found myself grateful that we are small. Funny how I can be self-conscious about how many people attend our services. At the same time I'm very grateful for the intimacy we are able to have because of our size.

"As you continue, I offer an 'old-timey' Protestant blessing that your journey be filled with 'traveling mercies': Love the journey, God is with you, come home safe and sound." The Reverend Gess's commitment and effort to Weave of Faith is staggering; it also takes courage for a lesbian to create an interfaith, inclusive community. She has been called, and she has listened carefully to where she must serve. She has made rejection a blessing by creating a new room in God's house.

JANICE MIRIKITANI

If you saw Janice Mirikitani striding along Market Street in San Francisco, you'd never guess her story. Although she is a professional dancer and an accomplished poet, she spends most of her time as executive director of the renowned Glide Memorial United Methodist Church in one of San Francisco's worst neighborhoods. In her thirty-eight years at Glide Church, Mirikitani has established education programs, a drop-in center, meals for thousands of children, a crisis center, workshops on domestic violence, AIDS/HIV testing, substance abuse programs for five hundred people a month, and job skills workshops. Five hundred women each month receive health services, and twenty-five thousand people serve as volunteers. Mirikitani oversees fifty programs, a staff of two hundred, and a budget of ten million dollars. In her large office, where we conduct the interview, she is interrupted continuously by staff members, each swearing to the urgency requiring her input. The office reflects the energy of a 24/7 church and woman.

Glide Church is an open door to a village where everyone is at home. All variety of households, all genders, believers and not-so-sures, poorest and richest, come on Sundays for what some say is the best church service in town. Bill Cosby, Maya Angelou, and Oprah Winfrey—old friends of Mirikitani and her husband, the Reverend Cecil Williams—occasionally stop in. But Glide would be famous without these celebrities. The 110-person gospel choir, stories of resurrected lives, and power-packed sermons delivered by Cecil and Janice make it known from coast to coast.

Beautiful, well-dressed, charismatic, and self-possessed, Janice Mirikitani's commitment to justice comes from never forgetting the injustice she suffered early in life. Her strength comes from believing in the ability to change. "I was born in Stockton, California, in 1941. In 1942 they shipped my family, along with 120,000 other Americans of Japanese ancestry, and me into camps. We were in Arkansas, and although I have no memory of it, I'm convinced that the experience of my people shaped my need for justice, and a sense that justice is a societal obligation."

211

Glide Memorial United Methodist Church is one of the largest human service providers in the San Francisco Bay Area. Janice Mirikitani's husband and Glide's pastor, the Reverend Cecil Williams, is African-American, and as a couple they model the rainbow family of their church.

It is near lunchtime, and the din of voices in the church foyer adjacent to her office grow louder and intrude upon our interview. She speaks up, offering a smile that mingles apology with pride. After the interview, she will step into the entry and be encircled at once by those who know that a word to Janice is what makes things happen. Few of them have any idea of how much personal understanding she has of their lives.

She says, "My mother didn't talk about the camps for forty years; she would change the subject. It was too painful, too humiliating to recall. We moved to Chicago after the war because of the anti-Japanese sentiment on the West Coast. My father divorced her and she married again and that was not a happy situation for me. We were very poor because of the incarceration.

"When she broke her silence in 1982, it was like a waterfall. She spoke out to get the reparations for Japanese-Americans for all the property and material losses. Breaking that silence was so freeing for me. I had been stuck in the camp for forty years imprisoned with, 'You're no good, you're worthless, you're ugly,' the racism of the camps. We were expendable because we were 'foreign' and economically threatening; Japanese farmers worked hard, and their white neighbors didn't like that. By the way, the Germans and Italians who farmed in California were never questioned, let alone moved. That's my life in two words: bringing justice."

She goes on, "I was also abused in childhood; a number of adult male relatives and a very close member of the family molested me for almost eleven years. I didn't reveal any of it until recently in my adult life, because it was so shameful. I knew that because when I tried to tell my mother, she couldn't hear it. It was too terrible to tell, so I kept it inside. Another silence." Janice's eyes fill. "Excuse me. It's part of my recovery." I wait, and ask from what. She takes a breath and says, "Recovery from racism, incest, abuse, voicelessness, shame, being invisible, being self-hating and self-destructive, recovery from alcohol, speed, a variety of chemical substances, and, most of all, recovery from violent

relationships and vio-
lent men. Addictions
come from how much
women internalize dam-

> "**I** kept myself contained within these walls shaped to my body and buried my rage." Janice Mirikitani, *Shedding Silence*

age done to them, and recovery is reclaiming the self.

"Silence is the disease that afflicts our society, and that is my mission in my books and poetry, in recovery circles, and in the programs we've created at Glide—to speak about the silence that imprisons. Not telling is a disease. Giving permission for people to empower their voices, particularly women, is the beginning of recovery and resurrection. It took me a long time to break the silence about my incest and abuse. I'd been at Glide for twenty years when I did it in public in front of fifteen hundred strangers in church. I don't know where the courage came from, except that I finally felt safe enough and inspired to do it." The words flow impeccably, not only because she is a frequent public speaker. These words are her truth, her teaching, and her lesson, and she found them by listening to others tell their stories and by watching how it healed them.

For a long time Janice shut down her past and willed herself to get through life. Graduated from the University of California at Los Angeles in 1963, she received a teaching credential from the University of California at Berkeley and taught high school for a couple of years in a white suburban school in the early sixties. She loved it until the principal fired her for talking about birth control and the Vietnam War. She took a job as a part-time special projects assistant at Glide, and that was when she met Cecil, with whom she has been in professional and marital partnership for twenty years.

"I worked with the gay-lesbian community and gay teenage hookers, transcribing police tapes of incidents involving their being abused and beaten by the police. Cecil began a revolution in this church. It became a shelter for gays and lesbians, and it accepted homosexuality, while United Methodist didn't and still does not.

"That work is what caused the walls protecting my secret to crash. Every way I knew to protect my secret crumbled as I began to engage people in their own pain. I met people who slept in the streets, kids who were starving and never went to school. I worked with people for whom secrets and rejection was a way of life. It shattered the old me, and I had to recreate myself. Cecil was with me every step of the way.

"As I became a new person I came to learn that the person in line for lunch here, who maybe doesn't smell so good, might be the one to knock on my door and tell me something I didn't know. If you think you can save people, you'll burn out here. What you can do is be there to be the glimmer, the hope.

"You cannot say, 'You people down there, you're crackheads, junkies, come up here and we'll bless you and you'll be healed.' That's a setup for the perpetuation of slavery. If you believe in justice, then you are the one in recovery who engages another and meets him or her as a messenger. I've learned from the woman who falls asleep on the sidewalk waiting in the lunch line. When I cover her naked bottom I know compassion. She is my equal, and that's my message. And she reminds me of the Power who keeps me in recovery. I can tell that woman that she deserves the best and that she has a choice about her life. That is justice and it's hard work.

"When he became pastor here, Cecil put this church into causes of justice. He took down the cross from the altar, fired the choir, and the thirty-five white people who were here left. He opened the door to young people and hippies and runaways, and he got so much criticism that I wanted to be his support system; I believed in his work. I brought a new perspective, that of a victim's perspective as a female, a person of Japanese descent, and an artist. We reached out to different communities and gave voice to many; it was about liberation theology, and it was radical. He had the message when I came here, and I've helped bring the action to the words.

"What's interesting in the partnership," she says about her work with her husband, "is that it has always been steeped in spirituality. Cecil puts his arms around the total person, and as an artist I also believe in that. It's been a good fit. The work we had been doing here has been strengthened by our marriage, but it's also been a challenge.

"One struggle we have in the mutuality and equality of gender is enacted at every moment of our lives. I'm stereotyped as an Asian woman to be demure with men, and I'm with an African-American man who has stereotypes in his relationship with women, too. The church has a vertical paradigm, and the struggle is to make our relationship more horizontal. We couldn't go to a PR firm to change people's image and expectation of Cecil and me in terms of power here.

"The change has to be internal. It's taken us thirty years to create ground where he will now finally say, 'You have to go to Jan because she's the Executive

Director.' This is very important, because 50 percent of our staff is hired from the street. We have guys who are ex-cons, very male dominant types, and they go running to the male minister all the time. So it's great that Cecil is in this place of transformation."

When asked if she has considered the ministry for herself, she says that she has. "But the title hasn't been as important as my own transformation to be more spiritual in my life. The Spirit couldn't be more present when a woman reveals to me her past, her pain, and her horror. My lack of enthusiasm to get ordained is that most of the people I know who have gone into it are the coldest and least able to help with messages; the church is the place of greatest denial. If I were talking to a newly ordained minister, I'd tell her to take off her frock, roll up her sleeves, and serve the ones most in need.

"The worst problem I have with people, whether they're ministers or top executives, is a sense of entitlement. Maybe women, being marginalized from birth, will understand what it means to serve with compassion. Of course I've met white women using robes who have acted just as entitled as white guys! Still, women are essential in making a difference in the world of faith, just as people of color make a difference in that world. Gays and lesbians are also essential. People don't change voluntarily, and the person who looks like you and thinks like you is not going to cause the pain that will make you change."

When local spiritual leaders Bishop Leontine Kelly and Reverend Cheryl Kirk-Duggan are mentioned, she says, "Phenomenal women. Yes, they change the face of the church and God. Bishop Kelly brought me some light that helped me to view myself differently. She made me feel that all is possible because of her own life. Maya Angelou is as spiritual as you can get. Toni Morrison is another.

"They have been sent by God to help us reveal ourselves to each other, and to mark the path for our new mission: to serve and help. No, not help. I mean that we are here to believe in each other. It worked for me. Cecil was the first to say that he believed in me. Then I began to see myself and say, 'I can do this.' As long as people said they would do something *for* me, it never did anything for me.

"I've seen women who are beautiful, strong, intelligent, and who destroy themselves. They get to a certain recovery point, and then they go back out on the streets, to the guy who beat them. I see wonderful kids, smart and talented, and we work on poetry together, and they perform it, and we lose them. I can talk about how much we give them, but it wasn't enough if we didn't get them to believe in themselves. I didn't work hard enough to find out what the next thing was, so I could create programs to address it.

"That's what the work is about, how to make people's lives work. We built the Cecil Williams Glide Community House, a residence of fifty-two units for anyone recovering from addictions, because I believe that to change the world, we have to make it better for kids. We have to provide the systems for those kids that will make them believe in themselves. Then, no matter what the drug dealer says, you can say no, I have a choice. It's harder, it doesn't have much money in it, but it's another thing I can do.

"I'm not saying I can save anyone. Everyone makes that choice with full responsibility. It's just that for some the journey is so dark—okay, we provided you tutoring, love, nurturing, a platform, new clothes, food for your family—and you didn't change. It's a matter of staying with you. You slipped and fell; I'm coming to get you. Let's see if there's something I can do, but maybe not. Sometimes a woman comes back after there was nothing I could do, five years later, and she's in college. You can't know.

"My greatest challenge is to be willing to continue to transform myself. I've never changed voluntarily; I was forced to, slapped in the face by something. The work of executive director is the hardest work for me, because it is not me. But it must be done; we have to raise nine million dollars this year to do the work. Every time we lost a child I dreamed of a building, and now we have it because I'm learning how to raise funds and to be a manager. That means I don't have to send a mother and her children back into the street.

"I work hard at growing my courage because I've sabotaged myself so often. But this job requires courage, and I just hired someone to help me grow into it. Managing a staff like this—the majority ex-cons and in recovery—is unique. This is how we repair not just a part of society but the total condition, by taking people off the streets to become healers of others. Here's where I need courage for decisions, and there are so many.

"Do I keep a person who can't write a coherent message? It would be so much easier if I got a bona fide secretary! What is the right thing? It's right for me to train this person to do a better job. It's more work, takes much longer, and not as efficient, but the right thing. Sometimes I get Ph.D.s in here who are experts but have no commitment to the organization. I let them go. That's the right thing, too."

5

Harvest

A new manifestation is at hand, a new hour is come.
When Man and Woman may regard one another as brother and
sister, able both to appreciate and to prophesy to one another.
A new manifestation is at hand, a new hour is come.
What Woman needs is not as a woman to act or rule, but as a nature
to grow, as an intelligence to discern, as a soul to live freely and
unimpeded, to unfold such powers as were given her.
A new manifestation is at hand, a new hour is come.

MARGARET FULLER

THE FINAL BOOK IN THE FIVE BOOKS OF MOSES IS A SUMMARY CHAPTER. BY completing the narrative that began with the creation of the world and repeating the story of the Israelites' journey from slavery to freedom, the dying leader of the generation of freed slaves prepares their children to enter the Promised Land. As inheritors with no memory of the bitterness and corruption of slavery, they are the harvest of a dream planted generations before them.

Women who have recently begun the work of spiritual leadership, especially in posts formerly reserved for men, cannot imagine what women clergy went through a generation ago. As beneficiaries of the pioneers who struggled to create change, they do not know this as the "new hour." They will find, however, that the struggle is not over and that disparity still exists. The commitment and accomplishment of the earlier generation may inspire them.

Besides the emergence of women of spirit, the latest phenomenon in American religion is the general spirituality movement led by individuals who, instead of following a single religion, borrow from many wisdom traditions to create inclusive, syncretistic teachings. The human potential movement, in its blending of psychology and spirituality, makes it difficult to distinguish between self-help counselors and spiritual leaders; several women in this section may fit into either category. Because this book is about recognized faith paths, if only as a point of departure, I have included only women who either are ordained leaders or base their teachings upon traditional sources. Their work is often not so much a regular service as intensive weekend or week-long gatherings devoted to a special theme such as forgiveness. These women are the harvest of the women's movement and the spirituality movement.

Iyanla Vanzant, a Yoruba priestess, ordained minister, writer, and speaker, catapulted to fame when she appeared on Oprah Winfrey 's television show to speak about her five books on human empowerment, personal growth, and spiritual healing. While her workshops and lectures speak primarily to women, her common-sense approach to spiritual strength and personal growth has attracted people of all backgrounds and ages. The Reverend Rebecca Cohen, recently ordained as a Unitarian Universalist minister, grew up as a minister's daughter. The Reverend Helen Cohen, her mother, who is also a Unitarian Universalist minister, had never seen a woman minister before she went to Harvard Divinity School.

Jean Houston, anthropologist and author of fifteen books, has woven many traditions to create seminars that have inspired and empowered thousands. On her deathbed, Margaret Mead instructed her student Jean to go out into the world and gather the best that each civilization has to offer. Perceiving this moment in history as a time when humanity will flourish or perish, Houston encourages her students to take advantage of global awareness and vast communication to access the wisdom of every civilization that has ever existed.

The Reverend Della Reese, best known as a singer and star of the television show *Touched By an Angel*, is the spiritual leader of a ministry she founded in Los Angeles. What began in the mid-1980s in her living room now fills a banquet room in a downtown hotel.

Marianne Williamson, until recently senior pastor of the Renaissance Interfaith Center in Detroit, Michigan, had her life saved by *A Course in Miracles*, a spiritual curriculum that has helped millions of people. Her book *A Return to Love*, based on the course, catapulted her to fame. A prolific author and popular lecturer, she is candid about her life, using it as an example to teach timeless ideas.

Iyanla Vanzant

When Iyanla Vanzant's syndicated television show, *Iyanla*, was on the air last year, comparisons to Oprah Winfrey were inevitable, because Oprah had put Iyanla on the map after reading her inspirational self-help guide to daily life, *One Day My Soul Just Opened Up*. Iyanla's frequent guest appearances on the *Oprah Winfrey Show*, which garnered stellar ratings, caught Barbara Walters's attention, and she invited her to host her own show. After initially refusing because she was satisfied with simply being a guest on Oprah's show, Iyanla changed her mind when she realized that it was her old demon, the fear of failure, that was stopping her.

Oprah and Iyanla may have in common a cultural history and a charisma, but the key difference between them is that while Oprah is a believer, she is essentially an entertainer and entrepreneur. Iyanla, on the other hand, is an ordained minister, an empowerment specialist, and a spiritual life counselor who blends African tradition, new thought, and old-time religion into a path of hope accessible to anyone.

When her show was not renewed, comparisons to Oprah came up again. Attending one of her workshops gave me insight into what had happened to her show. It was not that the revelations shared by workshop participants were too raw for television; that would practically be impossible. What took place between the wounded and the healer requires witness to appreciate: television, as primarily an entertainment medium, can reveal dramatic human interaction but not the way that a healer listens.

The workshop takes place at the Omega Institute, a human empowerment retreat center in Rhinebeck, New York. With the look and feel of a spacious, old-fashioned summer resort that serves wholesome and tasty vegetarian food, Omega was, until the early 1960s, a Yiddish summer camp. Where children once played volleyball, adults now meditate, thanks to New Thought philosopher and writer Ram Dass, who bought the defunct camp thirty years ago as a place for him and his friends to hang out. With the vision of cofounders Elizabeth Lesser and

Stephan Rechtschaffen, the gatherings grew into what Omega is today: a magnet for all who are looking for a respite and a better way to live.

Two hundred participants, about a third of whom are African American, have paid eight hundred dollars for a weekend seriously focused on forgiveness; this is less about rest than about revelation, and there are rules. We are to attend every session, and when in session we are to pay attention and not wander in the back of the room looking at pamphlets.

"We control the environment," Iyanla tells me later, "to create a space where people feel safe and comfortable, so that they can learn to sit through whatever comes up and move through it. We let them know that they won't die from it, turn into a frog, or turn blue. We take people into that place and show them that they can stand in it and be okay. The way we do that is to move people into a close space, get them all looking in the same direction, and pump the room full of love. We have certain techniques and exercises in every workshop, but each one is different." Instead of half-listening while checking out the room and deciding with whom to have lunch, the workshop is a meditation, with a practice that requires full attention to the moment.

Music begins the first session on Friday night. After a brief introduction by Iyanla, she tells everyone to stand up and say, "I am OPEN to the light and love of my soul." We say this 108 times with one hand on the heart and one on the forehead. We're instructed at specific times to massage our eyes and hands and to pat ourselves all over. After the ten-minute exercise ends with vigorous clapping, thirteen "angels," African-American women dressed in white, look around the room to see if anyone seems lost. Their responsibility is to keep everything running smoothly over the weekend. Stationed around the room, they remind you if you break a rule, offer tissues, and look to see who may need a comforting hand or a kind word.

Iyanla says, "Ask yourself why you're here and what it has to do with forgiveness." She invites people to come up to the two microphones in each aisle; perhaps because most of them know Iyanla's story, they can tell theirs. A fifty-year-old white woman clears her throat. She's shaking. "I'm here because I was sexually assaulted two weeks ago, and I want to forgive my attacker." Iyanla walks over to her and puts her arm around her. "Okay," she says softly. "Let it come up, feel it, feel bad, it won't kill you." I'm shocked to be in the presence of someone recently assaulted and astounded by her desire to forgive. What do you mean you want to forgive your rapist? Why? By the weekend's close, I will know the answer.

One after one they come up, each beginning with "I'm here because I want to forgive...." "My batterer, who killed my mother." "My brother, who murdered my son." "Myself for loving my addiction more than God." A man stands weeping and says he wants to forgive his wife for having an affair. Not all are bombshells. A very thin young woman whispers, "I want to forgive myself for not loving enough." Others say, "I'm here to forgive myself for being stuck in the past" or "I'm here to forgive my parents for not being better than they were."

Tissue boxes make their way around the room while people speak. Listeners nod through halting narratives, silently communicating that they understand; that they too have suffered the same thing. These people are not the same people who attend Jean Houston's workshops or Della Reese's services. They have not awakened after a comfortable first half of life with a vague feeling that they could be doing better with their lives. Many in this room look as if they don't know whether to thank or curse God for giving them another day, but their presence here speaks the hope that they, like Iyanla, can go through fire and will find the transcendent love that they desperately seek. As Iyanla says later, she is reaching poor women who are mostly of color, the ones overlooked by the spirituality movement.

When Iyanla leaves the podium to get close to the speakers and talks intimately to them, she holds the microphone so all can hear her gently probing questions and consoling response. When a woman sobs uncontrollably, Iyanla puts her hand on her shoulder and says, "Now take a really nice, deep breath. See how that makes room inside you, reminds you that you're alive?" The woman grows calmer and nods. Regardless of gender, color, or age, Iyanla speaks to each one as a beloved, as if no one else were in the room.

No matter how horrific an offense, she teaches, judgment is the wrong place to go, and that is what we ultimately must forgive ourselves for: our judgment of them. We must forgive, no matter what was done. At the same time, we acknowledge that whatever harm was done to us invalidated us. A young mother says that the person who invalidated her was her father, because he wouldn't let the family celebrate holidays or birthdays. When Iyanla tells her to find the pain of this in her body, she immediately points to her heart. "How could he have done differently?" Iyanla asks her rhetorically. "He didn't know how. You have a little boy. Your father was once a two-year-old child like him. Picture your father as your son, and say this: 'I forgive myself for judging my father and anyone else.'" The woman sits down with closed eyes, takes a breath, and her face relaxes.

If a clairvoyant may be described as one gifted with extra intuition, Iyanla's gift is extra empathy. While she has enough pizzazz to be an engaging talk show host, she is ultimately her name: Iyanla, "the Great Mother" in the Yoruba language. When the last person has spoken, she says, "I want to acknowledge those of you who spoke, for having the courage to stand up." The effect of hearing these petitions for forgiveness is powerful, as if we are in the presence of an ineffable collective truth. Twelve-step meetings also rely on the power of telling the truth to one another, but this is more like a dramatic tent revival; the difference is that this tent of meeting balances passion with solid common-sense psychotherapy.

Iyanla shifts from intimate healer to ebullient and energetic master of ceremonies, leading us through a repetitive chant: "I am open and ready to forgive myself and all others. We have all done the best we can." A Gospel trio clapping and moving to a doo-wop beat that feels like "You can do it, Baby!" intensifies and personalizes the exercise.

After the closing session on Sunday, a woman comes up to the circle surrounding Iyanla and, when it is her turn, asks if she received a doll from her. Iyanla shakes her head. "I get a lot of dolls," she replies. "If I got it, you should have gotten an acknowledgment." "I'll send another," the woman quickly says. Iyanla insists, "No. I got it if you sent it." The moment feels uncomfortable. The woman wants Iyanla to have the doll but she is told not to send another one, and she doesn't know whether Iyanla got the first one. She says softly, "The batterer who killed my mother," pausing for recognition from Iyanla, who nods, "also burned down my house, so I was homeless. I didn't have a job and didn't know what to do. I started making dolls and selling them. I'm no longer homeless," she says, looking down. Iyanla catches her eye, beams, and says, "That's great!" The woman walks away smiling.

A scheduling glitch erases our interview time. No one knows what to do until Iyanla offers to give up her lunch break. Her two daughters, dressed in angel white, accompany her to the interview, sitting on either side of her. We start talking about how strange it is that the most terrible events in life can be the greatest teachers. "Every experience of my life has had a divine purpose," she asserts. "No matter how destructive and dysfunctional somebody may be, they are really doing the best that they can. Even the uncle who raped me. He knew I was so hungry for love, and he gave me the only kind of love he knew and it was sexual.

"When I think about the depth of that experience, or being a teenaged mother, or being totally out of my mind, it's exciting, because if I got through those things with no awareness, now that I have some awareness I can't even begin to think what my possibilities are." While I understand her point, I stumble on the idea of everything being for a "divine purpose." What about a two-year-old with cancer? A church that hides the sins of its priests? Or the Holocaust? Rather than accepting the horrors of the world as God's mystery, I'd rather see God as the force that makes pain bearable by making it also a teacher.

I say nothing, however, because like Maryanne Lacy, Iyanla is a natural, intuitive healer who goes with the flow without worrying about inconsistency and exception. While women such as Nahid Angha, Marianne Williamson, and Laura Geller may regard inquiry, study, and investigation as holy, Iyanla's wisdom books have been her life experience and God's grace that helped her surmount a brutal childhood.

She goes on: "I still have challenges. My biggest one is learning that I don't have to do everything. It means learning how to really take care of myself on a new level. Writing is also a challenge, because I'm a face-to-face teacher. I teach when I write, but what I love best is a class of co-learners. The other challenge about writing is that I have to be still for long, long, long periods of time, and it is not my nature. As a child, the only time that I didn't hate myself was when I was dancing." Iyanla has written ten books. "Still," she says, "writing is my second love. No—shopping would be my second love if I didn't have to earn a living." We laugh. One of her books recounts her thrill at buying her first car less than ten years ago.

Answering a question about daily practice, she says, "I like to read Scripture. I open the book anywhere and usually end up in the Old Testament, which is a hard place for me to be, because I'm a New Testament person. But my most powerful lessons come from the Old Testament. It's my meditation every day of my life." When I ask if there is a Book with which she particularly identifies, she answers immediately, "Leviticus. Absolutely the law. That's what I teach, because

Yoruba is Nigeria's third largest ethnic group, numbering 22 million. Though some Yoruba are now Christians and Muslims, belief in their traditional religion, Santería, a syncretistic religion of Caribbean origin, continues. Santería integrates the worship of *orisha* (literally, "head guardian"); the beliefs of the Yoruba and Bantu people in southern Nigeria, Senegal, and Guinea Coast; and the worship practices of Roman Catholicism. Its origins date back to the slave trade when Yoruba natives were forcibly transported from Africa to the Caribbean, where they were routinely baptized by the Roman Catholic Church upon arrival, and their native practices suppressed. They kept their native practices alive by equating each *orisha* of their traditional religion with a corresponding Christian saint. The faith tradition was brought to America by immigrants from the Caribbean and Cuba, where it is estimated that 70 percent of all Cubans at least occasionally practice Santería. Music plays a large part in Santería ritual.

it is the law that I had to learn how to live.

"I can find the law of God in the Qur'an, in the Kabbalah, anywhere. God is consistent. Not the letter of the law but the spirit of the law. Women are finally getting over the 'Thou shalt nots' of the law that were against women and getting into the act. I say this because the feminine spirit looking at the law is going to save humanity. Let's tell the truth from a compassionate place, honor God in everything that we do, and honor each other in word, thought, and deed. Women speaking the word of God into the universe is what will change humanity." Iyanla is talking about white fire. Like Luisah Teish, another Yoruba priestess, she practices is an evolutionary religion, mixing East and West, black and white, and all dualities together.

"I am defiantly writing a new text for women, because we can honor the God of our ancestors, but our theology must evolve, and it's women who are going to do it. Men taught irresponsible theology that stated that half the population didn't have a right to make a decision. That's what God said? It's time to have a little talk with God. We're getting our tongues back. We all lost the ability to speak our truth, to ask for what we want. We lost it when we were raped, when our children were taken, and when we've been demeaned and demoralized.

"We are all afraid to say that we know the truth, and we don't support one another in that truth. When we begin to speak the truth of God, life, and love, all things are possible. That's when things are going to start happening," she says, as she takes the hand of her eldest daughter, Gemmia. "The women who have helped me to speak out are, first of all, my daughters. That they made it through what I did to them is absolutely incredible and a testimony to who they are as spiritual beings and women. Part of my mission is to help women find their tongues at home, and I use my magic tongue to do it. That is my gift. If I ever say anything to you, you will never, ever forget. It will be etched into your soul."

When asked about women who are speaking the truth, she says, "Oprah, of course. She's authentic; that's her greatest gift. She got thin, got fat again, and talked about it. I love her openness, how much fun she has on the show, and that she gets paid for it. And Mother Teresa. I'm her biggest fan. The gentleness and quietness of her spirit gave me a direction to hope to reach. She really encouraged me. And I also love Bella Abzug for her good heart. She was a feisty, fiery goddess who didn't take no for an answer. I like that.

"I'm cutting back on my speaking engagements and writing more, because the one thing sorely missing in the spiritual movement is to bring the experience of women of color to the table, and that's what my writing does. Not religion—there's enough of that—but just how to move through your day-to-day experience and come out whole. That's what women of color need to hear. That's what is missing—and Marianne [Williamson], I love her to death, but she can't get it.

"What does the Bible say about standing in line to get food stamps? Why do you need to do that if God provides? And what does it mean to honor your husband when he's coming home drunk and kicking your butt every day? It's all about applying God's law to your life, and the teacher has got to know your life." Perhaps that is why Marianne Williamson, Sylvia Boorstein, and Starhawk especially move me: as women from the Jewish middle class, however disparate their paths, they speak my language.

Before Iyanla's initiation, her godfather handed her a pile of books to read. He told her that she must read about all faiths to become a true healer. "I don't need to be a Baptist or a Jew or a Methodist, or a Yoruba," she says. "I don't need to be anything but a servant of God, and anything that can give me the tools is what I want. I do like living the Yoruba way of a matriarchal culture, because my

first concern is for the strength and the evolution of my daughters. In that tradition, my daughters inherit, not my sons."

We talk about celebrity. "I stopped autographing books when I saw people
were more interested in taking a picture with me than what the book was about.
They would stand in line arguing with each other and acting ugly, so I stopped
signing books. The celebrity thing keeps them from getting the message, and
that's what I want for them. I don't want them to run up to me in a restaurant, or
stop me when I'm shoe-shopping, or faint when they see me in Wal-Mart. That's
right," she says, perhaps thinking I'm surprised she didn't shop as Bloomingdale's,
"Target and JC Penney, too. I'm going to shop, wave, and smile and they're going
to get used to it. I'm going to live my life."

Yesterday, I Cried, the book that tells the by now well-known story of Iyanla's
early years in Brooklyn, describes her upbringing by a vicious and violent grandmother who favored her brother, Ray, and treated Rhonda (Iyanla's birth name)
as the scapegoat. If regular bloody beatings and emotional abuse weren't enough
of a test, an uncle raped her at ten; she was pregnant at fifteen and attempted suicide in the same year. Pregnant again at sixteen and at nineteen, she had her third
child by a man who tried to kill her.

After another attempted suicide, she ended up in Brookdale Psychiatric
Hospital, and it was there in the solitude of her room that she had time to think
and to listen to "guiding inner voices." She learned to pray, and her life took a
new direction. At twenty-nine, she went to college and became an attorney.
After learning the religion of her West African roots, she became a Yoruba priestess and began her true calling. As a spiritual counselor she changed her name to
Iyanla and began a weekly ministry that was so popular that it grew into a radio
show that led to books, seminars, and television.

How Iyanla overcame "learning life's worst lessons" and transformed herself
is a wonderful story, but that is not the end. She is an agent of change because she
is honest enough to reveal that no one with her legacy lives happily ever after
without daily effort and vigilance—and it is not "ever after," either. Like
Marianne Williamson and Joan Halifax, she shares how she has fallen more than
once, because no matter what she accomplished, no achievement stopped the
inner voices: "Fat and ugly! Whore! Misfit!"

At this point in her life, the voices are a faint whisper, and if her life is mercurial, it may have less to do with her past than her present: it is the nature of creative people to be a little less "on the ground." Add that ingredient to a woman of faith, and stand back.

THE REVEREND HELEN COHEN
AND THE REVEREND REBECCA COHEN

The Reverend Helen Cohen, minister of the venerable First Parish in Lexington Unitarian Universalist Church in Lexington, Massachusetts, shares my interest in the impact of women on religious life. In 1998 she sent a survey to 1,373 Unitarian Universalist ministers, both women and men, and received 565 responses evenly divided by gender. More reflective than scientific in its examination, it asked questions such as "Do men and women do ministry differently?" "Is Unitarian Universalism significantly changed by the influx of women?" "Is it changed for good or ill?" For her daughter, these questions are history.

The Reverend Cohen found her denomination "way ahead of the pack in having a gender-equal ministry." In 1968, 2.6 percent of their ministers were women; in 2000, over 50 percent were women. She writes, "The acceptance of change and evolution is part of what makes Unitarian Universalism attractive and unusual among religions, so many of which claim some once-and-for-all truth."

Helen and her husband, Don, live near the church in a modest and lovely book-filled home. Their daughter, Rebecca, is home for the weekend. I learn about the two ministers from the *New York Times*, which ran a story about them at the time of Rebecca's ordination. While families have always taken pride in multigenerational members of the clergy, we are beginning now to see daughters following in their clergy mothers' footsteps. I was also curious about two Unitarian Universalist ministers named Cohen, a Jewish name derived from

The Unitarian Church started ordaining women in the mid-nineteenth century. The Universalists were very advanced, and there were women who were able to find pulpits. In 1910 there was a backlash—the ministry needed to be more manly—so women were discouraged from becoming ministers. Just two percent of the ministers were women in 1970. Helen Cohen's class of seminary students in 1976 was one-third women. Rebecca Cohen's class was double that percentage.

Kohane, which means "priest" in Hebrew. Now that we meet, I see that Rebecca takes after her father's family, with a long mane of dark curly hair and blue eyes. Helen wears a long skirt and red tee shirt that sets off a blue stone pendant of a scarab. Her long, straight gray hair is pulled back, and she sits up straight as her daughter leans back comfortably, radiating a confidence.

Helen looks like an English professor or a minister's wife, bearing equanimity, depth of thought, and graciousness. Abundantly fulfilling the commandment of hospitality, she asks her husband, Don, to bring in a platter of bagels and lox. They raised their two daughters in both traditions, although Helen's connection to her tradition ran deeper and stronger than his. She says, "He had been Bar Mitzvahed and confirmed, but when we married he wasn't attending synagogue and I was not attending church. We were married by a minister and a rabbi, and we felt we could celebrate the whole range of holidays."

Rebecca Cohen didn't become a rabbi but finds her Jewish background helpful in her ministry. Rebecca says, "My openness to all faiths confirms that bringing religious traditions together can work. Eighty percent of my congregation comes from another religious tradition or no religion at all. UU [the insiders' way of referring to Unitarian Universalists] is about a mixing of those traditions, and growing up in this household makes that very natural for me.

"Judaism might be what helps me to appreciate ritual and tradition that is sometimes missing for us as Unitarian Universalists. Having grown up lighting the Hanukkah candles and doing a Passover Seder has helped me sense how important those rituals are and what they could mean in our lives even if we interpret them differently.

"When I do hospital work and people hear I'm Reverend Cohen, they think I'm Jewish. My search for a position made clear that congregations found me particularly attractive because of my Jewish background." Unitarianism has long been popular with rationalist, universalist Jews who like its message without dealing with Hebrew and anti-Semitism.

The Unitarian Universalist Association, formed in 1961, represents a merger of the American Unitarian Association and the Universalist Church Association. Their mission is "to cherish and spread the universal truths taught by the great prophets and teachers of humanity in every age and tradition, immemorially summarized in the Judeo-Christian heritage as love to God and love to man."

We talk about what it was like when Helen began her studies in the seminary in the mid-seventies. "Don had to deal with the initial shock of my becoming a minister, but he's been extremely supportive and has had to put up with the long hours and the weekends. He ended up with a lot of the child care because he was home working on a book."

Rebecca adds, "By the time I decided to go the seminary, he was incredibly pleased, and we didn't have to go through any adjustment. I felt more nervous about Mom's reaction at the very beginning, because we're very different. Dad's been very helpful with this because he knows us both so well."

Helen nods in agreement. She says, "I was ordained in 1980 when I was thirty-seven. I had been a college English professor at Yale before I entered Harvard Divinity School. I was disillusioned with academia and found a negative, insular attitude towards the world creeping into my blood. My worst gender experience was breaking into academia as a young college professor in an all-male school. I was introduced to a handsome white-haired professor who said, 'At Yale we've always approved of women, and lately we've been using them for more and more purposes.' I was twenty-six and just giggled in my intimidation. Years later, when I finally wrote a sermon about gender and relationships and this story was part of it, I cried as I wrote it. It took that long to realize how bad it was.

"I was raised in the Unitarian church and secretly wanted to become a minister when I was fifteen. Of course I didn't dare tell anyone, because I'd never seen a woman minister, so I followed my family footsteps into teaching." Her daughter Rebecca smiles.

"When I finally did apply to divinity school, I wasn't among the pioneers, to all of whom I am grateful for facing the initial painful barriers, rejections, and dismissals. But I still had not yet seen a woman minister and had frequent bouts of thinking that I was crazy. How could a woman, how could I, do this work?" This is a question Rebecca never had to ask herself. "It was only after I met two very successful women ministers in school that it made it easier for me to leap from my sphere.

"I always held myself back, but lately I've become more dramatic. For many years I didn't wear bright colors, even though I love them. I've worked hard to state opinions without needing everyone to agree or I'll feel stepped on. Let everyone have a right to express their opinions is what I struggle towards; this is very much a woman's issue. I was raised to believe that hanging out with men is more interesting than hanging out with women, so coming to value women fully was part of my learning.

"I've gotten to know many female colleagues, and we get together regularly to share our experiences. In the beginning there were so few women around that it was a challenge to find anyone to talk to, but now it's possible and an important part of who I am. After I'd been in the ministry seven years, a group of us got together and called ourselves Reverend Mothers. We all had children and would meet once a month to talk about how we were managing. We supported each other and sometimes advised each other, although none of us liked to get advice." She smiles.

Rebecca has never been part of a women minister's group and doesn't know if she will ever feel the need for it. "Being a woman is a big part of my identity," she says, "but I haven't thought as much about what that means as the generation before me. I haven't had to, or I feel like I haven't had to. I wonder whether the sisterhood bond of my mother's generation will stay with mine or we'll lose it, because we don't think we need it.

"As long as I can remember, I had the image of women up front and leading; it seems so natural. I only became aware of Mom's ambivalence and difficulties much later. I've never had to wonder whether it was okay to be a minister. On my interviews, some congregations had never had a woman minister, and they were specifically looking for one. They said they wanted someone who would care about them. The normalness of having a woman minister is getting pretty high in our churches."

"There's an organization called Ministerial Sisterhood of Unitarian Universalists," Helen says, "and they get together as a general assembly each year. I belong to it, but I haven't been active in it, because I don't identify myself in that way. Race is my generation's social issue. If I had time for that work, that's what I'd be doing rather than gender issues. I'm not a feminist."

She gently reminds her daughter, "The last thirty years have brought enormous change. I don't know how much it has to do with women ministers and how much it has to do with a cultural shift from an intellectual-oriented direction to what I think of now as a more holistic, emotional experience. It's probably circular—women feel at home in this atmosphere. I also think that ministers have less authority today, and so that may be less appealing for men.

"Eighty-five percent of the class at the UU seminary in Berkeley are women. In the survey, an older male minister

"The revolution within the church began with lay women. At the Unitarian Universalist Association's General Assembly in 1977, they created a resolution adopted by the church to move towards a more egalitarian, more relational, more valuing of the whole family, direction. They weren't concerned with women becoming ministers, but I think it moved women forward in the ministry by stressing less hierarchy." —Helen Cohen

responded that ministers are now just mother hens holding the community together, and he meant it as a putdown. This is what happens when there are so many women in the ministry; he experiences it as a conflict. I didn't survey congregants, and I would really like to know how they feel about the change. How are men feeling about being in a women-led institution? I certainly fear that if we were to go a whole lot farther in percentages, that would not be healthy."

Helen's caution causes Rebecca's eyebrows to rise, but she says nothing. I ask about what ministry Rebecca sees for herself. "At first I thought I'd be like Mom, with a strong worshipping/preaching ministry and an equally strong pastoral ministry. But when I did my pastoral training, I discovered that I didn't have the natural gifts that made pastoral care much easier for my mom, and then I knew that Mom and I are not the same.

"I have an up-front leadership in institutions, and that's my gift. Although our styles are different, we share a gift for preaching. When I first looked at congregations, I leaned towards congregations like Lexington but realized that they weren't the best match for me. She also has a larger congregation—three hundred and fifty—than I was looking for. Where I'm going is a new congregation, and it's looking toward building its identity and an organization. Both these goals are exciting for me and what I'm good at."

Helen worries about Rebecca. "It's a very demanding job, at least for me, personally. I love it, but it's very hard to have a congregation of people all of whom have different ideas. Doing things together and trying to meet all the different needs that people bring can be a challenge. We're not very set in a tradition, since the denomination itself is only two hundred years old; Catholicism didn't form for five hundred years, and Judaism obviously took longer.

"When I first started the work, I worked seventy or more hours a week with two young children. I was being torn apart constantly, and we didn't have relaxed time. I'd come home tired with a lot on my mind, so I wasn't present with them as I would have liked to be. I was torn between what the image of being feminine or being a woman was and what the image of leader was. I spent a lot of my life holding myself back—and we have the same genes."

Rebecca says, "One of the reasons I initially resisted the ministry is that I'd like to have a family, and I saw how hard it was for Mom to balance things. I wanted her around more on evenings and weekends. It looked like an impossible task to have a family and ministry. For a while I thought I'd wait to have kids and then enter the seminary when they were in junior high school. Then I realized that I'm not married, don't have plans to get married in the near future, so why should I put off what I wanted to do for people who didn't yet exist or may never exist?

"Having a family will be the biggest challenge for me in the future. I've certainly learned some things growing up in a minister's family, and I'll make different mistakes. I hear that the first couple of years are the most anxious. I hope they are, because if it gets worse, I don't know what I'll do! If I get these years out of the way by the time I'm a parent, it will make a difference."

Helen talks about the needs of the congregation changing. "It's become harder for people to be centered, grounded in a set of values that goes through their whole lives. Everyone is constantly active, constantly communicating, living on the surface so much of the time. I'm not a cell-phone person and sometimes want to be in places where I'm not in touch with people. So many live in a way where they're never alone.

"And we're constantly making decisions. Our culture gives us so many opportunities to make decisions, and that too becomes superficial. Look how long the cereal aisle is at the supermarket and how much time you spend choosing. That goes for buying cars, homes, videos, and how many televisions we have so each member of the family can choose what to watch.

"People aren't getting to experience the depth they have, and they don't have time to get centered and connected. People want to know that their lives mean something and that they are connected to something more than the work they do and the things they own. They want deeper connection; they sense it's there, but they don't know how to live it. They don't get to connect because there are so many people in their lives and so many roles. Church needs to be a place where people can be themselves, not playing a role. Here is the place to figure out who they are and how they can fit into the world. Authenticity is an important part of who I am as a minister, and what I'd like to reveal is myself—myself on the growing edge.

"People need to be held," Helen goes on. "The spirit is what holds us and makes us feel safe. I saw this at home with my mother, who held the family. I've had practice holding a child physically and metaphorically. I know what life's challenges are from having children; each child has a different temperament. What I bring from parenting is different from someone who hasn't done it himself or herself.

"We're all so busy, so competitive, so involved in active pursuits and the glorification of individualism and independence in our culture, and our particular religious faith has deprived people of many of the traditions, roots, and clear values that have helped us. To get people to sit still even for an hour is a challenge! Parts of the service are active and busy, and parts of it are quiet and meditative. To fit in all the different needs of the people in that hour is almost impossible.

"The Spirit, which makes us feel whole inside and is what connects us to all that surrounds us, is threatened and undercut by the way we live. Materialism is at the top of the threats. We don't have time for friendship, and hospitality is a very important part of the religious experience.

"Part of why I married Don was that I was drawn to the roots of his faith. The Seder is the one time of the year that I can feel continuity of tradition. Unitarian Universalism has gone back to emphasizing community, the generations past and future, too. If you have a religion that says the world is about to end all the time, there isn't much concern about your children and your children's children. But to me, that's what it's all about: making a better world for those who are to come." Even Unitarians draw the line somewhere.

MARIANNE WILLIAMSON

When I was in rabbinical school, my tutor, a fellow student, was a handsome, moody young man who had been raised in an ultra-Orthodox home and had studied at Yeshiva University, the main Orthodox seminary. Not knowing him well, I asked what he was doing at our liberal, transdenominational school. After a brief hesitation, perhaps to decide how much he could trust me, "Joseph" recounted a painful story of how his family had completely rejected him because he was gay. After an attempt at suicide that put him in the hospital, a nurse gave him a copy of *A Return to Love* by Marianne Williamson.

Her book, based on the teachings in *A Course in Miracles*, saved his life with a message that he had never found in all his yeshiva training: love is what we are missing, and it is the only path to peace. Perhaps for the first time in his life, Joseph felt connected to God, but not the God of his fathers. Williamson says, "Nothing is as fragile as a prayer without belief." While his Jewish prayer had shattered the day that he knew he was gay, because of her he was alive to wrestle with his sexual and spiritual identity. I don't know whether he knew that Marianne Williamson is Jewish.

As other leaders in this book have done, she has used her own pain as a learning and teaching tool, which assures her followers that she understands them because she is like them. They listen to her and think, "God, if she could get her act together, so can I." That she appears to have started out where they are offers encouragement and hope, but it is deceiving. Few people have had tea with Jacqueline Onassis, friendships with world political and spiritual leaders, and a golden tongue that helped birth the New Age movement. It is a pleasure to quote her because she is both profound and eloquent. For the past ten years her books have headed the *New York Times* bestseller list and have sold millions of copies. An updated version of *A Return to Love*, which first came out in 1992, features a glamorous, intense portrait of the author.

As she explains in the book, she was raised in a good-enough home in Houston, was a child of the sixties and seventies, and a "total mess" by her mid-twenties. She had read philosophers and self-help books, had done a variety of drugs, had gone from relationship to relationship and city to city, had tried psychotherapy, and still had no purpose or direction in her life. She writes, "What happened to my generation is that we never grew up. The problem isn't that we're lost or apathetic, narcissistic or materialistic. The problem is we're terrified." Internal and free-floating, we fear not getting things right, especially relationships and careers, and we have little self-respect. "We're more afraid of life than we are of death," she says. The deepest terror is not about dying but never finding out what you were supposed to do with your life.

Her parents begged her, "Just do anything." After a brief marriage and a return to Houston, she collapsed emotionally. "Nervous breakdowns can be highly underrated methods of spiritual transformation. They certainly get your attention," she notes dryly.

In 1977, Marianne found her path out of hell when she read A Course in Miracles, an inspirational book supposedly dictated by Jesus to Helen Schucman, an agnostic Jewish psychologist. Despite her initial alienation from its Christian terminology, the book gave answers to what she had thought was unanswerable and promised salvation by showing the path to love through forgiveness. She learned that a miracle isn't necessarily an external event but can be internal and as simple as a change of perception that returns us to our biological default, love. And Marianne finally learned that she needed more than herself for that miracle.

A Course in Miracles is a complete self-study spiritual thought system that teaches that the way to universal love and peace, or remembering God, is by undoing guilt through forgiving others. Grounded in traditional Christianity but expressing a non-sectarian, non-denominational spirituality, it focuses on the healing of relationships and making them holy. It was "scribed" by Dr. Helen Schucman, a clinical research psychologist, through a process of inner dictation she identified as coming from Jesus. It was first published in 1975, the year Schucman assigned copyright of the course to the Foundation for Inner Peace (FIP). There are currently over 1.5 million copies of the course in circulation worldwide, and it has been translated into nine languages. Eleven other translations are in progress.

Many friends were surprised when she left California in 1998 to move to Warren, Michigan, a suburb of Detroit, to become the spiritual leader of the Church of Today. But this is not a typical pulpit. Her sole responsibilities are to lead Sunday morning services and to teach "A Course in Miracles" weekly. Detroit is a touching place, she says. Despite its descent from once being a mighty city, its citizens blend a spiritual richness by loyally claiming it as their hometown. That a celebrity like Marianne would choose to live in Detroit is an affirmation for which the community has shown its gratitude by embracing her.

She prefers the title of spiritual leader rather than minister because she is not ordained and she is Jewish. The Church of Today, an affiliate of the Unity Church, is exactly that: a contemporary community that is enthusiastic without being evangelical about the good word, and they don't care who speaks it. Hospitality is a big part of the new message. When you arrive at the church, a friendly attendant helps you find a space in the crowded parking lot. Newcomers are greeted at the door and taken to a special room for a special welcome, an orientation, and a name tag that alerts church members that they are first-timers.

A gift shop sells everything needed for enlightenment, including clothes, incense, candles, and books, with a whole shelf devoted to A *Course in Miracles* and Marianne's books. A coffeehouse with a large-screen closed-circuit television makes prayer and cappuccino simultaneously possible; it also holds the overflow when the fifteen-hundred-seat sanctuary is filled. Speakers amplifying the service are everywhere, even in the bathroom. Before and after the service, they fill the church with soft-rock Christian and gospel music. The social action office has its door wide open for volunteers and those in need.

No wonder Marianne took the position: this place rocks, and she's made it rock more. After years of decline, attendance is higher than it has ever been, and the church has become more welcoming to Detroit's black citizens. Besides creating racial healing groups, she has replaced the church's "700 Club" soft Sunday music with a multiracial gospel choir, and roughly a third of those assembled are African-American. Iyanla Vanzant has said that Marianne cannot speak to people of color as she herself can, but Marianne's gift is that she can speak to anyone, from a gay Orthodox Jew to the black teenagers sitting together in the sanctuary.

We attend the second service at eleven that will be followed by our interview; it is the only day that she permits photographing, because she is in full makeup. The lights dim, and the service begins with a five-minute guided meditation led by Marianne in an appropriately hypnotic voice. Following it, first-time visitors are welcomed, and the choir sings "Amazing Grace."

For forty-five minutes, without a note in front of her, she strides back and forth across the pink-and-mauve stage that must have been cool in the 1980s and expands the ideas touched upon in the meditation. At turns insightful, funny, candid, and always engaging, she talks about self-hatred, ego, and consciousness, often from her own experience. Her energy is high, positive, and contagious, and people are rapt because she is telling the truth, the message is not simplistic, and she knows how to cut to the chase. "Some people can sing," she says later. "I can talk."

After the service, Marianne invites anyone who wants to stay for a special meeting to discuss the future of the church. For most clergy within institutions, this would be a risk, but Marianne's situation is unique. It is testimony of the community's respect and affection for her work that they have allowed her to create her own faith community within the structure of their institution. To the one hundred who stay, she says that she's about to consider signing a second contract with the church. If it stays as it is, she'll serve another year and step down, but if the church will consider a different model, she will reconsider.

She proposes that instead of inviting guest speakers once a year, the church could establish itself as a center that includes the speakers as ongoing teachers who return throughout the year. Such a place would be both a center and a school of higher consciousness. She would also like to change the name of the institution to be more inclusive.

We meet in her office. Sitting behind a vast paper-strewn desk with an ornate crucifix between us, she asks if we would like some water. We begin talking about Houston. I ask how her family feels about her being a Unity Church minister. "My father

Now called Renaissance Unity Interfaith Fellowship, the church supported Marianne's vision with events such as "Women, Love, and Power: Healing the World in the Twenty-First Century," a weekend with Oprah, Marianne, and other notable women in the spirituality movement. As of September 2002, Marianne resigned her post as senior minister of the Renaissance Unity Interfaith Fellowship.

passed away, and my mother is great, " she answers. "When I first started teach-ing the Course, though, my mother kept saying, 'Your father and I will be glad to send you to rabbinical school.'" She smiles. "I've always said that if I'd learned the mystical roots of my own religion when I was in Sunday school, I probably would be a rabbi today."

Too bad. We could use her. Frank pride consoles me, however, when I see a Jewish sister doing so much good.

"The way that it's always been done no longer works. All these Jewish kids are going to India, and everyone throws up their hands and says, 'What are they finding from an Indian guru that we didn't give them?'"

Marianne is pointing out that Jews have lost the scent of Judaism: that's why there are so many Jewish women in spiritual and healing circles that have noth-ing to do with Judaism. We are running in many directions to reclaim it, from Chabad (a fundamentalist Jewish outreach organization) to Jewish Renewal, but nothing is working well enough or fast enough.

"I used to have judgment about Jews going to India," Marianne says, "but now I understand the historical roots of what happened to Judaism. Many of the great rabbis in Eastern Europe died in the Holocaust. Their kabbalistic mystical teaching died with them." She pauses. "I used to be angry that I didn't know this part of Judaism, as if somebody had consciously withheld the information. By now, I know better."

Expanding upon the theme about becoming wiser as we grow older, she says, "my generation is getting older. The old part of the brain knows, as a generation, that we're no longer needed here—our egg and sperm days are over. We are either actively involved in the quest to be reborn or we are starting to die. We're also the first generation from whom nature would prefer fewer babies and more wis-dom, because if we don't become wiser, the children being born now are going to be in terrible, terrible trouble twenty years from now.

"So we have another reason live: to participate in a spiritual journey. We were born into our bodies; can we now be born into our spirit? American society is very rich, yet we're actively participating in the destruction of our own habitat, the earth. Can we become wise? People with their eyes open to what is happen-ing are tempted to be quite depressed, but pessimism is appropriate today only if you believe that there is a limited set of options for how to proceed. If you don't believe in miracles, you've got to be a pessimist. But a spiritual optimist is one who knows that there is more to the mind than the intellect."

Marianne's daughter, Emma, was born in 1991, the year of her rapid ascent into celebrity. I ask how she is being brought up. "Emma is Jewish and goes to a Jewish Sunday school. My mother would kill me if I didn't send her," she says, laughing. "I hope that she learns Hebrew and has a Bat Mitzvah." Eyebrows raised, I glance at the crucifix on her desk, puzzled. Marianne breaks up and practically doubles over. "Yeah, I can see your confusion," she says, "but this is an interfaith fellowship. The crucifix was a gift to me."

Marianne says, "The Jewish community here has been very kind and respectful. They write about me in the Jewish paper here. It's understood that this is an awkward situation." I mention Starhawk and Ma Jaya, also born Jewish, and Marianne laughs. "Well, once again this is, hello? Jews are spiritual, but all I learned in Sunday school was history. I knew more about Mesopotamia than I knew about God. So when rabbis say to me, 'You could have found it here,' I respond, 'You should have taught me.' Emma hears some things from her mother that she doesn't hear in Sunday school, but her Jewish education is important to her and to me. I'm satisfied with what she's learning, and I feel very strongly about being part of an ancient people who are very close to God, who are still here and still making a profound difference on the planet.

"What I'm most interested in is the mystical core of a religious congregation, whether it's a shrine, mosque, church, or temple. I'd be giving the same answers if I were a rabbi. I want this to be a place where Jews could come, but not instead of temple. Same with Muslims. I don't think it serves anybody to muddy the distinctions between the religious systems. Different flowers are beautiful; each is a discrete, complex, and sophisticated system. So, it's time for Jews to be Jews, Christians to be Christians, and Muslims to be Muslims. There is unity in diversity, and everyone culturally, religiously, and sexually needs to go back to their own roots and their own identity. Simultaneously, we must find the oneness that we all share. A Course in Miracles says instead that God's teachers come from all religions and no religion. I'd like to see more generic spiritual worship with a rich devotional practice. There is room for everyone."

While Marianne has freedom most women clergy would envy, she knows how much women struggle to gain their rightful authority and how much they have to put up with. "Most institutions resist a strong ministry, especially if we're talking about women. This is the last unchallenged oppression in America: the invalidation of women leaders. Our society suffers because it cannot accept leadership from women. The feminine principle is so needed now. The old patriarchal paradigm purports that somebody up top makes all the decisions and sends a memo out for everyone to follow. The new paradigm purports that the role of the leader is to hold the space for everyone's genius.

"The reason my work is a great career for me is because it's an opportunity to foster new life. All women are mothers—not necessarily biological mothers, but mothers of the next generation, of the planet, of the future. To be happy, women must play that role of bringing forth life. In our faith groups, we attempt to live the principles that we feel should guide civilization. This is wonderful work for a woman because it's like growing a family. We're fostering values that will outlive us. Women are naturals as facilitators of religious practice in this dawning age. The work is more about the capacity to put our arms around someone, understand, and love them, than speaking the word from on high. Even among men, the sensibility of the clergy is changing. This is not about going from men to women, but from imbalance to balance.

"Christianity sees the woman in a Mother/whore dichotomy, making Mary virginal and Mary Magdalene a slut, dirty in her sexuality. That imagery has violated the psyche of Western women on the deepest level. During the Inquisition, historians say nine million people were burned at the stake, eighty-five percent of whom were women. And do you know why? Because there was a systematic effort by the early church to eradicate the passionately freethinking woman. The current pope has apologized for this, by the way. Such a woman threatened the patriarchal system then, and she threatens them now. That is because she raises her children to be passionate and freethinking as well. Such people are impossible to manipulate and difficult to control. Neither feminine power nor spiritual power can be controlled. Because of this, many women, who embody both, walk through the fire of witch burning even now. "They used to call us 'witch,' now they call us 'bitch.' It's not all that different.

"This work carries tremendous responsibilities, like a therapist. There is a lot of transference that goes on. You have a responsibility not to be seductive to the people you serve, so I'm not suggesting an inappropriate throwing around of our sexual vibration. It's just a beautiful dimension of our being that doesn't cancel out our intelligence or our spiritual power." Among all the women interviewed, only she speaks of the sexual risk for women spiritual leaders.

Having heard her speak extemporaneously with grace and punch several times, I ask how she knows what to say. She responds, "Thoreau said something like, Anybody who speaks honestly from his own experience is describing a foreign land. I don't think I have anything new to say, but any time you speak eternal truths from the vantage point of your life experience, it's a gift to someone. I once heard author Arnold Patent say that if you genuinely have something to say, there is someone out there who genuinely needs to hear it." That is why each woman in this book can arrive at the same place and still tell a story never told before. "The key is in *knowing* that you don't have anything special to say," she goes on. "If you think you do, then that produces fear because you think people are going to find out that you don't. I always remind myself that I'm not the water; I'm just the faucet. Then I relax and whatever comes through, comes through.

"For me, speaking about God is like giving mother's milk: if it's time to come out and it doesn't, I feel the backup within me. All of us feel the need to give our gifts whatever they are. There's a Jewish proverb, 'Sad is he who dies not having sung his song.'"

She stifles a yawn; she is very thin. I wonder if she, like Laura Geller, pops nutrition bars at her desk in lieu of meals. Asked about how much she works, she replies, "I work very hard." And long? She nodded. "I'm almost fifty, and I get it now. Nature has the right idea: you have babies in your twenties when you're young, and then by the time you're ready to go out into the world, they're ready to take care of themselves. The life I live at the moment is hard. I hope by the time your book comes out this won't be my reality, but it has been for some time. I have so many things to do that I always feel I'm letting someone down."

I ask about the world she envisions for Emma, and she expresses concern about the same things that are worrisome to every parent. "Clearly we are at an extraordinarily critical juncture in human history. There is an intensification of darkness, but there is also an intensification of light. I try to teach my daughter to believe in God, to know that He is an actual, living presence in her life. She knows that her purpose is to become her greatest, most glorious expression of all that is good within her. As she tries to do that in her life, and all of us try to do that in our lives, a miracle will happen and this world will transform. It's the eleventh hour, to be sure, but it isn't midnight yet."

THE REVEREND DELLA REESE

Finding out about the Reverend Della Reese's Sunday morning service is just about impossible. After many phone calls, her daughter calls us back and tells us where they are meeting. We speculate that they don't want fans showing up. Best known as a singer and star of the television show *Touched by an Angel*, the Reverend Della Reese leaves her home in Salt Lake City every Friday to serve her 375-member congregation on Sunday morning in Los Angeles.

Della's church meets in the Hotel Nikko at 11:00 A.M. in a large conference room set up with rows of chairs with a wide central aisle. Upon entering we are given, along with information about the church, a packet of gifts: a flower for smelling, a smooth stone for touching, a tape for hearing, daily written inspiration for seeing, and a piece of candy for tasting. All this to honor our five senses, the first level of understanding the world.

The service begins with a rousing processional playing "Ain't No Stopping Us!" The gospel choir and a three-piece band are loud enough for earplugs. After the two male associate ministers lead the Lord's Prayer, guests are welcomed, and we turn to all those around us to shake hands, hug, meet. Unlike Dr. Suzan Cook's church where most of the congregants were black, we fit in because at least 40 percent of the congregation is white. After twenty minutes of warm-up singing and responsive readings, Della walks up the aisle, unsmiling, like a gruff old granny who gets on your case for your own good. "God loves you! I sure appreciate your being here! I got wonderful news for you this morning! God loves you!" she exults.

She calls up a sweet-faced black teenager who needs money for college. The kid has worked hard and now the church is helping her. The congregation claps with the joy of aunts and uncles. The girl is modeling what Della's church teaches: Go for it!

At almost two hours into the service that has been lead by an assistant minister, Della stands up to preach. The spiritual idea for the day is about power. Power is acting effectively, she says as she walks around the platform. Pointing out her own foibles regarding power, she concludes, "And I'm a minister!" She tells us that we create worlds with words, so watch your mouth! If you say nothing good can happen, nothing will. Tell God you're tired of this pain, you don't want it anymore. "You know why you don't have a Jaguar?" she asks pointedly. "Because you don't ask for it. That Jaguar is yours if you want it!" Her sermon inspires generous offerings as the basket is passed. I might have been more generous if she had sung instead of spoken.

We meet the Reverend Della Reese in her rented home in Sherman Oaks. In the living room is a photo of her with actor Redd Foxx along with other memorabilia of her long career. I put out my hand, and she brushes it aside for a hug, saying, "Shaking hands is a boy thing."

Despite the presence of several people passing in and out of the room, she offers us coffee and gets it herself. Before the interview begins, I ask if she will autograph my assistant's old LP album that Della cut in the sixties. While she is writing I tell her how much this will mean to Gail. She hands the album back, and her look makes me think that she would have made a formidable junior high school vice principal. I ask her about the new career in the ministry.

"I don't consider becoming a minister a new turn in my life. I would have done this earlier, but when I was growing up, it was almost a sin for a woman to be in the ministry. But I did it privately all the while anyway. I sang gospel from the time I was six to twenty-two. I've been involved with God and God's been involved with me since before I remember.

"I'm sixty-eight, and until recently a minister was a man's thing. It kept me from officially stepping into the pulpit, but it did not stop my ministry at all, because I worked, as I do now, with anyone who happened to be near me. I've had a relationship with God in the Baptist church, in the church of my bedroom, in the church of a hotel room, in the church of me.

"I was born and raised in Detroit. I used to ask questions as a child that you're not supposed to ask, because it means you're fresh. But I could not accept that I was made in the image of God and then accept that I was a wretch, and I would speak on it. 'Then God is a wretch, because I'm made just like him and I'm a wretch.' You're not supposed to question that in any way. I got put out of every church that I went to. They'd tell my mother I was fresh and

Della Reese was ordained in 1987 as a minister by the Universal Foundation for Better Living, founded by the Rev. Dr. Johnnie Colemon. What began with eight people around her dining room table now is a church with a weekly attendance of hundreds.

fast. No good was ever going to come from me, and I'd question that. If I'm God, then how come no good's ever going to come.

"I've always had a deeper interest than just the Word, I've always been interested in the power behind the Word—not the letter, but the spirit of it. Twenty years ago I was doing a play in Philadelphia, and my hairdresser and makeup artist was telling me his problems while he was fixing my hair. I would tell him what I thought, and when I finished he'd say, 'You sound just like Johnnie Colemon.' He told me she was in Chicago, so the next job I had was in Chicago, and my hairdresser was with me.

"He said, 'You've got to go, now you're here, I can show you what a Johnnie Colemon is.' And he took me to the church, and here was a woman saying what I had always believed and had never heard anyone else espouse so firmly. Here was a woman saying that God loved me and he was aware of my life and me. It was his good pleasure to give me the Kingdom and he thought I was magnificent, and secretly I always thought God thought that about me. So I started commuting from Los Angeles to Chicago to church any Sunday I could. I started taking classes and got involved.

"She came into my world and said, 'You're right; what you feel about God is right. He does love you; he does have something special for you, he is involved in your life.' She has a church of 4,500 people, the Christ Universal Temple, and she has twenty-two branches all over the world. It's interracial, interdenominational. You should talk to her for your book. She's been in this for forty-three years. She's building a school for this practice of the principles. You can become a minister, a counselor, a teacher, and there will be a section for children and teenagers.

"While I was doing this, my brain exploded and I realized I knew very little truth. I had the sensitivity of my spirituality, but to know what to do, what truth to use, I had no knowledge about that. When my brain exploded I suddenly knew that all the things that everyone said, all the bad things that were going to happen to me, went the opposite. I put my spirit in God's hands. That was in 1979, and now it's almost 2000. All those things that were supposed to be wrong never went wrong." The explosion that Della refers to was an aneurysm in her brain that caused her to collapse while she was performing on the *Tonight Show*.

"When I got up from this explosion, I wanted everyone to know that I had proved that you don't have to die because somebody told you that you have to die. You had the power to do with yourself what you wanted to do as long as it was for your highest self. I came up running! I started some classes in my home for my friends, and they started bringing their friends, and in time there were so many people in my house on Tuesday night my husband couldn't walk into the kitchen without being fully dressed.

"Franklin was wonderful about it, but I knew I could stop this now and have peace and harmony in the house, or I could do it one more day and the whole marriage thing could fall apart. I moved the classes out of the house, and they grew. One night a woman brought her husband who had terminal cancer. His anger was all-consuming. His wife brought him not to be healed but to get some peace in his mind. At first he was the skeptic. Classes are better than the church in that people have opportunity to speak. More than a church speaking to people, the class gave everyone a chance to say how they felt immediately. The man got involved with other people and stopped being stuck on himself every minute, and he came to a place of peace. He never expected to live, and that's probably why he didn't. But he came to a place where he loved his wife, and she had that as he was leaving.

"His wife wanted him buried in the essence of thought that he left in, so I wasn't allowed in the pulpit where they buried him. The minister of the church was sort of indifferent, and his widow was livid. The whole thing made me feel that I should have been equipped to help her more.

"Then a couple came to me to get married, and they didn't want to say 'until death do us part.' They wanted to say 'for as long as we live and love each other.' Fine with me—it's their wedding. So I did it, and then the minister came to do the benediction and says, 'Father, I didn't hear them say that they wanted to be together until death does them part.' The couple was disturbed, I was angry, and I said, 'Father, you need to send me a minister, someone who understands suffering, because there is no minister here.' I didn't get an answer, and God always answers. Finally He said, 'Do it yourself.' So I went back to school. I went to school for eight years and got a license to be a minister. That's how we started.

"People misunderstand when you are an entertainer. You walk into a strange place filled with people you have never seen before and possibly will never see again, and for a couple of hours, you become intimate with these people. You express what they feel, and they come in twos and fours and eights and twelves, and they leave that way. So after this marvelous, intimate experience, you're left alone in a hotel room somewhere, because you didn't come in twos and fours. You came alone and you go home alone." I think of Debbie Friedman and all her fans; yet, there is a loneliness to her life because people fall in love with her gift and their fantasy, not her.

"That's the time you need a spiritual feeling in you, to keep you from doing what you shouldn't be doing. You need God for that, to know He's protecting you. Most people live with their families in their homes, and they're surrounded with their people and their things. There's security in that. Entertainers—wanderers, you might call us—have to call on something from the depths of ourselves to survive.

"When I'm entertaining and when I'm teaching the truth, there is one subject matter. I'm doing an extension of my ministry on my television show, which is based on the principles of God. And many a night I've entertained and have sung a song that many might have thought was meant for a man, but it was between God and me. It was personal and private. If the spirit of God made me feel like I wanted to tap dance, I'd dance in the church, but it would be a different dance than the dance I'd do on the stage. The dance on the stage involves the people and the dance on the pulpit would involve God and me.

"I love all my work. I love to sing because of the vibrations in my body. I love to act because I can be somebody other than myself. I love the ministry because it's helping people in their lives. Let me tell you a story. One lady was sleeping on the street in a box with her three little daughters. She came to the church—I don't know how except by the grace of God—and I said, 'If you're suffering, it must be because you like it.' She said, 'Do you think I want to be like this?' And I said, 'Yes, because if you didn't, you'd get up and get out of there.' She went hostile on me, and in a week she came back and she wasn't as mad. To make a long story short, she now has a seven-room house, pool, and the kids are in private school. She started in a low job in an insurance company, she made suggestions, and now she's a vice-president. Look," she says, extending her arm, "it gives me little bumps on my arm to think about it. The work is exciting." Della is like Ma Jaya, a spiritual tough lover.

"I've been through the valley of the shadow of death three times, and once you've been there, things take on a difference. One lady said to me at a seminar, 'I like to talk to you, Reverend Della, because you've been through something. I don't want to hear nothing from nobody that ain't been through something.' I know how important every second is, because in a moment it could all be over. So I don't burden myself with things that are not to the glory of God. When I lead a service, it feels good. If I'm doing something that isn't good, I remove myself.

"Jesus Christ is my most important teaching and the way he left for us to live and the principles that God gave us. We have the key to life, and we think we only have the key to death. Everything's going to happen after we die over in the

Beulah Land, when the saints go marching in, and the streets are gold, and you drink milk and eat honey. Jesus said, 'The only time is now. The Kingdom is mine.' That Kingdom shouldn't have pain and sickness and poverty in it.

"**U**nderstanding Principles for Better Living is a teaching ministry geared toward meeting the needs of the total man/woman. We are among the mighty forces at work today to change man's thought about God. Through prayer, we reckon with the vital forces of spiritual hunger, shaking the foundations of all who come. We know that filling this hunger is the greatest need in the world today. We are the religion for the New Age." —from the welcome pamphlet at Della's church

"It doesn't matter whether the minister is a man or woman; the message is the same. We have two male ministers in our church. All that anyone can bring to a spiritual experience is the teaching of Jesus Christ. Each of us brings it our own way, whoever we are. Reverend [Cecil] Williams touches one way; I'll touch a different way. I think that women have been the rulers since the beginning of time. The problem has been man's ego—he needs to be the leader, to be in charge, the way hunters and warriors are.

"But it's always been the talk at the dinner tables, in bed at night, that gave men the energy and strength to get up the next morning and go try it one more time. It's the spiritual experience a woman gives her husband that he needs to do his work. She's always been there for support, but they only remember Eve and the apple. We've always had the ability to come out; we've just gotten the courage lately. We've been doing this work underneath all the time, and now it's out there. Mary Magdalene was the first preacher, so Jesus knew where to put the stuff. He didn't say, 'Go get Peter, James, Matthew.' He said, 'You go tell them.'" I wonder if Rebbetzin Jungreis watches *Touched by an Angel*. The moral values are virtually identical except perhaps on the issue of women.

"I don't know if everyone who comes to church believes in Jesus. I'm not responsible for that. I'm responsible for giving you information. God gives you the revelation. If the principles don't work for you, try something else. I know they work. That's what this millennium is about. It's not about the machines that are going to break down; it's about principles that have stood for two thousand years. I explain that, I invite you, beg you sometimes, just to try it. When you come face to face with the truth, whatever name it is—it could be called Blackberry—if it's true, it rings clear, you see? When you like the name Jesus, or you don't believe he's the messiah, if you'll listen to the truth, it will work for you, that's that. Love one another—that works whatever you are. If you have faith, it's going to work. Many paths lead to the same place. I don't care how you get to God, just get there.

"We have everyone at our service. Only people, not white, not black, not Spanish, not Greek. Our church is founded on love, and I'm talking unconditional love. I'm glad to see you. That's what our fellowship period in the beginning is. One Thanksgiving I was worried the service and dinner would be too long, so I cut out the fellowship, and I got talked about bad. They were upset because they came to share those moments of love, they came to hug, and they came to have physical contact with everybody.

"We meet for a celebration on Sundays, and we have classes during the week in Bible. We are a how-to church: how to make your life better. If you don't have expectation to get things, you won't get them. You're the only person thinking in there, and whatever you think becomes true. If you don't expect anything, the subconscious mind begins to shut doors and paths, so you get what you expect: nothing." As Iyanla Vanzant says, black women clergy are essential for women of color.

Of all her achievements, Della says, "What I'm proudest of in my life is my husband, my children, and my music. That I'm a loving person, I'm very proud of that. Someone who's been bounced around as much as I have could easily be cynical and angry and all those negative things. I've been lucky. Most of the people I've worked with were as spiritual as you could get. Redd Foxx has a bad rap. He was a Christian. I don't say he belonged to any church, but he couldn't eat if you were hungry. If you needed money, he'd reach in his pocket. He never had money because he constantly gave it away. If you needed a job, he'd help you. That's a Christian. Entertainment people *are* spiritual.

"I love my church. It's wonderful; we just need a place where people can feel permanent. I've been moving around all my life, but some people need a building that they can go to all the time. The character, ethics, the spirit, and the love in my church couldn't be better. I fly in every Friday night from Salt Lake City, and I'm in touch with the church all week long by phone.

"When God tells you to do something, He gives you everything you need to do it. If I didn't have the Sunday service, if I didn't have that, I don't think I could have done this for five years being away from home. It's a challenge to get up and catch the plane, but the compensation God gives me is worth it. Others see it as overwhelming, but it's not."

JEAN HOUSTON

When Jean Houston strides into a room, you feel like standing up. Nearly six feet tall and statuesque, with a mane of vigorous dark brown hair, her physical presence fits her ebullient and powerful persona. Past sixty years old and well-known as a leader in the human potential movement for over thirty years, she began her work as a student of human capacities. Later she began cross-cultural studies under the advice and inspiration of the great anthropologist Margaret Mead.

Before she died, Mead gave Houston an immense charge: "I was wrong to tell you to work with governments and bureaucracies to create change. Instead, travel all over the world to gather the collective wisdom of all peoples. Harvest the human potential, and get people to learn together, because we're in a time when we're going to grow in body, mind, and spirit. Write for those people so they can grow and make a difference in their communities."

Jean learned the wisdom of her mentor's words while serving briefly as a spiritual advisor to Senator Hillary Clinton when she was in the White House. To help the First Lady in her writing of the book *It Takes a Village to Raise a Child*, Jean suggested that she imagine what Eleanor Roosevelt might say about raising healthy children. Reporters jumped on the exercise, proclaiming Jean Houston as a New Age channeler, and years of Houston's serious work were dismissed overnight. The White House kept quiet during the flap.

Successful as a teacher, lecturer and author of eighteen books, anyone interested in Houston's ideas should attend one of her workshops to get the full measure of her gift. A visionary with youthful boundless energy and optimism, Jean is better than Prozac for those looking for the light in a dim world.

Jean now lives in Ashland, Oregon, but we meet her while she is still living at her home in Pomona, New York. She is a teacher of the importance of rich, sensory environments, and her house, built by the actor Burgess Meredith in the 1940s, illustrates the point. More like a theater or museum, the living room displays a mummy's case (I regret not looking inside), busts of immortal sages, statues, several large tapestries, and remnants of antiquity collected over a lifetime.

Her long-time assistant, Fonda Joyce, with whom I've spoken once or twice on the phone, greets us like old friends and seats us in the living room. Jean enters a few minutes later wearing slacks, blouse, vest, and Hush Puppies. Gay looks her up and down, dubious about how her wardrobe will work for the portrait. Jean doesn't notice and immediately launches into her remarkable story of being mentored by "people who have been sustained, high-level creators," as she calls them.

"I'm the child of a very hybrid kind of family. My father was an agnostic Baptist, and my mother was Sicilian Catholic. In order to marry my mother, my father promised the priest that he would raise the children Catholic, but he forgot until I was five years old." She delivers this line with a straight face. "My father had been writing for the Bob Hope show and was suddenly off the show for an excess of high spirits. We found ourselves broke and living with my mother's family in Brooklyn. When my grandmother reminded him of his promise, they sent me to Catholic school, but my father couldn't stop commenting on its absurdity, so he gagged the catechism.

"He got me to ask the most interesting questions to the poor little nun who was my teacher. Like 'Sister Teresa, I counted my ribs and I counted Joey's ribs and we have the same number.' Every child raised their undershirts to show that boys and girls had the same number of ribs. Or 'Sister Teresa, did Jesus ever have to go to the bathroom?' Well, that just brought down the house! She put up a big sheet of oak tag with Jean Houston's years in Purgatory. Every time I asked a question, like 'When Jesus rose, was that because God filled him with helium?' I got an X after my name; each X representing 100,000 years. By the end of first grade, I had 300,000 years in Purgatory, and I ran home crying to my father. He laughed and took me to see the movie *The Song of Bernadette*. While I was entranced by the appearance of the Virgin Mary, he got hysterical laughing. 'That's old Linda Darnell! I met her at a party in Beverly Hills. Hot dog! I knew she'd go far.'

"After the movie, I ran home to Chickie, our dog, who was in a closet with her newborn pups, and I threw myself down next to her, vowing to the Virgin Mary to give up candy for a week, anything, to be like Bernadette. I didn't see or hear anything different, but suddenly the world moved into meaning. I knew that

I was the fig tree in the yard, a plane in the sky, the pups—everything was present and interrelated in the universe of fellowship, and it was very good." As it says in the Creation story.

"I heard my father laughing—he was always laughing—and immediately the universe began to laugh. The joy that spins the universe that Dante writes about, that's what it was like. The experience stayed with me all my life, but I didn't stay in the Catholic church, in which I didn't have much of a future, as you can see.

"When I was seven, I began to pen-pal with people of different religions all over the world. My father bought me *The Hero with a Thousand Faces* when I was eleven, and I began to look at the mythic domains of the spiritual life. When I was fourteen, I literally ran into an old man on the street on the Upper West Side of Manhattan. He asked, 'Are you planning to run like that for the rest of your life?'

I answered, 'Yes, sir, looks that way.' He said 'Bon voyage.' I said 'Bon voyage,' and I kept on running to school. The following week I was walking my dog and saw the old man in the same place. He asked me where I was going, and I told him 'Central Park' and he said he'd go with me. He had a long French name but asked me to call him by the first part, which sounded to my American ears like Mr. Tay-er.

"He had no self-consciousness. He would fall to the ground and say, 'Jean, look! A caterpillar. Feel yourself to be a caterpillar. What will you be when you become a butterfly?' I was nearly six feet tall, but I tried. 'When I'm a butterfly I'll fly all over the world and maybe I'll help people.' We started to meet every week. One spring day he said, 'Jean, smell the air. It's the same air sniffed by Aristotle. Ah, Jean, be filled with Joan of Arc, be filled with the tides of history.' That afternoon I came home and told my mother, 'I met my old man again. When I'm with him I leave my littleness behind.' You couldn't be your normal nebbish self and be with him, because he looked at you as if you were the cluttered house that hid the Holy One.

"The last time I saw him was in 1955. He was very pale. I brought him a snail, and he began to talk about patterns, whorls, spirals in nature, the rose window at Notre Dame, brains, and that life was a spiral becoming. He said, 'All around us the Divine penetrates us, the cherry tree over there is the Divine bursting out of the ground.' He said that this was the most critical time of human history, and despite all the crisis and chaos it was a new world coming into being. I asked him what it would be birthed into, and he said it would be a new sphere of mind and a new sphere of interconnected deity. He said, 'Jean, you must touch upon every culture, every people,' and I said that I'd try.

"I asked him who he was. 'A pilgrim of the future.' He looked at me a long time and said, 'Deep things are calling us forward.' I said, 'Goodbye, Mr. Tay-er. See you Tuesday.' Chickie didn't want to go and whimpered. I waited for him Tuesday, but he didn't come.

"Years later, in graduate school, somebody gave me a book without a cover. As soon as I began to read it I knew that it was my path. Noesphere, metamorphosis! I asked my friend if she had the cover, and she did. It was *The Phenomenon of Man* by Teilhard de Chardin. It was my old man, Mr. Tay-er. That's who I walked with for a year and a half." Teilhard de Chardin was a Catholic priest who had looked over the wall of dogma, saw the universe, and gave Jean the same view. As a student and friend to many visionaries, she says that they all describe an early sense that something was guiding them and that they weren't alone. Jean is the only woman in this book without a traditional faith path: she is a syncretist, the blender and borrower that her teachers wanted her to be. She belongs in the book because she is a spiritual leader of spiritual leaders. She is a friend and respected colleague of Lauren Artress, Marianne Williamson, and Sylvia Boorstein, to name but a few who are grateful for her vast knowledge and creative application of traditions.

I ask about her spiritual practice. "I meditate and I still pray to God because that is ingrained in me, but God has both a feminine and masculine face plus much, much more. I'm connected with the whole universe." She pauses. "I learned something about how a life of faith works when I worked with Hillary Clinton. I asked her how she could stand the constant toxic projections, the criticism, and lack of privacy she received in the White House. She said, 'I practice gratitude. I think of all the people and things that I'm so deeply grateful for.' That woman is strong because she has a deep religious faith."

Several months after the interview, we attend Jean's Mystery School, now in its twentieth year. Nothing captures Jean's fertile and generous expression better than the words in her catalog: "Mystery School is a way of honoring ancient schools across the world and across history, where women and men gathered to explore and decipher the great mysteries and their resonance and application, in order to live more freely and more fully. The weekends are designed to provide rich experiences embracing sacred psychology: a synthesis of history, music, theater, the world's cultures, societies and peoples; philosophy, theology, comedy and laughter; science, fiction, and fantasy; metaphysics and general joy." When she speaks, you almost hear background music.

While nothing about Mystery School feels like a religious service in a formal sense, the conference room becomes a sacred space filled with music and silence, and soul-searching feels sacred. Jean holds and guides the students deep into themselves and into the giant cosmos first glimpsed as a child. Restoring body, mind, and spirit feels great, but the exercises and lectures are intended to do more than restoration. The weekend is a wake-up call to expand our life stories and to be of use to the world; the reason we have creativity, energy, and spirit is because they are the tools necessary to repair the world. Our workshop is called "Millennium Marvels and Mysteries: Becoming an Everyday Genius." We will look at the lives of geniuses such as Mozart and Einstein and learn new ways to creativity. A spiritual leader's task is to bring forth creativity in others. Jean will teach me how.

After a suitable wait for a star and the audience being warmed up by Jean's Mystery School partner, Peggy Nash Rubin, Jean comes out exuding the confidence that women desperately need in a world that sees them narrowly. She starts by asking questions: "Who was at Woodstock? Who was a former nun? Any Jubus [Jewish Buddhists]? Any Jews?" When she sees my raised hand, she moves closer, squinting because she's slightly near-sighted and doesn't wear glasses. Upon recognizing me, she whoops, "So you're straight Jewish, Rabbi! Well, maybe not so straight," she chuckles. No problem with being a lesbian here, but being a rabbi is something else. Because I am a lesbian, people assume that I am also religiously expansive. When a young Asian woman asks me whether I perform intermarriages, she is disappointed with my answer.

The vision of Jean's followers, who are well educated and mostly white, is to practice a single millennial path inclusive of everyone. Jean follows Margaret Mead's suggestion to harvest the wisdom of many traditions, although presence of Jewish tradition manifests less as wisdom than as schtick. She uses common Yiddishisms like "Oy" frequently and tells jokes like Woody Allen.

Like Suzan Johnson Cook, Jean uses her legacy of empowerment to empower others. Flexing her psychic muscle, she predicts that Gore will lose to Bush in the election in 2000. Whether this may influence the undecided in the room is the question. She laughs easily, and we laugh with her; as "Mr. Tay-er" taught her, so she teaches us. "This is a time in which the world mind is surely taking a walk with itself. This is jump time, a moment when we can access all traditions to evolve into a time of enlightenment and wisdom. That is why I've studied the spiritual technologies of many cultures, to look for what works in each. We're probably having more spiritual questing than at any other time in history, a time of a huge rise in spiritual deepening. There are dilettantes, but many are serious, and this is the only thing that will save us." This idea is like believing in God; I have to believe it, because I don't want to despair. What Jean is describing may be a new way to understand and recognize salvation.

"People today live maybe a hundred times the amount of sheer experience and stimulation of their ancestors even a hundred and fifty years ago, but we're not prepared to be anything but white males. We're all attending a wake for a way of being that has been ours for thousands of years. We are the people in the parenthesis between living and dying, at the end of an era and not quite at the beginning of the next.

"In Yeats's poem 'The Second Coming,' we are the rough beast slouching all over the place looking for the spirit to be born. I find this all over the world. One of the parts of my work has been to help indigenous cultures to re-appreciate their mental, intellectual, and spiritual traditions. I help them to recover them as they also move into the new millennium and become participants [in] what is certainly becoming a global civilization.

"There is great yearning and burning of the spirit because there is an ignorance about it, a generation grown up with no sense of it. It can come in the deepening of traditional practices, and it also can come out in the extraordinary new fusions that are happening. A student of mine is a Trappist monk who works with the Dalai Lama! They share spiritual traditions in different forms of contemplative and meditational prophecies."

For many people a single path is the appropriate one. We also live in a time of cultural fusion, and many people are enabled or feel compelled to explore many traditions. This was never possible before this time. Beatrice Bruteau with her Gospel Zen is a great example of this. It's about integrating traditions.

"This makes the men in traditional paths very nervous. Women priests and rabbis don't mix and match so much as garner the religious genius of millennia. What they're doing is using this to illumine pathways, the unread vision of the higher dream. It's a re-enchantment of their traditions, and they stay, some more and some less, within the structure of their faiths. There is more inclusion and harvesting among women. If men are hunters and women are gatherers, well, this is the all-time harvest of spiritual tradition.

"Women are the most interesting spiritual leaders in this time. They emphasize process rather than product, on making things cohere, develop, and grow. The spiritual path is really a path of process. It isn't going for the gold; it's the experience itself. I think the whole hierarchical notion where the man is here and the maidservants are there no longer works. Women today are offering a feminine face of the Divine, bringing the rising of Marys all over the world.

"Spiritual life, especially for women spiritual provocateurs, is hugely risky and requires more vigilance than other professions. I've known too many spiritual leaders who were emotional babies, and they got into a lot of trouble. Every day I take an inventory, and if I find a negative or toxic thought, I say, 'Stop!' If you're a public person, it requires extra self-examination and clarification. Every night, the last thing I say before I go to bed and when I wake up is, 'God, let me be a blessing to someone today.'

"It's also good to have a circle of really good friends. My closest friends and I are very different, but we hone each other in mutual sharing. When you're in constant demand, you can run yourself into the ground, and you can lose the depth and source of your strength. You feel inauthentic."

We talk about the erotic nature of the spirit and how it can lead so many spiritual leaders astray. It seems to be a great risk for male clergy. She says, "Spiritual eros in women is different from men. Mother Teresa once told me that the reason she could take care of so many people is because she was so deeply in love with Jesus. She was married to Jesus. She saw her Beloved in the faces of the dying, and she couldn't do enough for him. Men, on the other hand, may look to earth to express their passion, not heaven. Some of them get into trouble that leads to dangerous behavior, and scandals.

"The risk that women have as spiritual leaders is the risk of innovation, the pushing the membrane of the possible. The rise of the feminine that brings women into full partnership with men in the whole domain of human affairs frightens people, like maps of the world that show that it wasn't flat. Women are always charting new territory and are always catching more hell than men. I've certainly experienced it, and I'm sure you have," she says glancing at me. At the interview I told her my story of struggle. "If men are tempted by the power sexually, women's pitfall is low self-esteem and a sense of inadequacy. They just haven't had the support systems men have. Women are also hypersensitive, so they also have to be extremely strong." All my life I was told that I was too sensitive; I have found my sisterhood. "It takes constant mindfulness to keep sensitivity and strength in balance. I try to practice it, taking every moment as filled with Presence. I try to see it in the dogs out there, my husband, the little green plants I put in six weeks ago."

During the coffee break, I meet people who have been to other workshops. Many have attended a year of ten Mystery School workshops. All speak of Jean's warmth and wisdom and how their lives have been changed by her teachings. They are of all ages, from teenagers to octogenarians who do somersaults, which is one of Jean's exercises. There are ex–Peace Corps people, physicians, and teachers. What they share is disenchantment with traditional paths to the Spirit. Despite their affection, Jean isn't their guru; she is their guide.

Peggy gathers us to do a little singing and dancing. It's fun, and it's a way to change channels to solve problems. In joy, we sing to express joyful hearts. How often do most of us sing and dance? Thank God for weddings. A former Shakespearean actress and one of the directors of the Oregon Shakespeare Festival in Ashland, Peggy awakens us to the pleasure of reciting sonnets and leads great meditation.

Jean tells us that we are all healers and then proves it. We pair off, face each other, and put our right palms within an inch of each other. When we feel the heat between them, one partner tells the other where they are feeling pain, like a headache or backache. The healer takes her hand and places it close to the place of pain. The man I am working with puts his hand near the knot in my shoulder. He asks me, on a scale of one to ten, how intense the pain is. I say six.

It begins to diminish to three, and I tell him. Then we reverse the procedure, and I have the same effect on his "eight" backache, which reduces to two.

The weekend turned out to be more than research. Laughter, music, good people, wise teachings, and wonderful exercises rejuvenated us, giving us an elixir to free the spirit to birth new ideas and dreams, and we left riding on Jean's magic carpet of boundless possibilities.

Gay practically has to lasso Jean to get her photograph. Finally seated in a quiet place, she takes in her hand the only piece of jewelry that she wears in addition to her wedding ring and sends forth the message: the only mistake that we can make is to forget that she is Athena, and so are we.

About the Photographs

Beginning in 1973, when I began photographing people, I used the medium to learn what I didn't know or understand about human beings and myself. First I photographed my community of origin so I could develop my own sense of myself. I expanded that to other Jewish communities until 1987, when Malka Drucker and I began the research for our book, *Rescuers: Portraits of Moral Courage in the Holocaust*, about non-Jews who risked their lives to save Jews during World War II. From these people I learned the most fundamental lessons: how to know the meaning of our lives, to know that giving to others feels better than getting for ourselves.

In 1999, after Malka was ordained, she became passionate about a new idea: to interview other women spiritual leaders. Each time she researched a different woman, she found herself curious about what the woman looked like, so she asked me to collaborate. At first I wondered whether the women would be too much like performers. I love to photograph people exactly as I see them, and my previous subjects had been people who were not accustomed to having their pictures taken. They didn't pose with any intention of determining what my portraits would look like. Soon after the first sessions with these women spiritual leaders, however, my fears disappeared.

We began, as we had with *Rescuers*, by Malka conducting an in-depth interview that I videotaped, followed by my taking the photograph. I chose color for the original portraits for two reasons: first, because many of the women wore colorful ritual garments, and, second, because I did not want to abstract these people who were having a profound impact on the religious/spiritual life of this country. Although the photographs are reproduced here in black-and-white, the color portraits are part of an exhibit entitled "Photographers, Writers and the American Scene" being shown throughout the United States, beginning in 2002. The women were willing to allow me to make the kind of picture I wanted, and I credit them for that trust. After I printed the photographs and sent each one an eight-by-ten, most were pleased with the results. This speaks well for their level of comfort with themselves.

GAY BLOCK

Select Bibliography of
Women Spiritual Leaders

MOTHER AMMACHI

Ammachi: A Biography of Mata Amritanandamayi. M.A. Center, 1994.

Immortal Light: Ammachi's Advice to Families. M.A. Center, 1994.

Bess, Savitri L. *The Path of the Mother: With the Divine Guidance of the Holy Mother, Ammachi.* New York: Ballantine Wellspring, 2000.

DR. NAHID ANGHA

Angha, Nahid. *The Journey: Seyr Va Soluk.* San Rafael, Calif. International Association of Sufism, 1991.

_____. *Deliverance: Words from the Prophet.* San Rafael, Calif. International Association of Sufism, 1995.

_____. *Principles of Sufism.* Fremont, Calif.: Jain Publishing Co., 1995.

_____. *The Journey of the Lovers.* San Rafael, Calif.: International Association of Sufism, 1998.

_____. *Ecstasy: The World of Sufi Poetry and Prayer.* San Rafael, Calif.: International Association of Sufism, 1998.

_____. *The Nature of Miracle.* San Rafael, Calif.: International Association of Sufism, 1999.

THE REVEREND DR. LAUREN ARTRESS

Artress, Lauren. *Walking a Sacred Path: Rediscovering the Labyrinth as a Spiritual Tool.* New York: Riverhead Books, 1995.

_____. *The Sand Labyrinth: Meditation at Your Fingertips.* Boston: Journey Editions, 2000.

SYLVIA BOORSTEIN

Boorstein, Sylvia. *Don't Just Do Something, Sit There: A Mindfulness Retreat with Sylvia Boorstein.* San Francisco: HarperSanFrancisco, 1996.

_____. *It's Easier Than You Think: The Buddhist Way to Happiness.* San Francisco: HarperSanFrancisco, 1997.

_____. *Road Sage.* Boulder, Colo.: Sounds True, 1999. Audio.

_____. *The Courage to Be Happy: Jewish/Buddhist Teaching Stories on Gratitude, Compassion, and Mindful Awakening.* Boulder, Colo.: Sounds True, 2000. Audio.

————. *Pay Attention, for Goodness' Sake: The Buddhist Path of Kindness*. New York: Ballantine Books, 2002.

————. *That's Funny, You Don't Look Buddhist: On Being a Faithful Jew and a Passionate Buddhist*. San Francisco: HarperSanFrancisco, 1997.

DR. BEATRICE BRUTEAU

Bruteau, Beatrice. *Evolution toward Divinity: Teilhard de Chardin and the Hindu Traditions*. Wheaton, Ill.: Theosophical Publishing House, 1974.

————. *Worthy Is the World: The Hindu Philosophy of Sri Aurobindo*. Rutherford, N.J.: Fairleigh Dickinson University Press, 1972.

————. *What We Can Learn from the East*. New York: Crossroad/Herder & Herder, 1995.

————. *The Other Half of My Soul: Bede Griffiths and the Hindu-Christian Dialogue*. Wheaton, Ill.: Theosophical Publishing House, 1996.

————. *God's Ecstasy: The Creation of a Self-Creating World*. New York: Crossroad/Herder & Herder, 1997.

————. *Jesus through Jewish Eyes: Rabbis and Scholars Engage an Ancient Brother in a New Conversation*. Maryknoll, N.Y.: Orbis Books, 2001.

————. *Radical Optimism: Practical Spirituality in an Uncertain World*. Boulder, Colo.: Sentient Publications, 2002.

THE REVEREND DR. SUZAN JOHNSON COOK

Cook, Suzan Johnson. *Wise Women Bearing Gifts: Joys and Struggles of Their Faith*. Valley Forge, Pa.: Judson Press, 1988.

————. *Sister to Sister: Devotions for and from African American Women*. Valley Forge, Pa.: Judson Press, 1995.

————. *Sister Strength: A Collection of Devotionals For and From African-American Women*. Nashville, Tenn.: Thomas Nelson, 1998.

————. *Too Blessed to Be Stressed: Words of Wisdom for Women on the Move*. Nashville, Tenn.: Thomas Nelson, 1998.

————. *A New Dating Attitude*. Grand Rapids, Mich.: Zondervan Publishing House, 2001.

DEBBIE FRIEDMAN

Friedman, Debbie. *Blessings*. San Diego, Calif.: Sounds Write Productions, 1990. Audio.

————. *The World of Your Dreams*. San Diego, Calif.: Sounds Write Productions, 1993. Audio.

————. *Debbie Friedman Favorites: Arranged for Piano*. San Diego, Calif.: Sounds Write Productions, 1995. Audio.

————. *Renewal of Spirit*. San Diego, Calif.: Sounds Write Productions, 1995. Audio.

JOAN HALIFAX ROSHI

Halifax, Joan. *Shamanic Voices: A Survey of Visionary Narratives*. New York: E.P. Dutton Books, 1979.

_____. *Shaman, the Wounded Healer*. New York: Crossroad, 1982.

_____. *Shaman*. New York: Thames and Hudson. 1987.

_____. *The Fruitful Darkness: Reconnecting with the Body of the Earth*. San Francisco: HarperSanFrancisco, 1993.

_____. *Being with Dying: Contemplative Practices and Teachings*. Boulder, Colo.: Sounds True, 1997. Audio.

SISTER JOSE HOBDAY

Hobday, Jose. *Creation Stories of the Native American Traditions*. Boulder, Colo.: Sounds True, 1992. Audio.

_____. *Learning Solitary Prayer*. Kansas City: Credence Cassettes, 1994. Audio.

_____. *Morning Has Broken*. Kansas City: Credence Cassettes, 1994. Audio.

_____. *The Spiritual Power of Storytelling*. Kansas City: Credence Cassettes, 1994. Audio.

_____. *Food for Life*. Kansas City: Credence Cassettes, 1994. Audio.

_____. *Simple Living: The Path to Joy and Freedom*. New York: Continuum, 1998.

_____. *Stories of Awe and Abundance*. New York: Continuum, 1999.

JEAN HOUSTON

Houston, Jean. *The Search for the Beloved: Journeys in Sacred Psychology*. New York: J.P. Tarcher, 1987.

_____. *The Hero and the Goddess: The Odyssey As Mystery and Initiation*. The Transforming Myths Series, Book 1. New York: Ballantine Books, 1992.

_____. *Godseed: The Journey of Christ*. Wheaton, Ill.: Quest Books, Theosophical Publishing House, 1992.

_____. *Public Like a Frog: Entering the Lives of Three Great Americans*. Wheaton, Ill.: Quest Books, 1993.

_____. *Life Force: The Psycho-Historical Recovery of the Self*. Wheaton, Ill.: Quest Books, 1993.

_____. *A Mythic Life: Learning to Live Our Greater Story*. San Francisco: HarperSanFrancisco, 1997.

_____. *The Possible Human: A Course in Enhancing Your Physical, Mental, and Creative Abilities*. New York: J.P. Tarcher, 1997.

_____. *The Passion of Isis and Osiris: A Union of Two Souls*. New York: Ballantine Books, 1995.

_____. *A Passion for the Possible: A Guide to Realizing Your True Potential*. San Francisco: HarperSanFrancisco, 1998.

_____. *Jump Time: Shaping Your Future in a World of Radical Change*. New York: J.P.

Tarcher, 2000.

———. *Archetypes of the Collective Unconscious: The Seeker, Traveling the Path to Enlightenment*. New York: J.P. Tarcher, 2002.

Rebbetzin Esther Jungreis

Jungreis, Esther. *The Jewish Soul on Fire*. New York: William Morrow & Co., 1982.

———. *The Committed Life: Principles for Living from Our Timeless Past*. New York: Cliff Street Books, 1998.

The Reverend Dr. Cheryl Kirk-Duggan

Kirk-Duggan, Cheryl A. *African American Special Days*. Nashville: Abingdon Press, 1996.

———. *Exorcising Evil: A Womanist Perspective on the Spirituals*. Bishop Henry McNeal Turner/Sojourner Truth Series in Black Religion, Vol. 14. Maryknoll, N.Y.: Orbis Books, 1997.

———. *Refiner's Fire: A Religious Engagement with Violence*. Minneapolis: Fortress Press, 2001.

———. *The Undivided Soul: Helping Congregations Connect Body and Spirit*. Nashville: Abingdon Press, 2001.

———. *Misbegotten Anguish: A Theology and Ethics of Violence*. St. Louis: Chalice Press, 2001.

Janice Mirikitani

Mirikitani, Janice, ed. *Ayumi: Japanese American Anthology*. San Francisco: Japanese American Anthology Committee, 1980.

———. *Shedding Silence*. Berkeley, Calif.: Celestial Arts, 1987.

———, ed. *Watch Out! We're Talking: Speaking Out About Incest and Abuse*. San Francisco: Glide Word Press, 1993.

———. *We, the Dangerous: New and Selected Poems*. Berkeley, Calif.: Ten Speed Press, 1996.

———. *Love Works*. San Francisco: City Lights Foundation, 2002.

Mirikitani, Janice, Cecil Williams, eds. and Maya Angelou. *I Have Something to Say About This Big Trouble: Children of the Tenderloin Speak Out*. San Francisco: Glide Word Press, 1989.

Dr. Elaine Pagels

Pagels, Elaine. *The Gnostic Paul: Gnostic Exegesis of the Pauline Letters*. Minneapolis, Minn.: Fortress Press, 1975; Harrisburg, Pa.: Trinity Press International, 1992.

———. *The Gnostic Gospels: A New Account of the Origins of Christianity*. New York: Random House, 1979.

———. *Adam, Eve, and the Serpent*. New York: Vintage Books, 1989.

_____. *The Origin of Satan*. New York: Random House, 1995; New York: Vintage Books, 1996.

DELLA REESE
Reese, Della. *Coming Home*. N.p., 1997.

_____. *God Inside of Me*. New York: Jump at the Sun, Hyperion Books for Children, 1999.

_____. *Strength Is the Energy of God!* Charlottesville, Va.: Hampton Roads Publishing Co., 2001.

_____. *What Is This Thing Called Love?* Charlottesville, Va.: Hampton Roads Publishing Co., 2001.

Reese, Della, with Franklin Lett and Mim Eichler. *Angels Along the Way: My Life with Help from Above*. Boulevard, 2001.

STARHAWK
Starhawk. *Dreaming the Dark: Magic, Sex and Politics*. Boston: Beacon Press, 1997.

_____. *The Spiral Dance: A Rebirth of the Ancient Religion of the Great Goddess*. 3rd ed. San Francisco: HarperSanFrancisco, 1999.

_____. *Webs of Power: Notes from the Global Uprising*. Gabriola Island, B.C.: New Society Publishers, 2002.

LUISAH TEISH
Teish, Luisah. *Jambalaya: The Natural Woman's Book of Personal Charms and Practical Rituals*. San Francisco: Harper & Row, 1985.

_____. *Carnival of the Spirit: Seasonal Celebrations and Rites of Passage*. San Francisco: HarperSanFrancisco, 1994.

_____. *Jump Up: Good Times Throughout the Seasons with Celebrations from Around the World*. Berkeley, Calif.: Conari Press, 2000.

IYANLA VANZANT
Vanzant, Iyanla. *Acts of Faith: Daily Meditations for People of Color*. New York: Fireside, 1993.

_____. *The Spirit of a Man: A Vision of Transformation for Black Men and the Women Who Love Them*. San Francisco: HarperSanFrancisco. 1996.

_____. *Faith in the Valley: Lessons for Women on the Journey Toward Peace*. New York: Simon & Schuster, 1996.

_____. *One Day My Soul Just Opened Up: 40 Days and 40 Nights Towards Spiritual and Personal Growth*. New York: Fireside, 1998.

_____. *Working Through the Meantime: An Interactive Guidance Workbook*. Inner Visions Worldwide, Inc., 1998.

———. *Don't Give It Away*. New York: Fireside, 1999.

———. *In the Meantime: Finding Yourself and the Love You Want*. New York: Simon & Schuster, 1999.

———. *Until Today! Daily Devotions for Spiritual Growth and Peace of Mind*. New York: Fireside, 2001.

———. *Living Through the Meantime: Learning to Break the Patterns of the Past and Begin the Healing Process*. New York: Fireside, 2001.

———. *Up From Here: Reclaiming the Male Spirit: A Guide to Transforming Emotions into Power and Freedom*. New York: HarperSanFrancisco, 2002.

MARIANNE WILLIAMSON

Williamson, Marianne. *Return to Love: Reflections on the Principles of a Course in Miracles*. New York: HarperCollins, 1993.

———. *Illuminata: Thoughts, Prayers, Rites of Passage*. New York: Random House, 1994.

———. *A Woman's Worth*. New York: Ballantine Books, 1994.

———. *Illuminata: A Return to Prayer*. New York: Riverhead Books, 1995.

———. *A Return to Love: Reflections on the Principles of a Course in Miracles*. New York: HarperCollins, 1996.

———. *Illuminated Prayers*. New York: Simon & Schuster, 1997.

———. *Christmas Prayers*. White Plains, N.Y.: Peter Pauper Press, 2000.

———. *Enchanted Love: The Mystical Power of Intimate Relationships*. Touchstone Books, 2001.

———. *Miracle Cards*. Carlsbad, Calif.: Hay House, 2002.

Williamson, Marianne, and Emma Williamson. *Emma and Mommy Talk to God*. New York: HarperCollins Juvenile Books, 1996.

Further Reading

Bednarowski, Mary Farrell. *The Religious Imagination of American Women*. Bloomington: Indiana University Press, 1999.

Clinton, Hillary Rodham. *It Takes a Village and Other Lessons Children Teach Us*. New York: Simon & Schuster, 1996.

Eck, Diana L. *A New Religious America: How a "Christian Country" Has Become the World's Most Religiously Diverse Nation*. San Francisco: HarperSanFrancisco, 2001.

Fiorenza, Elisabeth Schüssler. *In Memory of Her: A Feminist Theological Reconstruction of Christian Origins*. New York: Crossroad Publishing Co., 1998.

Flinders, Carol Lee. *At the Root of This Longing: Reconciling a Spiritual Hunger and a Feminist Thirst*. San Francisco: HarperSanFrancisco, 1998.

Galland, China. *The Bond Between Women: A Journey to Fierce Compassion*. New York: Riverhead Books, 1998.

Sharma, Arvind, ed. *Women in World Religions*. Albany: State University of New York Press, 1987.

Spretnak, Charlene, ed. *The Politics of Women's Spirituality: Essays by Founding Mothers of the Movement*. New York: Doubleday, 1994.

Zikmund, Barbara Brown, Adair T. Lummis, and Patricia Mei Yin Chang. *Clergy Women: An Uphill Calling*. Louisville, Ky.: Westminster John Knox Press, 1998.

About the Authors

MALKA DRUCKER is a rabbi and award-winning author of nearly twenty books, including *Jacob's Rescue*; *The Family Treasury of Jewish Holidays*; and *Rescuers: Portraits of Moral Courage in the Holocaust*, another joint project with photographer Gay Block. She lives in Sante Fe, New Mexico.

GAY BLOCK, a portrait photographer since 1975, shows her work widely in the United States and Canada. A recipient of a National Endowment for the Arts Fellowship, she has exhibited her work at the Museum of Modern Art in New York, the Museum of Fine Arts in Houston, as well as many other locations. Her exhibit of the *Rescuers* photographs has traveled to more than seventy venues and was the basis for a Showtime television series. She lives in Sante Fe, New Mexico.

Notes

Notes

Notes

Notes

Notes

Notes

About SKYLIGHT PATHS Publishing

SkyLight Paths Publishing is creating a place where people of different spiritual traditions come together for challenge and inspiration, a place where we can help each other understand the mystery that lies at the heart of our existence.

Through spirituality, our religious beliefs are increasingly becoming a part of our lives—rather than *apart* from our lives. While many of us may be more interested than ever in spiritual growth, we may be less firmly planted in traditional religion. Yet, we do want to deepen our relationship to the sacred, to learn from our own as well as from other faith traditions, and to practice in new ways.

SkyLight Paths sees both believers and seekers as a community that increasingly transcends traditional boundaries of religion and denomination—people wanting to learn from each other, *walking together, finding the way.*

We at SkyLight Paths take great care to produce beautiful books that present meaningful spiritual content in a form that reflects the art of making high quality books. Therefore, we want to acknowledge those who contributed to the production of this book.

PRODUCTION
Sara Dismukes, Tim Holtz,
Martha McKinney & Bridgett Taylor

EDITORIAL
Rebecca Castellano, Amanda Dupuis, Polly Short Mahoney,
Lauren Seidman, Maura D. Shaw & Emily Wichland

COVER DESIGN
Bridgett Taylor

TEXT DESIGN
Susan Ramundo, SR Desktop Services, Ridge, New York

PRINTING & BINDING
Transcontinental Printing, Louisville, Quebec

Other Interesting Books—Spirituality

Lighting the Lamp of Wisdom: *A Week Inside a Yoga Ashram*
by *John Ittner*; Foreword by *Dr. David Frawley*

This insider's guide to Hindu spiritual life takes you into a typical week of retreat inside a yoga ashram to demystify the experience and show you what to expect from your own visit. Includes a discussion of worship services, meditation and yoga classes, chanting and music, work practice, and more.

6 x 9, 192 pp, b/w photographs, Quality PB, ISBN 1-893361-52-7 **$15.95**;
HC, ISBN 1-893361-37-3 **$24.95**

Waking Up: *A Week Inside a Zen Monastery*
by *Jack Maguire*; Foreword by *John Daido Loori, Roshi*

An essential guide to what it's like to spend a week inside a Zen Buddhist monastery.
6 x 9, 224 pp, b/w photographs, HC, ISBN 1-893361-13-6 **$21.95**

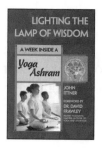   

Making a Heart for God: *A Week Inside a Catholic Monastery*
by *Dianne Aprile*; Foreword by *Brother Patrick Hart,* OCSO

This essential guide to experiencing life in a Catholic monastery takes you to the Abbey of Gethsemani—the Trappist monastery in Kentucky that was home to author Thomas Merton—to explore the details. "More balanced and informative than the popular *The Cloister Walk* by Kathleen Norris." —*Choice: Current Reviews for Academic Libraries*
6 x 9, 224 pp, b/w photographs, Quality PB, ISBN 1-893361-49-7 **$16.95**;
HC, ISBN 1-893361-14-4 **$21.95**

Come and Sit: *A Week Inside Meditation Centers*
by *Marcia Z. Nelson*; Foreword by *Wayne Teasdale*

The insider's guide to meditation in a variety of different spiritual traditions. Traveling through Buddhist, Hindu, Christian, Jewish, and Sufi traditions, this essential guide takes you to different meditation centers to meet the teachers and students and learn about the practices, demystifying the meditation experience.
6 x 9, 224 pp, b/w photographs, Quality PB, ISBN 1-893361-35-7 **$16.95**

Or phone, fax, mail or e-mail to: SKYLIGHT PATHS Publishing
Sunset Farm Offices, Route 4 • P.O. Box 237 • Woodstock, Vermont 05091
Tel: (802) 457-4000 Fax: (802) 457-4004 www.skylightpaths.com
Credit card orders: **(800) 962-4544** (8:30AM–5:30PM ET Monday–Friday)

Generous discounts on quantity orders. SATISFACTION GUARANTEED. Prices subject to change.

Spirituality

Who Is My God?
An Innovative Guide to Finding Your Spiritual Identity
Created by *the Editors at SkyLight Paths*

Spiritual Type™ + Tradition Indicator = Spiritual Identity

Your Spiritual Identity is an undeniable part of who you are—whether you've thought much about it or not. This dynamic resource provides a helpful framework to begin or deepen your spiritual growth. Start by taking the unique Spiritual Identity Self-Test™; tabulate your results; then explore one, two, or more of twenty-eight faiths/spiritual paths followed in America today. "An innovative and entertaining way to think—and rethink—about your own spiritual path, or perhaps even to find one." —Dan Wakefield, author of *How Do We Know When It's God?*
6 x 9, 160 pp, Quality PB, ISBN 1-893361-08-X **$15.95**

Spiritual Manifestos: *Visions for Renewed Religious Life in America from Young Spiritual Leaders of Many Faiths*
Edited by *Niles Elliot Goldstein;* Preface by *Martin E. Marty*

Discover the reasons why so many people have kept organized religion at arm's length.

Here, ten young spiritual leaders, most in their mid-thirties, representing the spectrum of religious traditions—Protestant, Catholic, Jewish, Buddhist, Unitarian Universalist—present the innovative ways they are transforming our spiritual communities and our lives. "These ten articulate young spiritual leaders engender hope for the vitality of 21st-century religion." —Forrest Church, Minister of All Souls Church in New York City
6 x 9, 256 pp, HC, ISBN 1-893361-09-8 **$21.95**

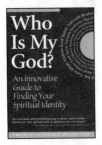 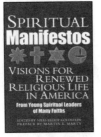 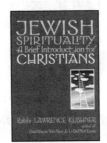 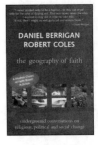

Jewish Spirituality: *A Brief Introduction for Christians*
by *Lawrence Kushner*

Lawrence Kushner, whose award-winning books have brought Jewish spirituality to life for countless readers of all faiths and backgrounds, tailors his unique style to address Christians' questions, revealing the essence of Judaism in a way that people whose own tradition traces its roots to Judaism can understand and enjoy.
5½ x 8½, 112 pp, Quality PB, ISBN 1-58023-150-0 **$12.95**

The Geography of Faith
Underground Conversations on Religious, Political and Social Change
by *Daniel Berrigan* and *Robert Coles;* Updated introduction and afterword by the authors

A classic of faith-based activism—updated for a new generation.

Listen in on the conversations between these two great teachers—one a renegade priest wanted by the FBI for his protests against the Vietnam war, the other a future Pulitzer Prize-winning journalist—as they struggle with what it means to put your faith to the test. Discover how their story of challenging the status quo during a time of great political, religious, and social change is just as applicable to our lives today. 6 x 9, 224 pp, Quality PB, ISBN 1-893361-40-3 **$16.95**

Spiritual Biography

The Life of Evelyn Underhill
An Intimate Portrait of the Groundbreaking Author of Mysticism
by *Margaret Cropper*; Foreword by *Dana Greene*

Evelyn Underhill was a passionate writer and teacher who wrote elegantly on mysticism, worship, and devotional life. This is the story of how she made her way toward spiritual maturity, from her early days of agnosticism to the years when her influence was felt throughout the world. 6 x 9, 288 pp, 5 b/w photos, Quality PB, ISBN 1-893361-70-5 **$18.95**

Zen Effects: *The Life of Alan Watts*
by *Monica Furlong*

The first and only full-length biography of one of the most charismatic spiritual leaders of the twentieth century—now back in print!

Through his widely popular books and lectures, Alan Watts (1915–1973) did more to introduce Eastern philosophy and religion to Western minds than any figure before or since. Here is the only biography of this charismatic figure, who served as Zen teacher, Anglican priest, lecturer, academic, entertainer, a leader of the San Francisco renaissance, and author of more than 30 books, including *The Way of Zen, Psychotherapy East and West* and *The Spirit of Zen.*
6 x 9, 264 pp, Quality PB, ISBN 1-893361-32-2 **$16.95**

Simone Weil: *A Modern Pilgrimage*
by *Robert Coles*

The extraordinary life of the spiritual philosopher who's been called both saint and madwoman.

The French writer and philosopher Simone Weil (1906–1943) devoted her life to a search for God—while avoiding membership in organized religion. Robert Coles' intriguing study of Weil details her short, eventful life, and is an insightful portrait of the beloved and controversial thinker whose life and writings influenced many (from T. S. Eliot to Adrienne Rich to Albert Camus), and continue to inspire seekers everywhere. 6 x 9, 208 pp, Quality PB, ISBN 1-893361-34-9 **$16.95**

Inspired Lives: *Exploring the Role of Faith and Spirituality in the Lives of Extraordinary People*
by *Joanna Laufer* and *Kenneth S. Lewis*

Contributors include *Ang Lee, Wynton Marsalis, Kathleen Norris, Hakeem Olajuwon, Christopher Parkening, Madeleine L'Engle, Doc Watson,* and many more

In this moving book, soul-searching conversations unearth the importance of spirituality and personal faith for more than forty artists and innovators who have made a real difference in our world through their work. 6 x 9, 256 pp, Quality PB, ISBN 1-893361-33-0 **$16.95**

Spiritual Practice

Women Pray
Voices through the Ages, from Many Faiths, Cultures, and Traditions
Edited and with introductions by *Monica Furlong*

Many ways—new and old—to communicate with the Divine.

This beautiful gift book celebrates the rich variety of ways women around the world have called out to the Divine—with words of joy, praise, gratitude, wonder, petition, longing, and even anger—from the ancient world up to our own time. Prayers from women of nearly every religious or spiritual background give us an eloquent expression of what it means to communicate with God. 5 x7¼,256 pp, Deluxe HC with ribbon marker, ISBN 1-893361-25-X **$19.95**

Praying with Our Hands: *Twenty-One Practices of Embodied Prayer from the World's Spiritual Traditions*
by *Jon M. Sweeney*; Photographs by *Jennifer J. Wilson*;
Foreword by *Mother Tessa Bielecki*; Afterword by *Taitetsu Unno, Ph.D.*

A spiritual guidebook for bringing prayer into our bodies.

This inspiring book of reflections and accompanying photographs shows us twenty-one simple ways of using our hands to speak to God, to enrich our devotion and ritual. All express the various approaches of the world's religious traditions to bringing the body into worship. Spiritual traditions represented include Anglican, Sufi, Zen, Roman Catholic, Yoga, Shaker, Hindu, Jewish, Pentecostal, Eastern Orthodox, and many others.
8 x 8, 96 pp, 22 duotone photographs, Quality PB, ISBN 1-893361-16-0 **$16.95**

The Sacred Art of Listening
Forty Reflections for Cultivating a Spiritual Practice
by *Kay Lindahl*; Illustrations by *Amy Schnapper*

More than ever before, we need to embrace the skills and practice of listening. You will learn to: Speak clearly from your heart • Communicate with courage and compassion • Heighten your awareness for deep listening • Enhance your ability to listen to people with different belief systems. 8 x 8, 160 pp, Illus., Quality PB, ISBN 1-893361-44-6 **$16.95**

Labyrinths from the Outside In
Walking to Spiritual Insight—a Beginner's Guide
by *Donna Schaper* and *Carole Ann Camp*

The user-friendly, interfaith guide to making and using labyrinths— for meditation, prayer, and celebration.

Labyrinth walking is a spiritual exercise *anyone* can do. This accessible guide unlocks the mysteries of the labyrinth for all of us, providing ideas for using the labyrinth walk for prayer, meditation, and celebrations to mark the most important moments in life. Includes instructions for making a labyrinth of your own and finding one in your area.
6 x 9, 208 pp, b/w illus. and photographs, Quality PB, ISBN 1-893361-18-7 **$16.95**

Spirituality

One God Clapping: *The Spiritual Path of a Zen Rabbi*
by *Alan Lew* with *Sherril Jaffe*

Firsthand account of a spiritual journey from Zen Buddhist practitioner to rabbi.

A fascinating personal story of a Jewish meditation expert's roundabout spiritual journey from Zen Buddhist practitioner to rabbi. An insightful source of inspiration for each of us who is on the journey to find God in today's multi-faceted spiritual world.
5½ x 8½, 336 pp, Quality PB, ISBN 1-58023-115-2 **$16.95**

The Women's Torah Commentary
New Insights from Women Rabbis on the 54 Weekly Torah Portions
Ed. by *Rabbi Elyse Goldstein*

For the first time, women rabbis provide a commentary on the entire Five Books of Moses. More than twenty-five years after the first woman was ordained a rabbi in America, these inspiring teachers bring their rich perspectives to bear on the biblical text. In a week-by-week format; a perfect gift for others, or for yourself. 6 x 9, 496 pp, HC, ISBN 1-58023-076-8 **$34.95**

  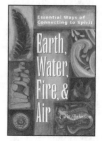

The Way Into Jewish Mystical Tradition
by *Lawrence Kushner*

Explains the principles of Jewish mystical thinking, their religious and spiritual significance, and how they relate to our lives. A book that allows us to experience and understand the Jewish mystical approach to our place in the world.
6 x 9, 224 pp, HC, ISBN 1-58023-029-6 **$21.95**

Earth, Water, Fire, and Air
Essential Ways of Connecting to Spirit
by *Cait Johnson*

Spiritual nourishment at its most basic— the elemental approach to spirituality

You can't help but be drawn into the elemental approach to spirituality so gracefully detailed in this book. It identifies the four basic elements as humanity's first ways of knowing Spirit and reminds us of their value as keys to self-healing and re-connection. Offers a fascinating look at element-based symbols, traditions, and ceremonies, with creative activity suggestions for both individuals and groups. 6 x 9, 224 pp, Hardcover, ISBN 1-893361-65-9 **$19.95**

SkyLight Illuminations Series
Andrew Harvey, series editor

Offers today's spiritual seeker an enjoyable entry into the great classic texts of the world's spiritual traditions. Each classic is presented in an accessible translation, with facing pages of guided commentary from experts, giving you the keys you need to understand the history, context, and meaning of the text. This series enables readers of all backgrounds to experience and understand classic spiritual texts directly, and to make them a part of their lives. Andrew Harvey writes the foreword to each volume, an insightful, personal introduction to each classic.

Bhagavad Gita: *Annotated & Explained*
Translation by *Shri Purohit Swami*; Annotation by *Kendra Crossen Burroughs*

"The very best Gita for first-time readers." —Ken Wilber

Millions of people turn daily to India's most beloved holy book, whose universal appeal has made it popular with non-Hindus and Hindus alike. This edition introduces you to the characters; explains references and philosophical terms; shares the interpretations of famous spiritual leaders and scholars; and more. 5½ x 8½, 192 pp, Quality PB, ISBN 1-893361-28-4 **$15.95**

  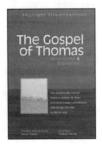

The Way of a Pilgrim: *Annotated & Explained*
Translation and annotation by *Gleb Pokrovsky*

The classic of Russian spirituality—now with facing-page commentary that illuminates and explains the text for you.

This delightful account is the story of one man who sets out to learn the prayer of the heart—also known as the "Jesus prayer"—and how the practice transforms his existence. This edition guides you through an abridged version of the text with facing-page annotations explaining the names, terms and references. 5½ x 8½, 160 pp, Quality PB, ISBN 1-893361-31-4 **$14.95**

The Gospel of Thomas: *Annotated & Explained*
Translation and annotation by *Stevan Davies*

The recently discovered mystical sayings of Jesus—now with facing-page commentary that illuminates and explains the text for you.

Discovered in 1945, this collection of aphoristic sayings sheds new light on the origins of Christianity and the intriguing figure of Jesus, portraying the Kingdom of God as a present fact about the world, rather than a future promise or future threat. This edition guides you through the text with annotations that focus on the meaning of the sayings, ideal for readers with no previous background in Christian history or thought.
5½ x 8½, 192 pp, Quality PB, ISBN 1-893361-45-4 **$15.95**

SkyLight Illuminations Series
Andrew Harvey, series editor

Zohar: *Annotated & Explained*
Translation and annotation by *Daniel C. Matt*

The cornerstone text of Kabbalah, now with facing-page commentary that illuminates and explains the text for you.

The best-selling author of *The Essential Kabbalah* brings together in one place the most important teachings of the *Zohar*, the canonical text of Jewish mystical tradition. Guides readers step by step through the midrash, mystical fantasy and Hebrew scripture that make up the *Zohar*, explaining the inner meanings in facing-page commentary. Ideal for readers without any prior knowledge of Jewish mysticism.

5½ x 8½, 176 pp, Quality PB, ISBN 1-893361-51-9 **$15.95**

 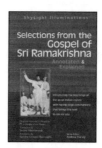 

Selections from the Gospel of Sri Ramakrishna
Annotated & Explained
Translation by *Swami Nikhilananda*; Annotation by *Kendra Crossen Burroughs*

The words of India's greatest example of God-consciousness and mystical ecstasy in recent history—now with facing-page commentary that illuminates and explains the text for you.

Introduces the fascinating world of the Indian mystic and the universal appeal of his message that has inspired millions of devotees for more than a century. Selections from the original text and insightful yet unobtrusive commentary highlight the most important and inspirational teachings. Ideal for readers without any prior knowledge of Hinduism.

5½ x 8½, 240 pp, b/w photographs, Quality PB, ISBN 1-893361-46-2 **$16.95**

Dhammapada: *Annotated & Explained*
Translation by *Max Müller*; Annotation by *Jack Maguire*

The classic of Buddhist spiritual practice—now with facing-page commentary that illuminates and explains the text for you.

The Dhammapada—words spoken by the Buddha himself over 2,500 years ago—is notoriously difficult to understand for the first-time reader. Now you can experience it with understanding even if you have no previous knowledge of Buddhism. Enlightening facing-page commentary explains all the names, terms, and references, giving you deeper insight into the text. An excellent introduction to Buddhist life and practice.

5½ x 8½, 160 pp, Quality PB, ISBN 1-893361-42-X **$14.95**

Meditation/Prayer

Finding Grace at the Center: *The Beginning of Centering Prayer*
by *M. Basil Pennington, OCSO, Thomas Keating, OCSO,* and *Thomas E. Clarke, SJ*

The book that helped launch the Centering Prayer "movement." Explains the prayer of *The Cloud of Unknowing,* posture and relaxation, the three simple rules of centering prayer, and how to cultivate centering prayer throughout all aspects of your life.
5 x 7¼,112 pp, HC, ISBN 1-893361-69-1 **$14.95**

Three Gates to Meditation Practice
A Personal Journey into Sufism, Buddhism, and Judaism
by *David A. Cooper*

Shows us how practicing within more than one spiritual tradition can lead us to our true home.

Here are over fifteen years from the journey of "post-denominational rabbi" David A. Cooper, author of *God Is a Verb,* and his wife, Shoshana—years in which the Coopers explored a rich variety of practices, from chanting Sufi *dhikr* to Buddhist Vipassanā meditation, to the study of Kabbalah and esoteric Judaism. Their experience demonstrates that the spiritual path is really completely within our reach, whoever we are, whatever we do—as long as we are willing to practice it. 5½ x 8½, 240 pp, Quality PB, ISBN 1-893361-22-5 **$16.95**

Silence, Simplicity & Solitude
A Complete Guide to Spiritual Retreat at Home
by *David A. Cooper*

The classic personal spiritual retreat guide that enables readers to create their own self-guided spiritual retreat at home.

Award-winning author David Cooper traces personal mystical retreat in all of the world's major traditions, describing the varieties of spiritual practices for modern spiritual seekers. Cooper shares the techniques and practices that encompass the personal spiritual retreat experience, allowing readers to enhance their meditation practices and create an effective, self-guided spiritual retreat in their own homes—without the instruction of a meditation teacher. 5½ x 8½, 336 pp, Quality PB, ISBN 1-893361-04-7 **$16.95**

Prayer for People Who Think Too Much
A Guide to Everyday, Anywhere Prayer from the World's Faith Traditions
by *Mitch Finley*

Helps us make prayer a natural part of daily living.

Takes a thoughtful look at how each major faith tradition incorporates prayer into *daily* life. Explores Christian sacraments, Jewish holy days, Muslim daily prayer, "mindfulness" in Buddhism, and more, to help you better understand and enhance your own prayer practices. "I love this book." —Caroline Myss, author of *Anatomy of the Spirit*
5½ x 8½, 224 pp, Quality PB, ISBN 1-893361-21-7 **$16.95**; HC, ISBN 1-893361-00-4 **$21.95**

Kabbalah

Honey from the Rock
An Introduction to Jewish Mysticism
by *Lawrence Kushner*

An insightful and absorbing introduction to the ten gates of Jewish mysticism and how it applies to daily life. "The easiest introduction to Jewish mysticism you can read."
6 x 9, 176 pp, Quality PB, ISBN 1-58023-073-3 **$15.95**

Eyes Remade for Wonder
The Way of Jewish Mysticism and Sacred Living
A Lawrence Kushner Reader
Intro. by *Thomas Moore*, author of *Care of the Soul*

Whether you are new to Kushner or a devoted fan, you'll find inspiration here. With samplings from each of Kushner's works, and a generous amount of new material, this book is to be read and reread, each time discovering deeper layers of meaning in our lives.
6 x 9, 240 pp, Quality PB, ISBN 1-58023-042-3 **$18.95**; HC, ISBN 1-58023-014-8 **$23.95**

Invisible Lines of Connection
Sacred Stories of the Ordinary
by *Lawrence Kushner* **AWARD WINNER!**

Through his everyday encounters with family, friends, colleagues and strangers, Kushner takes us deeply into our lives, finding flashes of spiritual insight in the process.
5½ x 8½, 160 pp, Quality PB, ISBN 1-879045-98-2 **$15.95**

Finding Joy
A Practical Spiritual Guide to Happiness
by *Dannel I. Schwartz* with *Mark Hass* **AWARD WINNER!**

Explains how to find joy through a time honored, creative—and surprisingly practical—approach based on the teachings of Jewish mysticism and Kabbalah.
6 x 9, 192 pp, Quality PB, ISBN 1-58023-009-1 **$14.95**; HC, ISBN 1-879045-53-2 **$19.95**

Ancient Secrets
Using the Stories of the Bible to Improve Our Everyday Lives
by *Rabbi Levi Meier, Ph.D.* **AWARD WINNER!**

Drawing on a broad range of wisdom writings, distinguished rabbi and psychologist Levi Meier takes a thoughtful, wise and fresh approach to showing us how to apply the stories of the Bible to our everyday lives.
5½ x 8½, 288 pp, Quality PB, ISBN 1-58023-064-4 **$16.95**

Spirituality/Meditation

Does the Soul Survive? *A Jewish Journey to Belief in Afterlife, Past Lives & Living with Purpose*
by *Rabbi Elie Kaplan Spitz;*
Foreword by *Brian L. Weiss, M.D., author of* Many Lives, Many Masters

Some surprising answers to what Judaism teaches us about life after life.

Do we have a soul that survives our earthly existence? To know the answer is to find greater understanding, comfort and purpose in our lives—and in our deaths. Here, Rabbi Elie Kaplan Spitz relates his own experiences and those shared with him by people he has worked with as a rabbi, firsthand accounts that helped propel his own journey from skeptic to believer. Spitz shows us that beliefs in these concepts, so often approached with reluctance, is in fact true to Jewish tradition.
6 x 9, 288 pp, Quality PB, ISBN 1-58023-165-9 **$16.95**; HC, ISBN 1-58023-094-6 **$21.95**

Bringing the Psalms to Life
How to Understand and Use the Book of Psalms
by *Rabbi Daniel F. Polish*

Here, the most beloved—and least understood—of the books in the Bible comes alive. This simultaneously insightful and practical guide shows how the psalms address a myriad of spiritual issues in our lives: feeling abandoned, overcoming illness, dealing with anger, and more.
6 x 9, 208 pp, Quality PB, ISBN 1-58023-157-8 **$16.95**; HC, ISBN 1-58023-077-6 **$21.95**

The Way of Flame
A Guide to the Forgotten Mystical Tradition of Jewish Meditation
by *Avram Davis* 4½ x 8, 176 pp, Quality PB, ISBN 1-58023-060-1 **$15.95**

Minding the Temple of the Soul: *Balancing Body, Mind, and Spirit through Traditional Jewish Prayer, Movement, and Meditation*
by *Tamar Frankiel* and *Judy Greenfeld*

This new spiritual approach to physical health introduces us to practices that affirm the body and enable us to reconceive our bodies in a more positive spiritual light. Focuses on traditional Jewish prayers and Kabbalah, with exercises, movements, and meditations.
7 x 10, 192 pp, Quality PB, Illus., ISBN 1-879045-64-8 **$16.95**;
Audiotape of the Blessings, Movements and Meditations (60-min. cassette), JN01 **$9.95**;
Videotape of the Movements and Meditations (46-min. VHS), S507 **$20.00**

Entering the Temple of Dreams: *Jewish Prayers, Movements, and Meditations for the End of the Day*
by *Tamar Frankiel* and *Judy Greenfeld*

Nighttime spirituality is much more than bedtime prayers! Here, you'll learn to combine prayer with movements and meditations to enhance your physical and psychological well-being before sleep. 7 x 10, 192 pp, Illus., Quality PB, ISBN 1-58023-079-2 **$16.95**

Children's Spirituality

Becoming Me: *A Story of Creation*

by *Martin Boroson*
Full-color illus. by *Christopher Gilvan-Cartwright*

For ages 4 & up

Told in the personal "voice" of the Creator, here is a story about creation and relationship that is about each one of us. In simple words and with radiant illustrations, the Creator tells an intimate story about love, about friendship and playing, about our world—and about ourselves. And with each turn of the page, we're reminded that we just might be closer to our Creator than we think!

8 x 10, 32 pp, Full-color illus., HC, ISBN 1-893361-11-X **$16.95**

A Prayer for the Earth
The Story of Naamah, Noah's Wife

by *Sandy Eisenberg Sasso*
Full-color illus. by *Bethanne Andersen*

For ages 4 & up

This new story, based on an ancient text, opens readers' religious imaginations to new ideas about the well-known story of the Flood. When God tells Noah to bring the animals of the world onto the ark, God also calls on Naamah, Noah's wife, to save each plant on Earth. "A lovely tale.... Children of all ages should be drawn to this parable for our times."
—Tomie de Paola, artist/author of books for children
9 x 12, 32 pp, HC, Full-color illus., ISBN 1-879045-60-5 **$16.95**

In God's Name

by *Sandy Eisenberg Sasso*; Full-color illus. by *Phoebe Stone*

For ages 4 & up

Like an ancient myth in its poetic text and vibrant illustrations, this award-winning modern fable about the search for God's name celebrates the diversity and, at the same time, the unity of all the people of the world.
9 x 12, 32 pp, HC, Full-color illus., ISBN 1-879045-26-5 **$16.95**

Also available in Spanish:
El nombre de Dios 9 x 12, 32 pp, HC, Full-color illus., ISBN 1-893361-63-2 **$16.95**

The 11th Commandment
Wisdom from Our Children

by *The Children of America*

For ages 4 & up

"If there were an Eleventh Commandment, what would it be?" Children of many religious denominations across America answer this question—in their own drawings and words. "A rare book of spiritual celebration for all people, of all ages, for all time." —*Bookviews*
8 x 10, 48 pp, HC, Full-color illus., ISBN 1-879045-46-X **$16.95**

Children's Spirituality

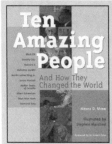

Ten Amazing People
And How They Changed the World

 For ages 6–10

by *Maura D. Shaw*; Foreword by *Dr. Robert Coles*
Full-color illus. by *Stephen Marchesi*

Black Elk • Dorothy Day • Malcolm X • Mahatma Gandhi •
Martin Luther King, Jr. • Mother Teresa • Janusz Korczak •
Desmond Tutu • Thich Nhat Hanh • Albert Schweitzer

This vivid, inspirational, and authoritative book will open new possibilities for children by telling the stories of how ten of the past century's greatest leaders changed the world in important ways.

8½, x 11, 48 pp, HC, Full-color illus., ISBN 1-893361-47-0 **$17.95**

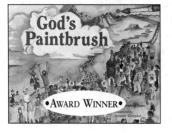

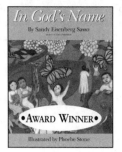

God's Paintbrush

 For ages 4 & up

by *Sandy Eisenberg Sasso*; Full-color illus. by *Annette Compton*

Invites children of all faiths and backgrounds to encounter God openly in their own lives. Wonderfully interactive; provides questions adult and child can explore together at the end of each episode. "An excellent way to honor the imaginative breadth and depth of the spiritual life of the young." —Dr. Robert Coles, Harvard University

11 x 8½, 32 pp, HC, Full-color illus., ISBN 1-879045-22-2 **$16.95**

Also available:

A Teacher's Guide 8½ x 11, 32 pp, PB, ISBN 1-879045-57-5 **$8.95**

God's Paintbrush Celebration Kit 9½ x 12, HC, Includes 5 sessions/40 full-color Activity Sheets and Teacher Folder with complete instructions, ISBN 1-58023-050-4 **$21.95**

In God's Name

For ages 4 & up

by *Sandy Eisenberg Sasso*; Full-color illus. by *Phoebe Stone*

Like an ancient myth in its poetic text and vibrant illustrations, this award-winning modern fable about the search for God's name celebrates the diversity and, at the same time, the unity of all the people of the world. "What a lovely, healing book!" —Madeleine L'Engle

9 x 12, 32 pp, HC, Full-color illus., ISBN 1-879045-26-5 **$16.95**

Also available in Spanish:

El nombre de Dios 9 x 12, 32 pp, HC, Full-color illus., ISBN 1-893361-63-2 **$16.95**

Where Does God Live?

For ages 3–6

by *August Gold* and *Matthew J. Perlman*

Using simple, everyday examples that children can relate to, this colorful book helps young readers develop a personal understanding of God.

10 x 8½, 32 pp, Quality PB, Full-color photo illus., ISBN 1-893361-39-X **$7.95**

Women's Ritual/Study

The Women's Passover Companion
Women's Reflections on the Festival of Freedom

The Women's Seder Sourcebook
Rituals and Readings for Use at the Seder

Edited by *Rabbi Sharon Cohen Anisfeld, Tara Mohr,* and *Catherine Spector*

Women's seders have recently emerged as one of the most meaningful and popular rituals in contemporary Jewish life. These two books bring together the voices of over 150 Jewish women—authors, scholars, activists, artists, political leaders, and students—to share new insights about Passover and to discuss the origins, evolution, and significance of women's seders.

The Women's Passover Companion is a complete exploration of the questions at the heart of this contemporary ritual. It presents an inspiring collection of Jewish women's writings on Passover, the Exodus story, and women's seders.

The Women's Seder Sourcebook is a practical guide to planning a women's seder, based on information from successful seder organizers around the world. It includes a wide variety of women's writings that can be incorporated into the family seder to bring women's voices to the table, and includes a formal curriculum of texts, discussion questions, and writing exercises for further study.

The Women's Passover Companion
6 x 9, 368 pp (est), HC, ISBN 1-58023-128-4 **$24.95**

The Women's Seder Sourcebook
6 x 9, 400 pp (est), HC, ISBN 1-58023-136-5 **$24.95**

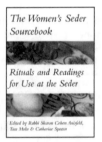

Moonbeams: *A Hadassah Rosh Hodesh Guide*
Ed. by *Carol Diament, Ph.D.*

This hands-on "idea book" focuses on *Rosh Hodesh,* the festival of the new moon, as a source of spiritual growth for Jewish women. A complete sourcebook that will initiate or rejuvenate women's study groups, it is also perfect for women preparing for *bat mitzvah,* or for anyone interested in learning more about *Rosh Hodesh* observance and what it has to offer. 8½ x 11, 240 pp, Quality PB, ISBN 1-58023-099-7 **$20.00**

Religious Etiquette/Reference

How to Be a Perfect Stranger, In 2 Volumes
A Guide to Etiquette in Other People's Religious Ceremonies
Ed. by *Stuart M. Matlins* and *Arthur J. Magida* **AWARD WINNERS!**

Explains the rituals and celebrations of North America's major religions/denominations, helping an interested guest to feel comfortable, participate to the fullest extent possible, and avoid violating anyone's religious principles. Answers practical questions from the perspective of *any* other faith.

Vol. 1: North America's Largest Faiths

VOL. 1 COVERS: Assemblies of God • Baptist • Buddhist • Christian Church (Disciples of Christ) • Christian Science • Churches of Christ • Episcopalian/Anglican • Greek Orthodox • Hindu • Islam • Jehovah's Witnesses • Jewish • Lutheran • Methodist • Mormon • Presbyterian • Quaker • Roman Catholic • Seventh-day Adventist • United Church of Canada • United Church of Christ 6 x 9, 432 pp, Quality PB, ISBN 1-893361-01-2 **$19.95**

Vol. 2: More Faiths in North America

VOL. 2 COVERS: African American Methodist Churches • Baha'i • Christian and Missionary Alliance • Christian Congregation • Church of the Brethren • Church of the Nazarene • Evangelical Free Church • International Church of the Foursquare Gospel • International Pentecostal Holiness Church • Mennonite/Amish • Native American/First Nations • Orthodox Churches • Pentecostal Church of God • Reformed Church • Sikh • Unitarian Universalist • Wesleyan 6 x 9, 416 pp, Quality PB, ISBN 1-893361-02-0 **$19.95**

Also available:

The Perfect Stranger's Guide to Funerals and Grieving Practices
A Guide to Etiquette in Other People's Religious Ceremonies
Edited by *Stuart M. Matlins*
6 x 9, 240 pp, Quality PB, ISBN 1-893361-20-9 **$16.95**

The Perfect Stranger's Guide to Wedding Ceremonies
A Guide to Etiquette in Other People's Religious Ceremonies
Edited by *Stuart M. Matlins*
6 x 9, 208 pp, Quality PB, ISBN 1-893361-19-5 **$16.95**

Other Interesting Books—Spirituality

God Within: *Our Spiritual Future — As Told by Today's New Adults*
Edited by *Jon M. Sweeney* and *the Editors at SkyLight Paths*

Our faith, in our words.

The future of spirituality in America lies in the vision of the women and men who are the children of the "baby boomer" generation—born into the post–New-Age world of the 1970s and 1980s. This book gives voice to their spiritual energy, and allows readers of all ages to share in their passionate quests for faith and belief. This thought-provoking collection of writings, poetry, and art showcases the voices that are defining the future of religion, faith, and belief as we know it. 6 x 9, 176 pp, Quality PB, ISBN 1-893361-15-2 **$14.95**

Releasing the Creative Spirit: *Unleash the Creativity in Your Life*
by *Dan Wakefield*

From the author of *How Do We Know When It's God?*— a practical guide to accessing creative power in every area of your life.

Explodes the myths associated with the creative process and shows how everyone can uncover and develop their natural ability to create. Drawing on religion, psychology, and the arts, Dan Wakefield teaches us that the key to creation of any kind is clarity—of body, mind, and spirit—and he provides practical exercises that each of us can do to access that centered quality that allows creativity to shine. 7 x 10, 256 pp, Quality PB, ISBN 1-893361-36-5 **$16.95**

Spiritual Innovators: *Seventy-Five Extraordinary People Who Changed the World in the Past Century*
Edited by *Ira Rifkin* and *the Editors at SkyLight Paths*; Foreword by *Robert Coles*

Pema Chödrön, Black Elk, H. H. the Dalai Lama, A. J. Heschel, Krishnamurti, Thomas Merton, Aimee Semple McPherson, Martin Luther King, Jr., Starhawk, Simone Weil, and many more.

Profiles of the most important spiritual leaders of the past one hundred years. An invaluable reference of twentieth-century religion and an inspiring resource for spiritual challenge today. Authoritative list of seventy-five includes mystics and martyrs, intellectuals and charismatics from the East and West. For each, includes a brief biography, inspiring quotes and resources for more in-depth study.
6 x 9, 304 pp, b/w photographs, Quality PB, ISBN 1-893361-50-0 **$16.95**;
HC, ISBN 1-893361-43-8 **$24.95**

Or phone, fax, mail or e-mail to: SKYLIGHT PATHS Publishing
Sunset Farm Offices, Route 4 • P.O. Box 237 • Woodstock, Vermont 05091
Tel: (802) 457-4000 • Fax: (802) 457-4004 • www.skylightpaths.com
Credit card orders: **(800) 962-4544** (8:30AM–5:30PM ET Monday–Friday)
Generous discounts on quantity orders. SATISFACTION GUARANTEED. Prices subject to change.